7.95

SOLI DEO GLORIA

RELIGION

SCIENCE

IMS

CULTURE

Brescia College Library
Owensboro, Kentucky

Presented By

Joseph Reninger

NO LONGER PROPERTY OF
BRESCIA COLLEGE LIBRARY

HEIRS APPARENT

BY CHING PING AND DENNIS BLOODWORTH

HEIRS APPARENT

BY DENNIS BLOODWORTH

ANY NUMBER CAN PLAY
AN EYE FOR THE DRAGON
THE CHINESE LOOKING GLASS

HEIRS APPARENT

What happens when Mao dies?

Ching Ping

&

Dennis Bloodworth

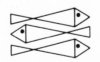

FARRAR, STRAUS AND GIROUX
NEW YORK

BRESCIA COLLEGE LIBRARY
OWENSBORO, KENTUCKY

Copyright © 1973 by Ching Ping and Dennis Bloodworth
All rights reserved
First American printing, 1973
Library of Congress catalog card number: 73-77199
ISBN 0-374-16898-9
Printed in the United States of America

951.05
B655

For Dominic, Bosco and John

Gift

49157

Contents

H.A.—1*

APPENDIXES

ILLUSTRATIONS

Success is the lurking-place of failure; but who can tell when the turning point will come?

Lao Tzu (as translated by Lionel Giles)

When anything reaches its limit, it must change. Germany produced Marx, and then Germany produced Kautsky and Bernstein who revised Marx's ideas. Russia produced Lenin, but Russia also produced Khruschev. And in our country someone will appear to revise Chairman Mao. If you do not believe me, after twenty years you will see.

Ch'en Yi (according to the Hung Ch'i Pao of 4 April 1967)

Indications

The object of this book is to examine the background to the often enigmatic Chinese political scene through Chinese eyes, and in Chinese terms, in order to discover who will guide a quarter of humanity when Mao has gone – and in what direction.

My wife, Ching Ping, is suited to the task. She does not live in Communist Peking or Nationalist Taipei, and she is not a propagandist or an apologist for either. Nor does she have the false belief in her own insight, based solely on blood and race, that afflicts Overseas Chinese emigrants ignorant of the land of their ancestors and Western-educated Chinese whose acquired alien concepts can be dangerously misleading when applied to a Chinese China.

She was born into an intensely political family in Peking. Her father was a Southerner and a close associate of Dr Sun Yat-sen, the true founder of the Chinese Republic, in whose day Nationalists and Communists cooperated within one movement. Between the death of Sun Yat-sen and the birth of the People's Republic of China, her own generation of the family played an active role in the political and military struggle for supremacy.

Uncommitted herself, Ching Ping has been able to draw much of the material for this book from personal friends and contacts with first-hand knowledge who cover the entire Chinese political spectrum. Some of them do not wish to be named. To these we can only offer our thanks anonymously, but we owe to them information about emerging Chinese personalities that has never been published in English before. In consequence, those who believe that a book is only valid if all it contains has demonstrably been borrowed from fifty other books may be disappointed, for we are not always able to quote our sources. It should be noted, moreover, that extracts taken from the Chinese press or from the speeches of Chinese leaders may not be identical with those published in English elsewhere, for in nearly all cases they have been directly translated from the Chinese, and not simply re-quoted from other English-language publications.

Footnotes, chapter notes and appendixes have been added, not only to serve those with a deeper interest in the subject, but to strip the text itself of distractions, because it is mainly directed at the reader-in-the-street. My part in it has been to produce and check an English adaptation of the Chinese manuscript, to insert any explanations that would make it easier to understand for a foreign reader with foreign ideas and no special knowledge of the Chinese political background or the Chinese political mind, and to add a postscript from Peking.

Perhaps the most important point to make in this context is that when a Chinese Communist declared that his country would never sit in the United Nations until Taiwan was expelled, he was saying exactly what he meant, and it is a pity that millions had to be spent before this was finally understood. When, however, he shouts "Chairman Mao is the Red Sun in my heart", he may be telling the metaphorical truth, or being careful to conform, or saving face all round, or covering up a political ploy, or speaking without thinking, or lying in his teeth. The Chinese, who never confuse reality with appearance, must often be judged by their acts rather than their words.

When a writer selects extracts from Chinese statements, therefore, everything depends upon his objectivity. It is possible, for example, to prove from speeches that the disgraced former President Liu Shao-ch'i (a) was the strongest advocate of Mao's "forward" policy in agriculture, (b) was its strongest opponent, or (c) eagerly put it into effect, but then deliberately sabotaged it by pushing it too far too fast. The underlying truth is that he privately opposed it but did not have to sabotage it – it collapsed by itself. And, as far as they can be determined, we have in this book tried to deal only in underlying truths. We have not complicated the text by presenting all versions of an event. We have analysed them ourselves and given our interpretation in the light of what our sources have said or written.

Ching Ping has nevertheless selected her facts with an end in view. *Heirs Apparent* is not a history of Chinese communism, of the "Long March" or of the "Cultural Revolution". The introductory chapter – "The Story So Far" – summarises all of these for the benefit of the ordinary reader, so that he can see events in their proper context when they are mentioned again or described more fully later. For the rest we are concerned with the heirs apparent themselves, not their dates of birth, the details of their schooling and their strings of titles and promotions – these can be found in standard reference works – but with their stories and their characters, their friends and their influences as these relate to what comes next. Of all the sketches, Mao's is the sketchiest, for by definition he dies before the last act. But his impact on all the others – winners and losers – is described in detail, since without that there would be no book.

We have tried to make the story as readable as possible. Since Chinese names are confusing, we have used nicknames wherever they are applicable,* and consigned all secondary characters to notes and appendixes. We have accepted the convention whereby the Chinese Head of State is erroneously referred to as the "President" rather than the "Chairman" of the Republic in order to distinguish him easily from Mao Tsetung, the Chairman of the Communist Party.

We have not used standard military terminology, and have written of the "Fourth Front Army" but of the "4th Field Army" in order to help the reader to differentiate between the two. The Chinese word *ch'un* really means an army corps but is often translated as "army", and we have conformed to this practice where there are precedents. Furthermore, as strengths and designations varied in the early days, Huang Yung-sheng could be a regimental commander in 1935 and deputy commander of a regiment three years later without having suffered any demotion.

All ages given are for the year 1972.

I have used the Wade-Giles system for transliterating Chinese names, as the Communists themselves use it in their English-language texts. While keeping the apostrophe that indicates an aspirate (*Ch'en* is pronounced as it sounds, but *Chou* – in Chou En-lai – is pronounced "Joe"), I have omitted the complication of the umlaut, which is often unnecessary anyway.

---

* In his book *The Red Army of China*, Edgar O'Ballance calls Hsu Hsiang-ch'ien "The Ironside" because he was a brigade commander in the "Ironside Division". But we have called Hsu Shih-yu "Ironsides" as this is a fair translation of his personal nickname.

The bibliography at the end of the book lists both Chinese- and English-language sources, and we should like to acknowledge our debt to William Whitson, formerly with the Office of Military History of the United States Army, and to Gordon A. Bennett, for material on Chinese army loyalty systems and on Vice-Premier Li Hsien-nien respectively (see List of Published Sources). Our thanks are also due to the editors of the *Observer* for permission to publish extracts from articles I originally wrote for the paper, to Sheila Colton for her critical reading of the manuscript and her invaluable comments, to Kang Sek Eng, Joseph Lee Tok Hwee, Andrew K. S'ng, and Wong Poh Kan, for their great assistance with the translation of the Chinese manuscript, and to Edward de Souza for typing and checking it so carefully.

DENNIS BLOODWORTH

Chronology of Relevant Events

1912–1920: The Manchu dynasty abdicates. Yuan Shih-k'ai is first President of the Chinese Republic. Southern revolutionaries in Canton repudiate the regime in Peking and set up their own government under Dr Sun Yat-sen in Canton. But most of the country is in the hands of local warlords.

May 1919: The "May Fourth" incident.

July 1921: The Chinese Communist Party is formed.

October 1923: Sun Yat-sen receives his first Russian adviser on party organisation, and a period of cooperation between Communists and Kuomintang (the Nationalist Party) begins which lasts until 1927.

June 1924: Sun Yat-sen inaugurates the Whampoa Military Academy in Canton with Chiang Kai-shek as Commandant and Chou En-lai as Political Director.

March 1925: Sun Yat-sen dies.

July 1926: Chiang Kai-shek sets out on his "Northern Expedition" to destroy the power of the warlords and unite the country.

April 1927: The Nationalists massacre Communist workers in Shanghai.

August 1927: The Communists organise the abortive Nanchang Uprising.

September 1927: The Communists launch the Autumn Harvest Uprising and make an abortive attack on Changsha.

October 1927: Mao Tsetung arrives on Chingkangshan, and establishes his first guerrilla base.

May 1928: Chu Te joins Mao Tsetung on Chingkangshan. The "Ma Huang" group leads peasant unrest in Hupeh. Oyuwan Soviet subsequently established.

June 1930: First Front Army organised in the Kiangsi Soviet, Second Front Army organised in the Ohsiang Soviet.

July–September 1930: Abortive Communist attempts to seize and hold Changsha and Nanchang.

October 1930: Mao establishes the "Kiangsi Soviet Government".

December 1930: Chiang Kai-shek launches the first of his "extermination campaigns" to wipe out the Communists.

Autumn 1931: Party Central Committee begins to move from Shanghai to the Kiangsi Soviet.

August 1931: Chou En-lai replaces Mao as Political Commissar of the First Front Army.

November 1931: The Party Congress elects Mao Chairman of the newly-proclaimed Chinese Soviet Republic.

November 1932: The Kuomintang (KMT) attack the Oyuwan Soviet, and the Fourth Front Army withdraws its main forces westwards into Szechuan Province. Ho Lung moves out of the Ohsiang Soviet, but, unable to link up with the Fourth Front Army, returns to make West Hunan his main base.

May 1933: Chou En-lai replaces Mao as Chief Political Commissar of the Red Armies.

March 1933–February 1935: Fourth Front Army sets up and consolidates a new Soviet on Tapa Shan in Szechuan.

October 1934: Under pressure of the fifth "extermination campaign" of the KMT, the First Front Army breaks out of the Kiangsi Soviet and begins the Long March.

January 1935: The Tsunyi Conference. Mao re-establishes his leadership.

May 1935: The First Front Army crosses the Tatu River.

July 1935: The First Front Army under Mao and the Fourth Front Army under Chang Kuo-t'ao meet at Maokung.

August 1935: The two forces split again at Maoerhkai.

October 1935: First Front Army reaches Shensi and subsequently establishes a guerrilla base centred on Yenan.

November 1935: Ho Lung and the Second Front Army break out of the Ohsiang Soviet.

June 1936: Ho Lung links up with the Fourth Front Army in Sikang.

July 1936: Second and Fourth Front Armies march north.

October 1936: Second Front Army unites with Mao's forces in the Shensi base, but the Fourth Front Army has been almost annihilated by the KMT after moving west rather than north on the instructions of Chang Kuo-t'ao. Li Hsien-nien subsequently takes the remnants of his column westwards into Sinkiang.

December 1936: The "Sian Incident". Chiang Kai-shek is kidnapped and coerced into negotiating an alliance with the Communists against the Japanese.

January 1937: The party's Central Committee arraigns Chang Kuo-t'ao for his mistakes on the insistence of Mao.

May 1937: Last stragglers from the Fourth Front Army arrive at the Shensi base.

July 1937: Full-scale Japanese invasion of China.

September 1937: An alliance is finally concluded between the Communists and the KMT. Communist forces are reorganised into the Eighth Route Army. Lin Piao ambushes a Japanese brigade at Pinghsingkuan.

1938: Chang Kuo-t'ao defects to the KMT. Chiang Ch'ing arrives at Yenan.

June 1938: New 4th Army formed.

1939: Li Hsien-nien returns to the former Oyuwan Soviet area in command of a column of the New 4th Army and builds up a guerrilla base.

January 1941: The KMT attack the rearguard of the New 4th Army after its combat troops have crossed to the north bank of the Yangtse.

February 1942: Mao launches a rectification campaign in Yenan to end "foreign formalism" and to "sinify" Chinese communism.

September 1945: The Japanese surrender.

November 1945: Lin Piao takes the nucleus of his future North-east Democratic United Army into Manchuria.

June 1946: The KMT launch an overt attack on a Communist base, and the civil war begins.

March 1947: KMT attacks force the Communists out of their headquarters at Yenan.

July 1948: Li Te-sheng engages in the battle for Hsiang Yang.

October 1948–January 1949: Communist forces are reorganised into Field Armies.

November 1948: Lin Piao takes the last KMT stronghold in Manchuria.

November 1948–January 1949: 2nd and 3rd Field Armies win the Huai-Hai campaign and take Suchow.

January 1949: Peking and Tientsin fall to the Communists.

April 1949: 2nd and 3rd Field Armies crosses the Yangtse River. Li Te-sheng subsequently takes Hwei Chow.

May 1949: Chiang Kai-shek retires to Formosa.

1 October 1949: Mao Tsetung proclaims the People's Republic of China. Mao is Chairman of the Republic and Chairman of the Chinese Communist Party. Chou En-lai is Prime Minister and Foreign Minister.

January 1950: The Communists occupy all China except for minor pockets of resistance, and plan the invasion of Hainan Island.

May 1950: Hainan Island assaulted and overrun.

October 1950: 18 Corps of 2nd Field Army moves into Tibet. Chinese "People's Volunteers" cross the River Yalu into Korea.

July 1951: Lin Piao inaugurates a new training programme for a million and a half men in Manchuria.

Early 1954: Kao Kang, head of the party and state apparatus in Manchuria, falls into disgrace, and Lin Piao narrowly escapes implication with him. Field Armies become static territorial "Fronts", their headquarters disappear, and they are replaced by a system of 13 (then eleven) military regions.

December 1955: Huang Yung-sheng becomes Commander of Canton Military Region.

February 1958: T'ao Chu is appointed Political Commissar of Canton Military Region. Ch'en Yi replaces Chou En-lai as Foreign Minister.

March 1958: Mao launches the "Great Leap Forward" and subsequently the campaign to organise the peasants into "People's Communes".

December 1958: Mao renounces re-election as Chairman of the Republic, following the failure of the Great Leap Forward.

April 1959: Liu Shao-ch'i is elected Chairman of the Republic.

August 1959: P'eng Te-huai criticises Mao at the eighth plenary session of the Central Committee at Lu Shan.

September 1959: P'eng Te-huai is replaced as Minister of Defence by Lin Piao.

November 1959: Ch'en Hsi-lien appointed Commander of Shenyang Military Region.

1960: The Soviet Union suspends all aid to China and withdraws its technicians.

1962–1965: Lin Piao is frequently ill or "resting", and his duties are then undertaken by Ho Lung.

October 1962: Chinese troops invade India, then withdraw.

The controversial play *Hai Jui Dismissed from Office* is staged for the first time. Mao confides to Chiang Ch'ing the task of reforming the Chinese opera.

1964: The "Big Military Contest" is introduced.

1965: Lin Piao resumes his active role as Minister for Defence, the accent is put increasingly on a "political breakthrough" in the People's Liberation Army (PLA), and troops concentrate on studying the "Thought of Mao".

September 1965: Military ranks are abolished. Lin Piao publishes his article "Long Live the Victory of the People's War".

November 1965: Mao Tsetung withdraws from Peking to Shanghai, following a meeting of the Politburo at which he was under fire. Yao Wen-yuan "fires the first shot" in the Cultural Revolution by publishing an article attacking *Hai Jui Dismissed from Office*.

Spring 1966: Lo Jui-ch'ing, Chief of Staff, is replaced by Yang Ch'eng-wu in an acting capacity.

April 1966: P'eng Chen and the old Peking party committee are dismissed.

May 1966: The first Red Guards are organised at Peking University.

July 1966: Mao Tsetung returns to Peking from Shanghai.

August 1966: The party's Central Committee lays down the objects of the Cultural Revolution in a "16-point Decision". Red Guards appear in public for the first time, and go on the rampage against "old culture and customs", etc.

October 1966: Red Guards attack President Liu Shao-ch'i and Party Secretary-General Teng Hsiao-p'ing by name.

December 1966: Ex-Chief of Staff Lo Jui-ch'ing (among others) publicly humiliated by the mob.

January 1967: Ho Lung denounced as a "bandit" and stripped of his positions as alleged accessory in an anti-Mao plot. A purge of "bourgeois reactionaries" in the PLA is organised. Wu Fa-hsien (Air Force Commander), Ch'iu Hui-tso (Director of Logistics) and Li Tso-p'eng (Political Commissar of the Navy) are deprived of office on the instigation of Chiang Ch'ing (but restored to their posts later in the year). The "January Revolution" breaks out in Shanghai, and the masses take over from the local administration.

February 1967: The "Shanghai People's Commune" is proclaimed. The commune administration is then modified to become a "Shanghai Revolutionary Committee" on which the local military commanders, the former civilian cadres, and the representatives of the masses are all represented. This "three-way alliance" is hailed by the press as the model for all China.

Early 1967: Li Hsien-nien is deprived of his post at the head of the Finance and Trade Office of the State Council (which controls four ministries devoted to finance and economy) but with the support of Premier Chou En-lai is reinstated after one month.

May 1967: Li Ch'ing-ch'uan, the "king of Chengtu", is dismissed from office. Liang Hsing-ch'u becomes Commander of Chengtu Military Region.

July 1967: The "Wuhan Incident". "Pockmark" Ch'en Tsai-tao kidnaps two emissaries of the Cultural Revolution from Peking.

August/September 1967: Hsiao Hua, Director of the General Political Department, and five of his immediate deputies lose their posts on the instigation of Chiang Ch'ing.

September 1967: A directive is issued empowering the PLA to carry out arrests and use force if necessary to prevent "rebels" from stealing or keeping weapons.

March 1968: Yang Ch'eng-wu is dismissed as Acting Chief of Staff and replaced by Huang Yung-sheng.

August 1968: Yao Wen-yuan publishes his article "The working class must exercise leadership in everything" which heralds the introduction of workers' and soldiers' "Mao Thought Propaganda Teams", and the Red Guard era officially ends.

September 1968: Revolutionary Committees are formed in all of China's 29 provincial divisions.

April 1969: The Ninth Congress of the Chinese Communist Party approves a draft constitution appointing Lin Piao as Mao's successor, and elects a new Central Committee and Politburo with strong PLA representation.

August 1970: A second plenary session of the Ninth Congress is held, and foreshadows the downfall of Ch'en Po-ta, head of the Cultural Revolution Group.

September 1970: Li Te-sheng first appears as Director of the General Political Department of the PLA.

February 1971: The *Red Flag* warns against "Sham Marxist political swindlers", meaning Ch'en Po-ta.

April 1971: An American table-tennis team visits Peking. Ping-pong diplomacy begins.

June 1971: Lin Piao is seen in public for the last time.

July 1971: It is announced that President Nixon will visit China.

August 1971: New Communist Party committees are formed for all of China's 29 provincial divisions.

September 1971: Huang Yung-sheng, Chief of Staff, is seen in public for the last time. A Chinese air force Trident jet crashes in Mongolia. The National Day parade on 1 October is cancelled.

October 1971: Radio and press attacks develop against an unnamed "ambitionist", identifiable as Lin Piao. The People's Republic is elected to represent China at the United Nations in place of the Nationalist "Republic of China" (Formosa).

January 1972: Ch'en Yi dies. Chi P'eng-fei becomes Foreign Minister.

February 1972: President Nixon visits China.

1 July, 1972: 51st anniversary of the founding of the Chinese Communist Party.

28 July, 1972: The Chinese officially announce that Lin Piao was killed in an air crash in September 1971 while fleeing to the Soviet Union, after having tried to assassinate Mao Tsetung and seize power.

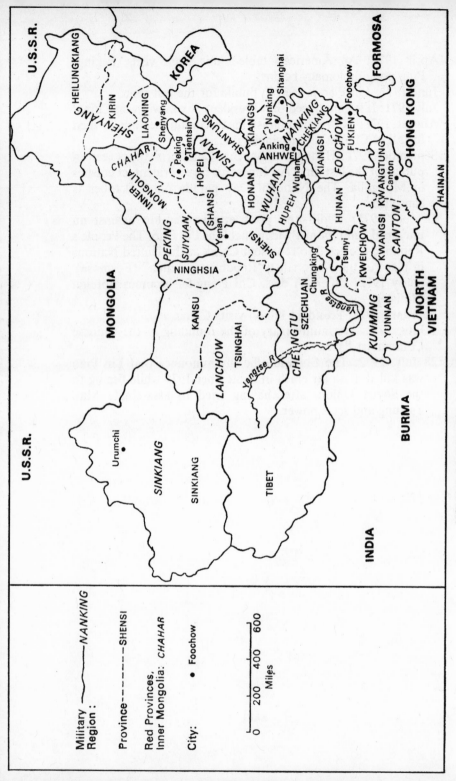

CHINA'S PROVINCES AND MILITARY REGIONS

Military Region: ——— *NANKING*

Province: - - - - - SHENSI

Red Provinces, Inner Mongolia: *CHAHAR*

City: ● Foochow

0 200 400 600
Miles

The Story So Far

What happens when Mao Tsetung dies? Who becomes master of China's eight hundred millions? That is our theme. But since, unlike a Chinese opera, it will not be unfolding before a Chinese audience that will know the players and the plot and need no programmes or scenery, we must first provide the setting for the actors.

The story begins with an ending, just as it must end with a beginning, for the fall of a ruler is always both. After more than two thousand years of imperial sway, the last dynasty in China was overthrown and a republic proclaimed in 1912. The provisional President,* who was the former Chinese commander-in-chief, only intended this to be democratic scaffolding, for he proposed to make himself the first emperor of a new dynasty. But he had not reckoned with his generals, who now realised that he was utterly dependent upon them, and that they held the real power. Within a few years, therefore, this pretender was dead and most of China was divided up among regional warlords who knew no chief.

The true republicans had not been silenced, however, and they formed what they claimed to be the legitimate government of China under the presidency of Doctor Sun Yat-sen in the southern city of Canton. Their revolutionary movement was reorganised as the Kuomintang (KMT) or Nationalist Party, and in 1923 it began accepting not only Russian Communist advisers and aid, but individual Chinese Communists as Party members.

The Chinese Communist Party was officially formed in 1921 under ominous conditions that held the seeds of future cliques and conflicts for, while it was inaugurated in Shanghai, there were groups of Chinese Marxists in France and the Soviet Union moulded by alien influences unknown to their parochial comrades at home, to whose central authority they were nonetheless called upon to defer. Today it is worth remembering

---

* Yuan Shih-k'ai.

where some of the men who later rose to power in Peking were at that time:

Mao Tsetung was a founder member of the party in China, and, except for two visits to the Soviet Union, has never been abroad. He is chauvinistically Chinese.

Chou En-lai, China's "moderate" Prime Minister, was a founder member of the party branch in France. He has travelled widely, and is regarded as a communist of "international" outlook.

Liu Shao-ch'i, former President of the People's Republic of China, was in the Soviet Union and joined the Chinese communist organisation while in Moscow. In the sixties Mao hounded him out of office and into dishonourable retirement as leader of the "Russian revisionist" clique within the party.

Those who were abroad soon returned to China, however, and when in 1924 the Nationalist General Chiang Kai-shek opened the Whampoa Military Academy in Canton with himself as Commandant, the Director of its Political Department was Chou En-lai. The Academy was the military kindergarten of many outstanding Nationalist and Communist commanders, among them Lin Piao, who was destined to become Vice-Chairman of the party and Mao Tsetung's heir-designate.

In 1925 Sun Yat-sen died, and the following year Chiang Kai-shek led his KMT forces on a "Northern Expedition" in order to win over or wipe out the warlords and unite all China under the Republic. The expedition itself was conspicuously successful from the start, but Chiang Kai-shek, who had never trusted the Communists, became alarmed by the power they were acquiring within the KMT government. In the spring of 1927 the Nationalists therefore massacred Communist workers who had seized control of Shanghai in order to hand the city over to them as they advanced north, harried, arrested and killed local Communits leaders elsewhere, and shed their Russian advisers. The KMT–Communist alliance snapped in two, and the Communists went underground.

In August, Communist and left-wing elements of the KMT briefly seized the town of Nanchang in what is known as the "Nanchang Uprising", and in the following weeks Mao Tsetung raised forces in the province of Hunan for an attack on its capital, Changsha. This equally famous revolt has gone down in Chinese communist history as the "Autumn Harvest Uprising" and it, too, failed.

However, its failure proved a turning point in the fortunes of the Chinese Reds. Mao led the remnants of his army, already badly mauled by the KMT, to an inaccessible bandit lair on the forbidding heights of Chingkangshan to rest, reorganise and rethink. That was the true beginning of the peasant revolution that was to prove Mao's winning formula. In the years that followed he carved out of the wild hills to his east the Kiangsi Soviet, a red base in rough country within which his guerrilla army was taught to move among the people "like a fish in water".

By the end of 1931 there were three important rural Soviets in China, but Mao's formula was not to be implemented without much argument. The Central Committee of the party tended to accept without question the Russian doctrine that the urban workers must lead the communist revolution, and Soviet advisers urged that the most important targets to seize were the towns. However, attempts to put Russian theory into Chinese practice repeatedly failed, and in 1931 the Central Committee itself finally moved to the Kiangsi Soviet. But in the meanwhile Chiang Kai-shek had begun mounting a series of "extermination campaigns" to destroy the Red bases, and by 1934 the KMT had forced the Communists out of their strongholds. Mao's subsequent migration is what is known as the "Long March", for his forces fought their way over some 6,000 miles of difficult terrain to the site of a new base in Yenan in north-west China, where the armies from all three of the abandoned southern Soviets were finally reunited in 1936 under his leadership.

In 1937 war broke out between China and Japan, and the Communists entered into an alliance with the KMT to fight the common enemy. But although their forces were regrouped into the Eighth Route Army, which was nominally under the supreme command of Chiang Kai-shek, Red generals devoted much of their time to the basic, almost compulsive occupation of winning over the peasants and setting up more Soviets for themselves. By 1938 the Communists had five such enclaves in the north and the New 4th Army on the Yangtse Kiang. This New 4th Army, made up of stay-behind rearguards from the southern Soviets, rapidly expanded its territorial base, provoking bloody clashes with KMT who stood in its way, and at the beginning of 1941 the Nationalists retaliated by attacking it in the rear on the south bank of the river. The killing that followed, like the Shanghai massacre in 1927, ended any real semblance of active cooperation between the Communists and the Nationalists.

After the Japanese surrender the KMT and the Communists turned to the serious business of fighting each other for the control of all China. Lin Piao moved into Manchuria, the industrial north-east of the country, which now became the first major objective in the race for territory. In 1948 Stalin advised Mao against trying to kick the Kuomintang out of China altogether, but Mao ignored him. Lin Piao overran Manchuria, Peking yielded, and the Red armies pushed southwards until they had driven the Nationalists overseas to the island of Formosa.

The People's Republic of China was proclaimed on 1 October 1949, and its future Chairman, Mao Tsetung, set about transforming it into a classless communist society. Between 1950 and 1953 China occupied Tibet, sent "volunteers" to fight in Korea, launched the first campaigns against class enemies, and instituted land reform on a nation-wide basis (liquidating landlords and distributing the land to peasant families). From 1953 to 1958 the Communists executed their first Five-Year Plan with massive assistance from the Russians, who sent whole industrial plants to China and thousands of technicians to teach the Chinese how to build and run them. Meanwhile the peasants were progressively organised into agricultural cooperatives, and the land which had earlier been given to them was gently but firmly taken away again so that it could be pooled and worked by their collective labour.

Now Mao had wrenched all China from the Kuomintang, despite the massive American military aid given to Chiang Kai-shek, with under-armed but dedicated guerrilla forces that depended heavily on a politically conditioned population. His experience had convinced him that not modern machines but the spirit of man in the mass moved mountains and won wars. Communist indoctrination was therefore more important than technology, men's aims were best achieved by revolution – and the enemies of revolution were evolution, reform, revision, and the rest of the gently-does-it.

So in 1958 he called for a "Great Leap Forward" in industry

and agriculture, a tremendous jump in output to be achieved not by Russian mechanisation, but by the collective effort of native Chinese millions organised into new "People's Communes". This frenzied burst of ill-directed energy brought the economy to its knees, and relations between China and the Soviet Union meanwhile froze over. Stalin, whose historic role Mao acknowledged, had died. Nikita Khrushchev, whom Mao disdained as an inferior, had succeeded him. Khrushchev was contemptuous of the Great Leap Forward and the communes, and was not amused by the implications that China must become self-sufficient to rid herself of reliance on Russia, and that Peking could create a true communist society before Moscow.

Khrushchev claimed that other communist states should recognise the primacy of the Soviet Union. Mao retorted that they should all have an equal say in all things. Khrushchev advocated peaceful coexistence with the capitalist world. Mao considered this blasphemy, and urged that the first duty of a communist country was to help all those in the underdeveloped continents engaged in armed revolutionary struggle to overthrow their imperialist oppressors. In 1960 the Russians stopped all aid to China and withdrew their technicians.

China's external quarrel with Moscow was reflected in an internal conflict that had already come to the surface in August 1959, when the Central Committee of the party held a plenary session at Lu Shan and the Minister of Defence, P'eng Te-huai, denounced the ruinous follies of the Great Leap Forward and the unworkable people's communes as "petit bourgeois fanaticism". P'eng was dismissed from his post as Minister of Defence and replaced by Lin Piao, but on his side Mao had already resigned from his position as Chairman of the Republic (while remaining Chairman of the Party) and the Russian-trained Liu Shao-ch'i had succeeded him as Head of State.

In the sixties Mao fought back against the cautious and critical "moderates" who sought to hold his revolutionary impatience in check. Successive campaigns were launched to cleanse the masses of anti-Maoism, to inspire them with the true ideals of selfless socialism, to kill their materialistic instinct, to purge them of their bourgeois habits of thought. Meanwhile, with Lin Piao as Defence Minister, Mao could place greater faith in the armed services than he could in the party and administration. The People's Liberation Army (PLA)* moved back towards Mao's concept of an indoctrinated revolutionary force. It was the army that first studied the earliest version of the little red book of Mao's "Thoughts", the army that the whole country was urged to emulate in order to become "one great school of revolution", and it was Lin Piao whom the Chairman was soon to appoint as his successor.

When Lin abolished ranks within the PLA in September 1965, China was on the eve of the "Great Cultural Revolution". After a meeting of the Politburo that same month at which he again found himself under attack by the "moderates", Mao set out with Lin's help to shatter China's entire party and administrative apparatus in order to rid it of all who opposed him, and his wrecking-hammers were the masses themselves. Led by young "Red Guards" drawn from schools and universities, Mao's "rebels" unrolled an offensive across the country in 1966 that uprooted the entrenched Communist bureaucracy and culminated in the overthrow and disgrace of Liu Shao-ch'i, the "revisionist" President of the Republic.

The revolutionaries could make no move and carry no weight unless all knew that the troops were with them, and at first the PLA was ordered to stand aside when the youthful mobs went into action and to let them have their head. However, rival factions of Red Guards and proletarian "revolutionary rebels" were soon fighting each other for local supremacy in the streets, Maoist against "Maoist" (for while all professed loyalty to the Chairman, some were in reality anti-Maoists who were only paying him lip-service). The PLA was therefore instructed to come forward and actively "support the left". But many provincial commanders were far from sharing Lin Piao's ostensible enthusiasm for the Cultural Revolution and, exasperated by the young Maoist upstarts who were trying to usurp their local authority, deliberately backed the wrong side. Then, in July 1967, the Commander of Wuhan Military Region openly defied the leaders of the revolution in Peking. He was soon removed, but although this mutiny prompted a short-lived campaign against the PLA, it sobered the Maoists in the capital, and in September the army was given a mandate to restore order.

Since the old structure had been destroyed, however, another

---

* The PLA includes not only China's ground troops, but also the navy and the air force.

had to be put in its place. Between 1968 and 1971 new administrative "revolutionary committees" and new Communist Party committees were elected in all provinces, and the pattern of power then stood out boldly. For all were dominated by the local military. Rebel factionalism was suppressed, and rebel heroes of yesterday who protested were denounced as "petit-bourgeois" leftists and anarchists.

The Cultural Revolution was over. A new era was dawning. The moderate Premier Chou En-lai had introduced ping-pong diplomacy. President Nixon was to visit Peking. An apparently domesticated China was received into the comity of nations. Mao's opponents and their arguments still lived, but Mao himself was moving into the late seventies well ahead of the world.

When the Manchu Empire fell, the general who had inherited power in Peking found himself challenged by the left wing, jostled by the right, and at the mercy of warlords who carved China up among themselves. When Mao became history, would Lin Piao hold his empire together? Or would left-wing extremists come to the fore? Or "Russian revisionists"? Or right-wing counter-revolutionaries who would put an end to the communist experiment? Or would the country fall among warlords again? These were the questions the world then asked and to which we must now try to give the answers, for China is fast becoming a nuclear power, and those answers will determine whether we are living with a cooling volcano, or a time-bomb.

PART ONE

THE CIVILIANS

1
Ladies First

A Japanese writer who made a tour of Communist China said afterwards: "The men and women are like a colony of crabs. You cannot tell them apart from their external appearance. To do so, you have to turn them over." The People's Republic is the sartorial home of unisex, for during most of its short history the millions, male and female, have worn the same, simple, heavily-patched tunic-and-trousers, and the women have stopped using cosmetics, for make-up is considered a weapon of capitalism. But some would also call it the spiritual home of Women's Lib, claiming that feminine power in Peking was amply demonstrated during the Great Cultural Revolution when the fourth wife of Mao Tsetung, Chiang Ch'ing, was lifted as if by a red gale to the very Gate of Heavenly Peace in Peking, from which point her commands to the Red Guards spread apprehension and even alarm throughout China and the world.

Chiang Ch'ing has had almost as many names as she has had "companions", and it was as Lan P'ing or "Blue Duckweed" in the thirties that she embarked upon the chain of liaisons that would eventually make her First Lady of a nation of eight hundred millions. A second-rank film actress in Shanghai, she enhanced her image by wedding a prominent writer and critic* who was thereafter energetic in his praises of her despite a stormy married life, and who happened to belong to the left-wing faction of literary society in China. Through the prominent critic, however, she met an even more prominent director† whose films – including a Chinese version of *Romeo and Juliet* – had already won him wide acclaim. Anxious to become a star, Lan P'ing begged this man to help her, and he gave her the lead in his next production. Their mutual interests multiplied, and two years later she broke with her unhappy writer-husband,

---

* T'ang Na. † Chang Min.

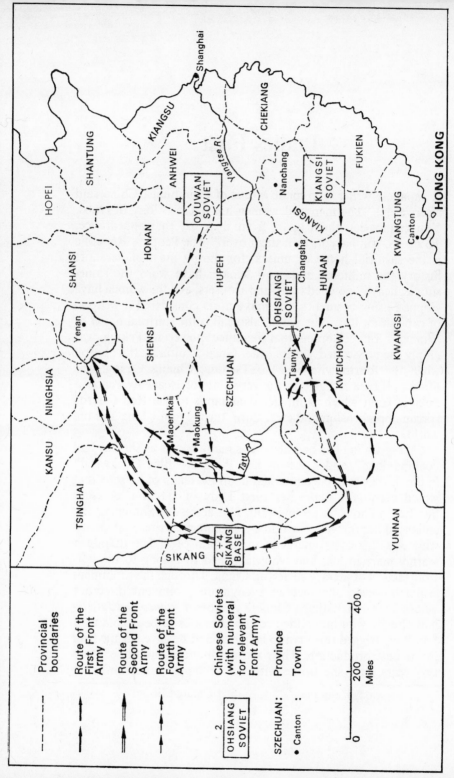

MAP OF THE LONG MARCH

Provincial boundaries

Route of the First Front Army

Route of the Second Front Army

Route of the Fourth Front Army

Chinese Soviets (with numeral for relevant Front Army)

OHSIANG SOVIET

SZECHUAN: Province

Canton : Town

0   200   400
        Miles

who gave a live performance as an unsuccessful suicide in a hotel room.

Despising him even more for this weakness, Lan P'ing then lived openly with her director. He was already married, but she was only concerned with fighting her way to the top, and the wife, who was a primary schoolteacher without pretensions, obligingly faded into the background without protest or public tears. However, others in the left-wing film world were indignant at Lan P'ing's behaviour and openly criticised her, and the more she was criticised the more resentful she became. Ambitious and imaginative, fearful that she had reached a dead-end in Shanghai, Lan P'ing took a logical decision and set off (if somewhat indirectly) for the headquarters of the Communist movement on whose cultural fringe she had been hovering.

Mao Tsetung had made his Long March from the Kiangsi Soviet to Yenan, which was now the holy centre of Red resistance to the foreign invader. Pro-Communist or simply patriotic young Chinese were flocking to it, and Lan P'ing in turn arrived with the intention of enrolling in the Anti-Japanese Military and Political University there. The film director was reunited with his schoolteacher wife. The prominent writer, brokenhearted, abandoned literary life for commerce, and subsequently opened a restaurant in Paris.

Yenan, Chinese Communist capital during the Sino-Japanese war which began in 1937, is in a valley surrounded by mountains of friable yellow soil through which a turbid river flows eastwards. The land rises to a plateau north of the walled city itself, and it was on this that Mao Tsetung established his headquarters, while down in the plain were an airstrip, and a club for the handful of Russian advisers attached to him and for those of his followers who had influence or money.

In the valley beyond the east gate of the town stood two wooded outcrops whose lower slopes were carpeted with soft, luxuriant grass. These were pitted with man-made caves, hollowed out of the hillsides in rows like pigeonholes and lined with brick. The Anti-Japanese University was lodged in an old temple outside the gate and in the nearby caverns. The students were young, keen and energetic, and after work in the evenings embarked on endless discussions or sang lustily, their voices echoing down the valley. They were for the most part soldiers, for the university had grown out of the Red Army School, and

3

they made do with rocks for tables and chairs in these holes in the ground within which they worked, ate and slept.

Lan P'ing apparently decided that this was not quite what she wanted, for she applied to join the Communist Party School instead. She was fortunate, in that the head of the organisation department of the party and the director of its intelligence service was a fellow-provincial from Shantung who called himself K'ang Sheng, and while she was waiting to be accepted by the party school, he used his influence to have her appointed as a lecturer at the Lu Hsun Academy of Arts on the strength of her experience as an actress.

The Academy was a centre for training propagandists, although some of its star students were later transferred to the secret service. The main subjects taught were socialist literature, drama, music and art, and many left-wing writers and scholars came at one time or another to Yenan from different parts of the country to work in it. But Lan P'ing was still nervous about the future, for although she had been given a senior post, she was aware that her technical knowledge was limited, and the environment was strange.

However, the school was run by an elegant and handsome fellow called Hsu Yi-hsin. Hsu, destined to be a diplomat, had cultivated a refined but not displeasing smile, and passed for a charming and intelligent person. Lan P'ing herself was no beauty, but she had a pair of large, brilliant eyes and a wide, disarming smile of her own, and her army uniform, with a tight belt at the waist, showed off her figure admirably. Among the rough, sunburned, yellow-skinned women of Yenan she stood out like a gem, and she spoke and carried herself well, as if on the stage, so that for a time Hsu was infatuated with her and gave her much comfort and guidance. In any case, the ratio of males to females in Yenan was eighteen to one, and no young woman who entered this community could expect to live a quiet and solitary life.

It is hot and muggy during the summer in north Shensi, and both sexes would strip off their clothes and jump into the Yen River to bathe. Beside the river was a hill covered with thick bushes and here, during the cooler nights, pair after pair of comrades could be remarked upon the ground, engaged in a pastime popularly known as "guerrilla training" whose climax was the inevitable "liberation". Officers held regular nocturnal

4

poker sessions, and there was an unofficial traffic in soldiers' rations, which could be exchanged for fresh mutton and kaoliang wine.

Yenan was not without corruption and love of the good things of life, therefore, and one party veteran* was moved to denounce this dark side of the "holy centre" and the uncommunist inequality that prevailed there. "Clothes are divided into three classes," he complained, "rations into five. The senior ranks enjoy many luxuries and the NCOs have their own perquisites. But our sick comrades cannot even get a bowl of noodle soup to drink, and young trainees only have two meals of thin gruel a day. Even so, if they hope to become party members, they must always give the exemplary answer 'I have enough'." This indiscreet champion of egalitarianism was sacked from the party, and later lost his life. But Lan P'ing suffered no hardship, and was even inspired, it seems, to try and become an even closer follower of Mao Tsetung.

Mao had always written poetry, and now that he had a little peace and leisure he was keen to mix again with literary people. He lectured to the Academy of Arts, and one day Lan P'ing, dressed in her neatest uniform, was sitting in the front row of the audience. Mao's entrance was greeted with loud applause. He did not have an intimidating or forbidding air, nor did he condescend or make others feel small. His appearance was reassuring, if unimpressive. He was of medium build, already slightly plump, and he had a yellowish, unhealthy-looking complexion. He wore a soiled and faded grey cotton uniform with the collar unbuttoned, but no cap, and with his long, uncombed hair he scarcely looked like a man of political authority and military power. He spoke quietly, with a Hunanese accent, and stopped frequently to cough. Nonetheless his exceptionally broad shoulders and long arms, taken with the wart on his chin, were said by soothsayers to denote a man of noble destiny.

Lan P'ing, who had been clapping or taking notes all along, stood up to ask questions when he concluded. He answered her slowly, complimenting her for being so attentive. His third marriage had been broken by the ordeal of the Long March. His wife was a sick woman, and Mao had packed her off to Moscow for mental treatment. He was living alone.

Not long after this first encounter, Lan P'ing's latest pro-

* Wang Shih-wei.

5

tector in the Academy of Arts fell in love with a Chinese woman writer who had just returned from the Soviet Union. Lan P'ing told others coldly that it was all one to her, and her meaning became clear when K'ang Sheng arranged for her to leave the Academy and look after Mao's archives. She appeared to be delighted to be able to exchange Hsu Yi-hsin, who was nearly ten years older than she was, for Mao, who was twenty years older, and she was soon very pregnant.

Lan P'ing ceased to exist. Mao gave her the name of Chiang Ch'ing ("River Green"), and from 1940 onwards they lived together openly. She bore him two daughters who were called Li Na and Li Min (she herself had started out in life as Li Ch'ing-yun). But hers was a sweet-and-sour triumph. She had reached the top, yet once again those around her resented her latest liaison, for Mao had been much criticised for jettisoning his previous wife, and other party leaders had first to be cajoled and then almost bludgeoned into agreeing that he could marry Chiang Ch'ing. Apart from K'ang Sheng, she had almost no friends. Her acquaintances in literary and art circles looked down on her and called her bogus behind her back.

Her trouble was that as the companion of a Communist leader who had fought for the southern Soviets and then made the gruelling Long March to Yenan, she was out of her league. Men measured her against women like the wife of Chu Te, "Father of the Red Army", who as a Communist Youth cadre organised her own guerrilla band of young people armed with axes and sickles at the age of sixteen, and rallied with it to her future husband's forces when he joined Mao Tsetung in the hills of Kiangsi. After her marriage, this backwoods Boadicea still took personal command of operations against the KMT, and accompanied Chu Te on the trek north. She was to become political commissar for the headquarter units of the Red Army that fought the Japanese, and later national director of the work department of the All-China Federation of Democratic Women; at Yenan she had an air of untamed toughness that seemed to reduce the integrity of the starlet from Shanghai to cardboard.

At the other end of the scale was the wife of Li Fu-ch'un, later a vice-premier of the Communist government in Peking, who had been trained in Moscow and was now in charge of all women's organisations in Communist-controlled China. She was a robust, determined, practical, very outspoken intellectual, capable of putting up with the harshest conditions, and she was nicknamed "The Female Tutor".

Then there was the wife of Chou En-lai, a plump, untidily-dressed woman with short hair and a warm smile, whose appearance concealed a cool, calculating mind. She had worked underground with Chou in China in her teens, had accompanied him to Paris and helped found the party there, and had been with him on the Long March. She was by now Vice-Chairman of the All-China Federation of Democratic Women, and she was to go further. She had a shrewd brain and a natural talent for politics, and many say that today she is frequently behind the skilful and agile diplomacy of her husband in party and international affairs. With these three grand revolutionaries around her, Chiang Ch'ing inevitably felt a certain constraint and a frustrating sense of inferiority.

Two years after the Japanese surrender in 1945, the Chinese Nationalists seized Yenan itself, and the Red leaders were forced to disperse and flee. But less than three uneasy yet exhilarating years after that, the KMT were defeated, the Communists were masters of all China, and Chiang Ch'ing found herself installed in an elegant quarter of Peking reserved for party chiefs. Life was to continue to be frustrating, however. While her own days were uneventful and even dull, Chiang Ch'ing could only watch as Mao organised the successive campaigns to reshape and discipline Chinese society which slowly eroded his popularity among many of his own prestigious comrades, including Liu Shao-ch'i.

The "two different lines" in the Chinese Communist Party sprang from disagreements over ideology and policy between Mao and Liu. But Liu was at that time the rightful and accepted heir of Mao, and his challenge, therefore, must not be construed as a bid for power. According to Marxist doctrine, the capitalist state must first pass through a socialist stage before this in turn gives way to the final classless communist society. Liu Shao-ch'i's theory was that the capitalists should be allowed to develop industry to a point of over-productivity, from which socialism would then emerge as naturally as "water goes down a drain and the ripe melon falls from the stalk".[1] But Mao protested that this would simply slow down the revolutionary process.

In the countryside, Liu urged that China should emulate the Russian system of agriculture which was the product of long years of experience in the Soviet Union, and create highly-mechanised collectives all over the country, so that the modern machinery would "lead the peasants by their noses".[2] The impatient Mao, on the other hand, held that agricultural cooperatives should be formed first without waiting for the machines, which could come later. He described any cautious lingering in the capitalist stage as a sign of backwardness, as "fearing wolves in front and tigers behind", or as progressing like " a woman swaying about on bound feet".[3]

Liu Shao-ch'i's policy had the approval of the majority in the Central Committee of the party, but in 1958 Mao launched his ill-conceived Great Leap Forward in industry and agriculture. In small towns and villages throughout the country uninstructed workers were obliged to leave their fields and files in order to make backyard "steel", hammer out spades and hoes, even laboriously copy foreign cars, piece by piece. In factories men and machines were overtaxed to a point of collapse as the urban cadres strove to increase output every month, and the fields were over-ploughed, over-sown and over-fertilised until many eroded as the rural cadres tried to multiply the usual yield by three, four, even five. The country was soon choked with phoney statistics, reject pig-iron, and mounds of rusting rubbish waiting to be moved by an inadequate transport system that was cracking apart under the strain.

Meanwhile the new network of "people's communes" was spreading rapidly across the country, for Mao wanted the entire population to be organised into these vast collectives within which peasants would eat in communal mess halls, march to and from their fields in brigades, and live in barracks instead of homes (once they were built). Private possessions would be pooled – even family cooking-pots would be melted down to make cauldrons for the canteens. The entire output of the commune would belong to the commune.

Mao was trying to take a short cut to both industrial power and the communist Utopia. A new, selfless, emancipated man would arise who would be farmer, backyard metal-worker and soldier all in one, so that the communes would be not only classless, but self-reliant. And as the peasant was to be an artisan and a soldier, a militiaman who would take his rifle to his work

8

and be trained to defend his commune, so the soldier must also be a comprehensive communist – ready to haul in the harvest, build irrigation canals, work on the bench.

But Mao was asking for angels. Deprived of all personal incentive, the Chinese peasant too often behaved like a peasant, and slacked off. The Chinese soldier, faced with some back-breaking civilian chore for which he had not joined the army, too often thought in the words of a soldier. Natural calamities aggravated the ruinous decline of the economy, and after the first lean, dangerous year Mao, bitterly criticised by his colleagues for having tried to do too much too soon, had to agree to call a halt and let Liu Shao-ch'i clear up the mess. The "revisionists" – often hypocritically deferential to Mao's face – proceeded to build up their own bureaucratic strength in the party apparatus while unpicking much that Mao had done.

The revolution slowed down. The huge, clumsy agricultural communes became communes in name only. The peasants worked collectively in smaller and more practical production brigades, and were allowed to cultivate their own plots and to rear pigs and poultry on the side, selling their produce in local free markets. Fixed quantities of grain had to be supplied to the commune, but the farmers were given a direct stake in the marketing of the rest of the crop, sharing the profits – or bearing the losses. Material gain was once more the incentive for increased production. The peasant, listless under a system that had demanded selfless communal service, was back in business and went to work with a will.

Mao was a visionary and an idealist, and his opponents were not anti-communists, but pragmatists. They were not anti-Marx, but anti-Mao – not Mao the leader, but Mao the idea. The revolution was important and a communist society their ultimate aim, but times had changed since the days of Ching-kangshan. They therefore believed that at this stage:

the revolution should not be hastened at the expense of the economy;
political indoctrination should not be so intense that work, technical training, and production suffered;
workers and peasants needed incentives and a modicum of material prosperity;
the defence of China should depend on professional and

modern forces – not on a "hostile sea" of underarmed
infantry and peasant militia;
China should be friendly with the Soviet Union and be
prepared to co-exist with the rest of the world. She needed
foreign aid and foreign know-how.

Mao's other adversary was the generation gap. A new China
was growing up which had no memory of the blood-and-iron
days of guerrilla war, of the iniquities of oppressive landlords
and the evils of the Kuomintang. The young did not know how
much worse things had been before, but only how unsatisfactory
they were now. They wanted jam today, and they threatened to
grow up as natural allies of the pragmatists.

But from where Mao stood, Liu's policy was as backward as
Soviet "revisionism", and a betrayal of the revolution. To
uphold his own ideology and dignity and to make his "Thought"
the only orthodox text for the Chinese Communist Party, he
set out to discredit Liu Shao-ch'i completely. Once more Peking
was to be the centre of a "policy struggle" that the world would
inevitably misname a "power struggle".

These were anxious days for Mao, but there was nothing that
his politically lightweight consort could do for him. Moreover,
while other leaders took their wives on visits abroad or
tours of China, sight-seeing during the day, banqueting at
night, always welcomed and applauded by adulatory officials
and drummed-up crowds, Chiang Ch'ing went nowhere. The
gregarious life she would have enjoyed so much was denied her,
and Mao himself, it seemed, was slipping. Chiang Ch'ing's
bitterness towards his detractors and their upstage wives can
be imagined. But it was also evident that Mao must strike back
at his opponents, and soon he found his point of attack.

A dramatist had written an historical play called *Hai Jui
Dismissed from Office*, whose hero was obviously the counterpart of the disgraced Defence Minister P'eng Te-huai, and
whose villain was therefore obviously meant to be Mao (in
China writers often call in the past in order to chastise the
present). Mao seems to have decided that it would be pointless
to ban the offending piece, and that what was needed was a
general "rectification" of the theatre. He had an expert in the
family, for Chiang Ch'ing had been trying to revolutionise
drama even in the early fifties, and at the end of 1962 he set

10

her the task of cleaning up the opera. Armed with her husband's political coaching, Chiang Ch'ing threw herself into the work impetuously like one released from a trap. Gathering young actors around her, she once cried: "Why is it that no one wants to see you act? In your plays are there any red scarves, any young students? No, all the characters are about forty years old. On the stages of a socialist society we are acting plays about emperors and aristocrats. Where is our ideal of democracy? You must accomplish what others have not done before," she urged them, " you must cut your way through these brambles!"[4]

After years of hard work, of persuading young people in the world of the theatre of the validity of Mao's thoughts, Chiang Ch'ing managed to uproot the "poisonous weeds" of bourgeois drama, and to cultivate in their place a few rectified "fragrant flowers". By 1970 two ballets and four modern Peking operas – new, or revised to include suitable Maoist content about revolutionary struggle – were being successfully staged across the country (despite dry lyrics and monotonous music). Earlier, Chiang Ch'ing took Mao to see the ballet *The Red Detachment of Women* in which at one point the actors sing "The Red Sun rises from the East, Mao Tsetung puts on his green uniform. The more you look at him, the more magnificent he is, his whole body filled with strength . . ." while a red sun like a burning ball rises behind the backdrop. Mao gave it his enthusiastic approval, but literary circles in the capital complained "these modern operas are like plain water" (without taste). When this reached her ears, Chiang Ch'ing retorted: "Such people are really naïve. What is wrong with plain water? Only with plain water can tea be brewed or wine distilled."[5]

People found her energy and enthusiasm somewhat overpowering – even downright irksome. According to one Peking opera star: "She spends sleepless nights studying every sentence of the dialogue and singing the lines very carefully, committing them to memory while someone takes notes beside her. She thinks minutely about what dresses we should wear, even where the patches on them should be. The jacket of Auntie Chang and the trimmings of her trousers do not escape her attention, and the shoes with red woollen balls on them worn by soldiers of the New 4th Army on the stage are Chiang Ch'ing's creation."

In the initial stages of this reformation, the Peking party

committee and propaganda department tried to sabotage Chiang Ch'ing's campaign. Difficulties would suddenly arise about the suitability or availability of actors for her plays. The Communists regard the pen as complementary to the sword, however, and the party's propaganda department in Peking, responsible for all literature, art, and publicity media, was a formidable weapon in its own right. In Mao's eyes, therefore, those who misused that weapon had to be destroyed.

In the autumn of 1965 Mao and Chiang Ch'ing moved to Shanghai, the only place where the "rectified" modern operas had received wholehearted support, for anti-Maoist control of Peking was now said to be so fingertight that there was no room for Mao "to put in a needle". From Shanghai, assisted by Lin Piao, the Chairman plotted the nationwide showdown with his "revisionist" adversaries that was to be called the Great Cultural Revolution, and before long the party was openly split between the "Proletarian Headquarters" of Mao and the "Bourgeois Headquarters" of Liu Shao-ch'i.

The coming offensive was heralded, significantly, by an attack in November 1965 on the author of *Hai Jui Dismissed from Office*, and by May of the following year Mao had smashed the Peking party committee and eliminated its "anti-Maoist chief",* who was accused of sponsoring the iniquitous playwright and of trying to establish his own "impenetrable independent kingdom" in the capital. Mao was able to turn the tables all the more promptly on his adversaries, because in the spring of 1966 President Liu ill-advisedly went on a tour abroad, whereupon Lin Piao arranged for troops he trusted to move in and dominate Peking, and the Chairman and his wife themselves returned to the city.

But it was in August 1966 that Mao's wider strategy became clear. Since the young of China were in danger of falling under the influence of Russian "modern revisionism", whose product was a Soviet society led by a new bourgeoisie more interested in washing-machines than world revolution, they had to be revitalised politically. Accordingly, they were turned into "Red Guards" and given licence to go out on the rampage as the spearhead of an offensive by the revolutionary masses against the "black gang" of anti-Maoists who were "taking the capitalist road".

* P'eng Chen.

Millions of fervent, discontented Chinese students itching for action were organised into a gigantic force to confront the great bureaucratic pyramid at the top of which stood President Liu and his immediate lieutenants. All educational institutions from primary school to university were shut down throughout the country so that the young could pour out into the streets to "make revolution" and overthrow the old order. Mao confided the manipulation of this mass movement to a "Cultural Revolution Group" in Peking, and the group was dominated by Chiang Ch'ing, who was officially its deputy director and – a little later – "adviser" to the parallel organisation within the PLA.

The teenage Red Guards of China began their revolutionary careers in a frenzy of destructive hatred aimed at all things bourgeois – foreign, religious, artistic, or traditional. Sexagenarian white nuns were bullied and baited, temples defiled, treasures of China's imperial past torn from their settings and broken up. But then the Guards were joined by workers organised as "revolutionary rebels", and together they turned upon the main targets of the onslaught – the cadres and bureaux throughout the provinces that made up the administrative and political framework of the republic.

The country was plastered with posters and wall-newspapers denouncing the "revisionist" leaders under Liu and all their minions, and at eight mass rallies in Peking eleven million Red Guards from all over China roared their allegiance to Mao, waved the little red book that contained his Thoughts, and swore damnation to his ideological enemies. Looking down on the vast, ever-moving sea of faces, the great portraits of Mao, the slogans and the flags, Chiang Ch'ing appeared almost intoxicated by the awesome sense of power and the earsplitting waves of adultation. At the eighth rally the temperature was below freezing point, but she still took part in a tour of the huge mob spread out across the centre of the city, standing up in an open command car and whipped by a piercing north wind but flushed with obvious elation. She was mistress of this colossal movement, of which the hundreds of thousands of young people assembled at that moment in Peking represented only a fraction.

A Russian who watched her at a student rally at this time wrote afterwards: "Chiang Ch'ing's slim-waisted figure, dressed in a close-fitting green army uniform, was constantly in motion.

13

The army cap and the large spectacles she wore gave her an imposing and serious look. But she appeared very youthful. No one would think she was already past fifty. Hiding behind a courteous tone, she would constantly interrupt speakers with her own remarks, manifesting in every way her 'revolutionary zeal'. Her own speech twisted the audience around her little finger until it was absolutely incandescent. Crudely flattering the young people, exploiting their lack of experience and their thirst for activity, Chiang Ch'ing evoked from them delusions of their own importance, their position, and their role."[6]

Her stifled ambitions to act were suddenly released, and she showed a very real flair for whipping the young into blind and bloody-minded fury, so that in the end her appearances had to be rationed. "What are you afraid of?" she once yelled. "At the worst you will only suffer from knife-cuts or bullets." The texts of her speeches could afterwards be produced as false evidence of her own sweet reasonableness, but they had a serpentine quality of their own, for while she would smoothly preach moderation at first in order to allay the fears of the pragmatists, she would often conclude by suddenly stinging her audience into violent action. In this way she incited the Red Guards to seize the wife* of President Liu Shao-ch'i, for while Mao might speak to these "little red devils" of the need for nationwide class struggle, it soon became evident that Chiang Ch'ing also had a personal score or two to settle.

The excited Red Guards lured the unsuspecting Madame Liu from her house by telephoning her to say that her daughter had been seriously hurt in a car accident. She was then seized and taken to Tsinghua University for "trial", insulted and bullied, accused of being an American spy, and forced to dance in a "bourgeois" cheongsam. She was younger, more attractive and better educated than her jealous tormentor, who had publicly called her a prostitute and a capitalist and the daughter of a toady. Several of the great ladies of Red China, including the "Female Tutor", simply went to ground at this time, but at the home of Chu Te, Red Guards found a few pots of Chinese orchids which had been raised by his wife, whereupon Chiang Ch'ing accused that tough old revolutionary amazon of bourgeois corruption and frivolous depravity, and had her dragged out into the street for another public "trial".

---

* Wang Kuang-mei.

14

These were not the only ones to suffer. The "revolutionaries" ransacked, looted and sometimes half-wrecked the homes of senior officials and their wives. Other victims had dunces' caps clapped on their heads and placards hung around their necks reading "I am a counter-revolutionary", and were then forced to run through the streets, hitting themselves as they went, or to kneel down to the Red Guards and beg for forgiveness. Among those who received this treatment was Chiang Ch'ing's former boy-friend, the film director.

There was one other woman in the ascendant at this moment, and she was, moreover, the wife of the man with whom Chiang Ch'ing was inevitably developing a bitter if furtive feud – Lin Piao, Mao's heir-designate and "closest comrade-in-arms". Her name was Yeh Ch'un, but although she was to become a full member of the Politburo in Peking, she appeared to have neither the ability of the wife of Liu Shao-ch'i nor the daring and malice of Madame Mao. When seen in public, her movements were often clumsy and uncoordinated, as if she were a lifeless robot, and on one occasion during the Cultural Revolution at which Chiang Ch'ing was addressing representatives of the "rebel" masses, she shouted "Protect Chiang Ch'ing" seventeen times over, and earned herself the nickname of "The Slogan-shouting Expert".

Yeh Ch'un was only important because Lin Piao was important, however, for in spite of the much-advertised equality between men and women in China, most wives rise and fall with their husbands. Chiang Ch'ing was a senior member of the Politburo by 1972, but will she still be a piece on the board once Mao dies?

During the Cultural Revolution she aroused a cold hostility in Lin Piao, Mao's appointed heir, when she turned her "rebels" against PLA commanders who stood in her way. But among Chinese the balance-sheet of grudge and debt can always be gracefully adjusted, even fudged, and several scapegoats have since been sacrificed to atone for the excessive zeal of Chiang Ch'ing. It must also be recalled that in the past she has collaborated closely with the military. The army under Lin Piao put Maoist doctrine before military drill, and the political education of the troops through "cultural work" became particularly important in the mid-sixties, when the whole country was urged to "Learn from the PLA". Chiang Ch'ing

15

was therefore made adviser to the forces, and took a hand in everything from "revolutionising" their literature to arranging for the best Peking opera company to be inducted into them.

Any prediction about Chiang Ch'ing must take into account that she is not just one attractive, vivacious, quick-witted, spiteful little woman with a chip on her shoulder, and she is not just a wife who may inherit the aura of her husband if she becomes a widow. She will be the leader of the left-wing, of the true Maoist revolutionaries who despise the *status quo*, whose loyalty belongs to the "proletarian headquarters", and whose spiritual home is in many ways not Peking but the great city of Shanghai, where power was still held in 1972 by the Brain and the Trigger-Finger that had detonated the Cultural Revolution in the first place.

The Brain and the Trigger-Finger

It was Shanghai that first acclaimed Chiang Ch'ing's proletarian stage productions, it was to Shanghai that she and Mao Tsetung withdrew to plan the assault on President Liu Shao-ch'i and the revisionists in 1965, and it was in Shanghai that the "January Revolution" of 1967 exploded. This was no coincidence, for Mao has always regarded the great port and city in which he attended the first congress of the Chinese Communist Party half a century ago as a citadel of urban revolt against the "bourgeois-reactionaries".

In January 1967 the Red Guards and "revolutionary rebels" in Shanghai took over the city's three main newspapers and launched a savage offensive against the municipal government and party committee, accusing them of conspiring with Liu Shao-ch'i. "In accordance with Chairman Mao's teaching that it is right to rebel," announced the local *Wen Hui Pao* in an inflammatory editorial on the sixth of the month, "the revolutionary rebels raise high the great revolutionary flag against those party persons in authority who are taking the capitalist road, striking them with speed and violence, for they swear to defend Chairman Mao with their lives. For him they would climb a mountain of swords, cross a sea of fire, having no fear of Heaven, no fear of the earth, no fear of devils, no fear of gods, no fear of being surrounded, no fear of being attacked . . ."*

This high-flown piece of rhetoric was the clarion call from the Maoist leadership for the masses to seize power, and from Shanghai it rang out across all China. On the day the editorial appeared, a million rebels rallied in the city to overthrow the administration, and one month later their leaders proclaimed a "Shanghai People's Commune", which was to be organised "in line with the Thoughts of Chairman Mao and conforming to the principles of the dictatorship of the proletariat".

---

* Condensed.

49157   951.05   Brescia College Library
BG55   Owensboro, Kentucky

Shanghai had pointed the way, and by 22 January the *People's Daily* in Peking was already urging the masses everywhere: "Seize power, seize power, seize power. Smash the old bureaucratic system. Workers and peasants, revolutionary intellectuals and revolutionary cadres must be their own masters and set up a new proletarian order." The jacks-in-office of the Communist establishment were to be flung on the dustheap not only in government and administration, and in cities and county towns, but in every farming commune and factory. The model for the rebels was to be the brief, ill-starred Paris Commune of 1871 which burst into existence when the French mob seized the capital, threw its administration out of office, and proceeded both to hire and fire their replacements by popular vote. "The spirit of the Paris Commune boils down to direct elections on a mass scale with 95 per cent participation," Premier Chou En-lai explained.[1]

The Shanghai Commune was an achievement of historical importance. For why had Mao called his own group the "revolutionaries" and his opponents the "powerholders"? And if the powerholders were only a "small handful", as he had said, why did he not simply evict them from office by constitutional means? The explanation seems to be that Mao wished to put the blame for the failure of his "Three Red Flag" campaign (national construction based on the Great Leap Forward, the people's communes, and the general revolutionary line of Mao Tsetung) on to President Liu and the "revisionist" hierarchy. To do this he had to show that he himself had been deprived of authority, that Liu and his friends had held the real power in China and had mismanaged and even sabotaged his programmes.

Mao therefore began by ostensibly representing a minority opposed to a majority. The Cultural Revolution was to ensure that the minority expanded into a majority, and that the majority shrank to a minority – the "small handful taking the capitalist road". The Maoists could only achieve this by triggering an insurrection of the millions. Accordingly, the masses "seized power" in Shanghai and it was for the rest of the country to emulate them.

Mao and Lin Piao soon seem to have had second thoughts, however. The "rebels" were destructive, incoherent, split into factions, while the strength of the revisionists had been under-

18

estimated. If the practices of the Paris Commune were adopted, and officials could be sacked and replaced any time the mob willed, there could be no guarantee that a majority of Maoists would be elected everywhere. The whole process now threatened to become too democratic for comfort. The "Shanghai Commune" therefore became the "Shanghai Revolutionary Committee" – a product of a "three-way alliance" of representatives drawn from the "rebel" mass organisations, the local military, and the "revolutionary" (meaning politically acceptable) cadres of the old bureaucracy. There was no more talk of "95 per cent participation" of the people in general elections to decide who would belong to it. Instead, there was "democratic consultation" among the immediately interested parties – in short, horse-trading and compromise at the top.

The Shanghai Revolutionary Committee thus became the prototype for a nationwide mesh of similar bodies that replaced the old discredited system of provincial government. Not surprisingly, it was slow to come into being. The rebels were bumptious and divided among themselves, the local military commanders had no intention of letting this ragtag rule them, and the old cadres were distrusted by the revolutionaries, yet were needed for their expertise. The "January Revolution" had nonetheless set the example for all China, and behind that revolution were the two men at the top of the Shanghai committee who had acted respectively as Brain* and Trigger-Finger. The trigger-finger was Yao Wen-yuan, an editor of the *Wen Hui Pao*, a member of the Cultural Revolution Group under Chiang Ch'ing, and a man about whom Chinese speculate more than any other individual.

Before the Cultural Revolution, Yao was known as a young and dynamic literary critic with a ruthless pen and an unswerving belief in Mao's ideas. As an official of the Shanghai Writers' Association, he was a key man in the organisation through which the Communists controlled literary output, and during the fifties and early sixties he also wrote for two periodicals† whose role was to mould the thinking of intellectuals, as well as for the *Liberation Daily*, the organ of the Shanghai party committee, of which he also became editor.

He was feared for his sparkling, vehement articles, in which

---

* Chang Ch'un-ch'iao. See further.
† *Literature and Art Journal* and *Literature and Art Monthly*.

he attacked bourgeois habits and belaboured individuals in literary and artistic circles for their political sins, for those at whom he struck soon found themselves undergoing "reform-through-labour" in mines, farms and factories. Some called him "The Big Club", because at one stroke he could kill the career of a victim who had incurred his ideological wrath. Spitefully prudish, he was a writer who made his reputation by black-guarding other writers, and he was widely hated. His vitriolic condemnation of the anti-Maoist play *Hai Jui Dismissed from Office* was to be described as the first shot fired in the Cultural Revolution. He also denounced the works of the doomed T'ao Chu,[2] who had climbed to fourth position in the party hierarchy only to plunge back into political oblivion.

Yao had little to do with the party organisation before the Cultural Revolution, and his political strength lay in his pen. In particular he acted as the literary right arm of a mayor of Shanghai* who was early involved in a fierce struggle with the local phalanx loyal to President Liu Shao-ch'i. The mouthpiece of this staunch Maoist, who called Liu an opportunist and accused him of plotting rebellion within the party, Yao was therefore above reproach himself. He had never written a line on behalf of Liu or his chief henchman, the Party Secretary-General Teng Hsiao-p'ing, and when Mao wanted a trustworthy mob-rouser in Shanghai, Yao was the obvious choice. He took his cue from Chiang Ch'ing from the outset, yet he was one of the few members of the Cultural Revolution Group in the party whose dismissal Lin Piao did not encompass during his feud with Mao's wife.

This feud was part of a pattern of personal rivalry and political dispute at the top that was projected on to the map of China as a perplexing tangle of violence and disorder, until Mao realised that the licence granted to the young Red Guards must finally be cancelled. In August 1968, therefore, he instructed Yao Wen-yuan to write an article in the authoritative *Red Flag* indicating that youth had had its fling, and that the destiny of China must now be shaped by its adult proletariat.

Yao's article was headlined "The Working Class must exercise leadership in everything", and it was the signal for "Mao Tsetung Thought Propaganda Teams" to move into all organisa-

---

* K'o Ch'ing-shih.

tions from schools to steel-plants in order to control students and intellectuals and to teach all men to "combat selfishness and repudiate revisionism". It naturally pleased the local soldiers, who were sick of having their authority flouted by iconoclastic teenagers in the mass and soon dominated the propaganda teams themselves. Yao thus won the approval of the military as well as of Mao, and that may partly explain why he has survived where all but three others of the prominent figures around Chiang Ch'ing have seemingly sunk without trace.

But only partly. Yao seems to have a special relationship with Mao, and apart from Chiang Ch'ing he is the only member of the party's Central Committee who can go directly to the Chairman himself for his personal endorsement and signature on documents. His closeness to Mao has given rise to many strange tales. Chinese-language broadcasts from Moscow have claimed that he is the husband of Chiang Ch'ing's daughter Li Na,[3] and so Mao's son-in-law. Others insist that Yao is the son of Mao. But the story of Mao's marriages and offspring is as bewildering as it is sad.

According to one account, when Mao was still very young his father obliged him to wed a girl of his parents' choice who was four years older than himself. He left her after two childless years, but in 1919 married the daughter of a famous left-wing professor in Peking, and they had three sons – Mao An-ying, Mao An-ch'ing and Mao An-lung. When An-ying was eight years old, he and his mother were caught by the Kuomintang and throw into prison in Changsha. His mother was executed, but he was released, and relatives sent him to Shanghai together with his two brothers to live with an uncle. In 1932 the Nationalists carried out an intensive search for Communists living underground in the city, and the children were forced to take to the streets and become vagrants, selling newspapers, collecting cigarette ends and sleeping on pavements. However, the youngest boy, An-lung, was smuggled out to safety, and when Communist agents finally found An-ying and An-ch'ing and took them to Yenan to join their father five years later, he was not with them.

An-ying was sent to the Soviet Union to study but was subsequently killed in Korea. An-ch'ing was mentally sick. At the Lu Shan conference in 1959 Mao remarked bitterly of his sons "one of them is dead, and one of them is mad".[4] But he did not mention the youngest, An-lung. Many now say that Yao Wen-yuan is in fact Mao An-lung, and although this confident, broad-shouldered writer, with lustrous eyes and a pen like a dagger, is formally recognised as the son of a left-wing writer named Yao Feng-tzu, the story goes that it was to this man that Mao confided him during the dangerous days of 1932, and that Yao Feng-tzu brought him up as his own child.

In 1969 the "Peking United Revolutionary Rebel Headquarters" suddenly gave it out that the real An-lung, lost for more than thirty years, had been located, and had returned to Mao's native village in Hunan after working in a commune in Kiangsu. But many Chinese remain convinced that Yao is the son – legitimate or otherwise – of the Chairman. He is a member of the Politburo, and the fact that, contrary to the usual Communist practice, no attempt has been made to publicise and glorify his past in spite of his high position in the hierarchy, is taken as confirmatory evidence.*

However, they scoff at Western conjecture that when Mao dies Yao may take his place. For even if Yao is Mao's blood-relative, they cannot see him in the role of Malenkov, who inherited Stalin's mantle in the Soviet Union. It is always dangerous to draw comparisons between the Russian and Chinese communist revolutions. The Russian revolution was led by the proletariat in the towns, but when the Chinese Communist Party was formed in 1921 the level of technology was low and industrial workers were few. The party was formed by a handful of intellectuals, and it gained power by mobilising the peasantry for armed struggle. In post-revolutionary Russia (as in any Western democracy) the army was kept firmly in its place, and when Stalin died, a series of civilians – Malenkov, Khrushchev, Brezhnev – became the new masters of the Kremlin. But in China success had from the first depended on the soldiers, and men who succeed Mao without his mystique must rely on firm backing from commanders of the PLA.

The situation was reflected in the delicate interplay between the Maoist leadership and the army in Yao Wen-yuan's own city. Hsu Shih-yu, Commander of the Nanking Military Region that includes Shanghai, wanted the cachet of Mao's approval, but not the inconvenience of his revolutionary instructions.

---

* See Appendix to this chapter (page 208).

22

On his side, Mao needed the support of the army, and in particular he and Chiang Ch'ing wanted to safeguard the revolutionary crucible of Shanghai. By 1971 a tacit understanding had been reached. The commander did not suppress the "rebel" masses more than he felt strictly necessary, but he did not carry out Mao's orders to support them more than seemed strictly necessary either. And there was no outcry. Chiang Ch'ing urged the man who had been the Brain behind the "January Revolution" to keep an eye on the commander and try to woo him further, and the commander for his part put one of his most trusted officers* into the Shanghai party committee in order to keep an eye on the Brain, having first posted away from the city those subordinates who were too prone to sympathise with the Cultural Revolution.

By 1972 Shanghai was otherwise a conspicuous exception to the general rule that the military prevailed in the new party committees in China's 29 provincial divisions. The first secretary was the Brain, Chang Ch'un-ch'iao, the second secretary was the Trigger-Finger, Yao Wen-yuan, and they were both, like Chiang Ch'ing herself, full members of the Politburo in Peking. These "extremists" of the Cultural Revolution Group were still to the fore, therefore, and Shanghai remained their stronghold. But what role the city would play in the future might depend on the slightly equivocal loyalties and tactics of the Brain.

Chang is in his early sixties, but his precise date of birth is not known and his story is obscure. He was a member of the left-wing Shanghai Writers Association in the thirties, and he worked as a propagandist in one of the Red guerrilla Soviets of North China during the war. Once the Nationalists had been defeated, he returned to Shanghai, where he established the local *Liberation Daily* and took over the offices of the Central News Agency for all East China. His ruthless witch-hunting for "rightists" earned him valuable notoriety, but he carefully cultivated young writers loyal to the message of their master in Peking, of whom by far the most important was Yao Wen-yuan. These were the foundations of his cultural empire, which eventually extended over not only the local press, but literature, the theatre, general education, and the propagation of the Thought of Mao. By 1964 he was a secretary

---

* Chou Shun-lin.

of the Shanghai party committee and director of its propaganda department.

Then came what was to prove his real break. Rebuffed in Peking, a resentful Chiang Ch'ing brought her first reformed Peking operas to Shanghai, and Chang the Brain at once gave her unstinted support (he helped her to revise one of them twelve times). Once Mao had moved from Peking to Shanghai in 1965, Chang also helped Yao Wen-yuan to polish his attack on the play *Hai Jui Dismissed from Office*. It was hardly surprising, therefore, that Chang should subsequently turn up in the capital as a deputy director of the Cultural Revolution Group and a member of Mao's fourteen-man "proletarian headquarters".

Back in Shanghai once again at the beginning of 1967, he was the mind behind the "January Revolution", and the proclamation of the "Shanghai Commune". He emerged from the ferment as Chairman of the Shanghai Revolutionary Committee and political commissar of the Nanking Military Region. To the astonishment of many observers, he now came under fire from the left, and was denounced as a renegade and a materialist who was trying to consolidate his own independent kingdom in Shanghai, and was reversing the stern verdicts the revolutionary rebels had passed on those "taking the capitalist road". Yet Chang himself was tirelessly urging fellow-intellectuals to develop a "world proletarian outlook" and to serve the workers, peasants and soldiers. The accusations plainly appeared unjust. Were they? It has been suggested that once he became local Chairman, Chang had something to conserve rather than something to destroy, and no longer wanted others to "seize power". But that is not all.

There is another side to this long-faced, myopic man with the cold, contemplative air. He is cautious and calculating, and during the Cultural Revolution he not only did the bidding of the Maos, but energetically denounced the bourgeois tendencies and the revisionism of the benighted Russians, as was then fashionable. Yet he had not always thought along these lines. After a tour of the Soviet Union in 1945 he produced *A Notebook of Observations and Experiences in Russia* in which he extolled their affluence and the benefits of bourgeois living. "In the Soviet Union," he wrote, "workers change their clothes after work and it is as if they had been transformed into different beings. In a cultural hall in one of Stalin's car factories, we came across a group of teenagers having a party. They were all dressed neatly and prettily and they were dancing gaily. Communists are not born lovers of poverty, a socialist state is not necessarily a poor society. In fact, on the contrary, we are born to create a rich communist society."

On his return to Shanghai after one such visit, he told factory workers: "Let us build up heavy industries, and when our production has increased, we shall all prosper together. Then we, too, can line up for the things we manufactured ourselves, the watches, the radios, the carpets, and so on." Every member of the group with which he had visited Russia had in fact been given a watch and a radio, so that, as one of their Russian hosts told them slyly, "Whenever our Chinese comrades think of us, they will be able to switch on the radio and hear the voice of Moscow." The Brain also regarded Khrushchev with reverence, and during the Cultural Revolution his enemies collected his favourable comments on the Soviet Union and sent them to Mao, accusing Chang of being a revisionist. But Mao's trust in him was not shaken, and he remained master of Shanghai.

Whether he will heed Mao's exhortations to "be unafraid of hardship" and to refrain from "dabbling in economism" (dealing in material rewards and incentives) once Mao himself is no longer there is open to question. By 1971 he was already playing his cards carefully. He was not becoming involved directly in squabbles between the revolutionary mass organisations and anti-Maoist groups whom he knew to have the covert backing of local military commanders. He merely passed on instructions from Mao and the Central Committee in Peking at formal meetings in Shanghai, leaving all dangerous discussion to Yao Wen-yuan. He appeared to have no desire to rise higher in the capital, or to be closer to Chiang Ch'ing. He was taking pains to remain on good terms with the regional army bosses, because his main object was evidently to keep his position at the top of the pile in a Maoist or "Maoist" Shanghai, the position he inherited when his predecessor, the former mayor and trusted agent of Mao, died in 1965.

Yao had set his sights higher. While retaining his post in Shanghai his object was almost certainly to worm his way to the top in the party centre in Peking as the champion of Maoism. By 1968 he had become "the person responsible for

Mao Tsetung's office" and one of the fourteen members of the "proletarian headquarters' which had replaced the old, contaminated Politburo. Between October 1968 and January 1969 he rose from 198th position in the hierarchy to eighth position, and in April 1969 he was made a member of the new Politburo. Still only in his forties, he is talented and ambitious, and it remains to be determined whether the revolutionary line-up led by Chiang Ch'ing, and backed by the Brain, the Trigger-Finger and the potentially explosive masses behind them will have real weight, or just nuisance-value, or simply fall apart when the Chairman is gone.

The future of China obviously does not depend on a straight fight between the "revolutionaries" and the soldiers. For one thing, it is impossible to speak simply of "the soldiers", and other forces are also inextricably involved – including most notably the State Council, the Chinese government under the "moderate" Premier Chou En-lai.

3

The Five Smiles of Chou En-lai

After the strident Chiang Ch'ing and the rampaging Red Guards, an apprehensive world observed with relief the emergence of the urbane, practical, wholly plausible Premier Chou En-lai as the obvious man to restore sanity to a sick China exhausted by the paroxysms of the Great Cultural Revolution. The "Smiling Diplomat" has been a reassuring figure since he opened the way to a compromise in Korea, affably extended his hand to John Foster Dulles at the Geneva Conference in 1954 (to have it ignored), and enchanted apprehensive delegates at the Afro-Asian Conference in Bandung the following year with his championship of the "Five Principles of Peaceful Coexistence".

But Chou En-lai has reduced his role as China's moderate, warm, conciliatory, understanding negotiator with the distrustful foreigners beyond her borders to a performance of almost scientific precision, and even his smile is carefully calculated. A Chinese author wrote some years ago: "The five smiles of Chou En-lai are famous within the Politburo. When he meets a Soviet 'elder brother' he gives him a beaming welcome with outstretched arms; when he sees Mao or Liu Shao-ch'i, he gives them a broad grin but his hands remain slack at his sides; when he greets diplomats from capitalist countries his smile is a little aloof as befits a prime minister; when he encounters other members of the Politburo or colleagues of some standing, he offers them a half-grin that moves the upper part of his face only; and when he greets lesser members of the Central Committee or leaders of other parties, the facial muscles relax, but only the skin smiles."[1]

Chou started young as an amateur actor – if he may be described as an amateur at all – and even at school won enthusiastic applause for a performance as a girl. His talent has served him well in difficult circumstances. After the Communists and the Kuomintang had formed a fragile alliance against the Japanese in 1937, Chou played the cordial collaborator at Chiang Kai-shek's headquarters. In 1946 he was still in Chungking, ostensibly trying to preserve the partnership and avert civil war, although Mao had already denounced Chiang as a "Fascist ringleader, autocrat and traitor" from Yenan, and Communist troops had begun to clash with the KMT.

Throughout those uneasy years Chou showed a touching desire to cooperate with the Kuomintang, while Mao struggled against them, and when the exasperated Nationalists questioned him about the apparent contradiction between his smiles and Mao's frowns, Chou overwhelmed them with protests of his sincerity, sometimes shedding tears. His act was convincing, and he won the trust and sympathy of several of the KMT and many Chinese "democrats" whose softened attitude towards the Communists later hastened the final disintegration of their own side.

Chou has always had a deceptively tolerant, cosmopolitan air and beguiling good manners that have made him attractive to foreigners. He studied in Paris, he speaks passable French, Russian, and English, and has a notable head for scotch. When younger, he was a good ballroom dancer, and if he entered a room every woman turned to look at him. He loves music and the theatre, and at 74 is a man of nice wit and lively gestures, who often speaks emotionally, and so gives an impression of being frank and intimate in conversation. But Chinese see him as almost a stage-mandarin, with his histrionic wedges of eyebrow and his warm, dangerously sharp eyes. "You make friends," he once said revealingly, "in order to isolate your enemy."

This ruthless flexibility is one of his secrets of survival. When he was in Chungking a mob of students, who were demonstrating against the Russians for plundering Manchuria after the Japanese surrender, turned their fury upon the local Communist mission, and Chou En-lai's office was besieged. "We must be patient," Chou told his staff coolly. "We must be ready to give in to them, and we must at all costs avoid bloodshed. Otherwise we shall be falling into the trap of the enemy. If they break in, we retreat. If they enter the front gate, we withdraw to the hall. If they come into the hall, we go upstairs."[2] His voice held no emotion on this occasion. His decision was reached as coldly as if he had ordered the guards to machine-gun the demonstration instead.

28

Apart from his flair for tactical agility, for adapting to all situations, Chou has a strong sense of the possible, and in fifty years of brutal struggle and sometimes vicious intrigue within the Chinese Communist Party, he has not actively plotted to become master of the movement himself. On the contrary, he has played the lieutenant to a series of leaders, passing nimbly on to the next when the last has fallen from grace. In consequence he not only became Prime Minister and manipulator of China's powerful government and state bureaucracy, but has survived to hold the job for more than twenty years.

Chou comes from Shaohsing in the province of Chekiang, a county renowned for its officials as well as its wine. He was born into a well-bred Confucian family with generations of Imperial mandarins on its ancestral tablets, and his background was feudal, intellectual. His mother read modern books, and he was called En-lai – "Advent of Favour" – to mark his father's success in the civil-service examinations. He was educated at the Westernised Nankai University, where he first plunged into politics and was arrested during the "May Fourth" anti-Japanese student demonstrations in 1919. In 1920 he travelled to Paris under a "work and study" programme organised by a group of Chinese scholars, and was a founder-member of the French branch of the Chinese Communist Party the following year.

He returned to China in 1924. He was already a leading member of the "international" group in the Chinese party, and he was only 26 years old when he was appointed Director of the Political Department of the Whampoa Military Academy of which Chiang Kai-shek was Commandant. It was he who organised the insurrection which enabled Chiang to take Shanghai without trouble during the Northern Expedition to eliminate the old warlords, and when Chiang treacherously ordered the KMT to liquidate the Communists in the city, Chou narrowly escaped execution.

This was the period during which the Comintern was blindly insisting that the industrial proletariat in the towns must lead the revolution. Chou En-lai took part in the Nanchang Uprising, after which he was forced to flee to British Hongkong, and three years later he was in Moscow explaining the failure of a second abortive attack on Changsha. But while successive party leaders were consigned to political oblivion as scapegoats for the dismal consequences of this misguided policy, Chou En-lai got away with no more than a confession of errors at the beginning of 1931 which still left him Director of the Military Affairs Department within the party.[3]

With other members of the Central Committee in Shanghai, he then joined Mao in the mountains of Kiangsi, where a Chinese Soviet Republic was proclaimed, and soon afterwards replaced him as political commissar of the army. Mao had lost control of his troops to this astute newcomer, who was to keep it for more than three years and until they were well embarked on the Long March. However, Chou's military authority was purely formal, derived from a committee decision and the support of the so-called "Twenty-eight Bolsheviks" who propagated the Moscow line. Mao's military power was real. At a conference at Tsunyi in south-west China in January 1935, therefore, Mao asserted himself, and Chou stepped down gracefully – possibly by private arrangement – to give his allegiance to the new master.

From that moment on, Chou progressively abandoned his military role and devoted himself to politics, government and diplomacy. This often meant playing the Kuomintang like a hooked shark after Chiang Kai-shek had been kidnapped at Sian in 1936 and, to gain his own freedom, had been obliged to accept terms for a Communist–KMT alliance against the Japanese from the man he had tried to kill in Shanghai nine years earlier. When the Reds overran all China in 1949, Chou was appointed Prime Minister and Minister for Foreign Affairs. He has been premier ever since.

Behind his amiable exterior and his erstwhile reputation as a formidable drinking companion, Chou En-lai is both physically and mentally tough, an almost indefatigable worker who has been described as "the busiest man in China". He takes no holidays, and frequently rises at dawn to attend an early rally. If he gets up later he will still be in play in the small hours of the following morning – working, negotiating, entertaining, or interviewing until his exhausted interlocutors are ready to drop. For Chou En-lai is a dedicated man, and his deceits must be seen as part of his dedication.

He is the head of the bureaucracy, but no one could accuse him of office-bound "bureaucratism". His spare time is spent in live contact with the masses – workers in factories, young

30

people in university, players backstage. He and his wife have given all their adult years to the party, and they renounced having children until it was too late in order to devote themselves to the business of revolution.

The comparison has already been made between Teng Ying-ch'ao, this small, dowdy, active woman of 69 whom Chou has known since the stormy days of the "May Fourth" incident in 1919, and Mao's wife Chiang Ch'ing. Falling sick with tuberculosis, Madame Chou made the Long March on a stretcher, but after recovering in Yenan, she slipped into Peking to direct the women's underground, escaping in the disguise of a maidservant when the Japanese arrived. She is known to all as "Big Sister". She does not simply bask in the reflected revolutionary glory of her husband, but has been a member of the Central Committee of the party in her own right since 1956.

Her illnesses left her barren, and she and her husband lead a quiet, restricted private life. But although they have no offspring of their own, they have adopted as "godchildren" at least two of the ten born by the formidable and fecund wife of Chu Te. Two other "god-daughters" of Chou, who is an opera and ballet fan, are respectively a well-known singer and an actress.[4] Chou En-lai and his wife have been described as China's "model couple", the "ideal revolutionary pair", and although the malicious have whispered of acrimonious marital exchanges involving the name of a young secretary of the premier, it can be taken that in such matters Chou has been constrained to be prudent by his consideration for his wife, his concern for his reputation and position, and his loyalty to party and state.

Even as a young man, Chou En-lai firmly put revolution before romance. His future wife was with him when he studied and plotted in France, but afterwards Chou also studied and plotted in Germany, and there he fell in love with a German girl who bore him a son. On his return to China, however, he simply set this episode in his life aside as if it had not happened, and a year later he married his communist comrade, Big Sister Teng. They were both devoted to the Chinese revolution. They had "similar aspirations and ideals". Critics condemn Chou for this affair, but he was simply getting his priorities straight – and proving that he had the true "party nature".

To have the "party nature", say the communists, is to recognise clearly that nothing comes before the struggle for socialism. A cadre with resolute "party nature" must work unremittingly to achieve the revolutionary goal, and must closely correlate communist theory and practice when dealing with all problems, so that his thoughts, words and actions are in complete accordance with party principles. This means that it is absolutely impermissible for him to entertain or tolerate in others any "soft-hearted humanism".

The engaging Chou En-lai combines unyielding party nature with a strict sense of the pragmatic, and he demonstrated these qualities in the International Settlement of Shanghai in 1931 when an important secret agent of the Communists was captured and then recruited by the Kuomintang authorities.* The turncoat was a machinist who had been trained in espionage and subversive activities in Moscow. He was also one of the most popular magicians in Shanghai, and a talented actor with a humorous line of patter who enchanted people with his imitation of a white *taipan*, for which he put on a long false nose and whiskers. His gifts were many, for in addition to concealing his true figure and appearance permanently from all but his close comrades-in-clandestinity, he devised a method of shooting a man in a closed room so that those outside heard nothing, and of strangling a man with his bare hands so delicately that no trace was left on the neck.

This remarkable performer had been working in Shanghai since 1927 as head of intelligence under the direction of Wu Hao, then leader of the underground movement, and together they had organised a special "Red Squad"[5] which was responsible for the security of the party's clandestine headquarters in the city and for the punishment of traitors. No one knew how many "comrades" had died at the hands of the magician, who carried in his head the darkest secrets of the party.

As soon as Wu Hao could confirm that this man had betrayed the underground, therefore, he took immediate revenge upon his entire family by having every single member of it executed – his wife, his three children, his brother-in-law, sister-in-law, and parents-in-law, eight persons in all. The corpses were tied together in pairs, head to foot, and buried ten feet below the courtyard of an empty house in a secluded residential area in

---

* Ku Shun-chang.

32

Shanghai's French Concession. Shanghai newspapers carried detailed reports when the bodies were nonetheless found. At the same time the Communists put it about that whoever betrayed the party or Wu Hao's organisation would receive the same treatment, for only if transgressors were most rigorously punished could discipline be preserved, and the cause furthered with maximum efficiency. This was an exemplary demonstration of the "party nature" of Wu Hao, otherwise known as Chou Shao-shan, or Chou En-lai.

Chou En-lai's performance during the period of the Cultural Revolution was true to his own nature as well as that of the party. Before the revolution broke out, he supported the revisionist line of President Liu Shao-ch'i and the Party Secretary-General, Teng Hsiao-p'ing. During the upheaval itself, he faithfully echoed the opposite line of the Chairman's "Proletarian Headquarters" in denouncing it. And when regional army commanders subdued the Red Guards and took over the provincial administration, he became the vital middleman between Lin Piao and these "Red warlords" who looked askance at a Defence Minister that had from the outset connived at the Maoist campaign inciting "revolutionary rebels" to seize power in their fiefs.

The warlords were to be the stepping-stones that would take Chou safely over this turbulent passage in the Chinese revolution. When Huang Yung-sheng, then Commander of the Canton Military Region and leader of the "warlord clique", was violently attacked by Mao's Red Guards, it was Chou En-lai who saved him from humiliation and negotiated his appointment as new chief of staff of the People's Liberation Army. This promised to be the beginning of a most satisfactory alliance for, as head of the government and the third man in the Politburo after Mao and Lin Piao, Chou controlled much of the political and administrative musculature of the country, while Huang could command the loyalty or collusion of much of the PLA. And they had a common objective – an end to the revolutionary convulsions provoked by Mao and Chiang Ch'ing, and a return to practical policies that would make China stable and strong.

Chiang Ch'ing, who believed that the revolt of the Red Guards and revolutionary rebels would carry her to power and glory, incited them to throw the old cadres out of administrative offices ultimately responsible to Chou En-lai, and to attack and seize weapons from the PLA for the purpose of "making revolution". The military, under orders not to intervene in the early stages, could only grin and bear it all and keep their powder dry. But the children of cadres now under fire from Chiang Ch'ing's mobs organised their own fighting factions, proclaimed their own honourable intention of "seizing power" as the masses had been instructed to do, and were soon slugging it out with the extremists.

Chou En-lai, it is believed, discreetly encouraged this rivalry and then stepped in to arbitrate. He did not make the mistake of rebuking the rivals and so incurring their hostility, but pointed out that their conflict could in itself provide a foundation for future compromise. "For," as he very aptly quoted, "unless you fight each other, you cannot know each other."[6] Chou stood between Maoist and "Maoist" revolutionaries, just as he was to stand between Lin Piao and the Red warlords, for the Chinese believe that in any struggle between two forces it is the indispensable mediator who is at once the most powerful and least vulnerable figure.

In 1967 he nonetheless came under attack, because he had protected some of his own cadres when the Red Guards had tried to consign them to limbo. He was described as "the second Khrushchev of China" (Liu Shao-ch'i being the first), as "the time-bomb buried beside Chairman Mao", and as "the rotten boss of the bourgeoisie, toying ambidextrously with counter-revolution". But within a few weeks Chou En-lai had rallied to his support the provincial commanders with Huang Yung-sheng at their head, soldiers sick of the mobs and mess and relieved to find the "Advent of Favour" himself behind them. And after some stiff talk in Peking, evidently, the Cultural Revolution Group was obliged to proclaim: "The Prime Minister is the Chief of Staff of Chairman Mao and Vice-Chairman Lin Piao. The Prime Minister is not to be toppled . . ."[7]

Chou En-lai's counsels had prevailed. The street violence was to stop. When Chou received "rebel" representatives he told them: "Whoever is the majority should extend a welcome to the minority now. Do not nurse past grievances. Why should you be resentful? You are the majority, you must unite with the minority, for even if the minority is wrong, you are not absolutely right either." He was primarily concerned with the

34

restoration of peace and unity, but he was not going to allow Chiang Ch'ing to profit from the martyrdom of her young left-wing hotheads. In September 1967 her Cultural Revolution Group in Peking was obliged to endorse the directive that authorised the army to crack down on any attempt by the "rebels" to seize weapons in order to make more mischief. Chiang Ch'ing herself was chosen to make a public declaration on the same day praising the PLA and warning the Red Guards that they must surrender their guns and stop attacking the army. "Learn from the directives of Chairman Mao," Chou then stressed. *"Learn from the speeches of Comrade Chiang Ch'ing."*[8] The extremists were isolated from their mistress, and subsequently an "anti-leftist" drive swept them into the background.

It would be a mistake, however, to imagine that Chou En-lai was the victor in this untidy battle, that he had decisively defeated Mao and Lin Piao and all the other advocates of the original commotion. He was Secretary-General of the Ninth Party Congress when it convened in the spring of 1969, and seemed to be at every reception and social gathering assembled in the months that followed, while Mao and Lin remained in the background. But Mao withdrew in order to win wider allegiance for himself and his chosen heir. He had theoretically eliminated the anti-Maoists during the nation-wide witch-hunt against President Liu and the "revisionists", but the quarrel between Lin Piao and Chiang Ch'ing, and the mistrust of Lin Piao prevalent among many of the military had created new contradictions. These had to be resolved, for the "revisionists" must not be given a chance to counter-attack. The Mao–Lin group was therefore compelled to seek a compromise with the suspicious soldiers who now formed a new clique of "power holders" and who included the Red warlords controlling several military regions. Mao had to give way, for the man to achieve that compromise could only be Chou En-lai. But Chou was not a rival of Mao.

That is not to say that Mao and Chou En-lai see eye to eye. It would hardly be possible, for Chou is the boss of a huge bureaucratic machine and a weakly-articulated national economy that have often threatened to jam under Mao's more impatient manipulations in his revolutionary quest for a classless Utopia. In 1955 Chou's State Council wanted to slow down and "consolidate" the over-hasty process of collectivising

35

China's peasantry, but Mao denounced this cautious policy and demanded that the number of farming cooperatives be doubled (and they were). Three years later the Prime Minister only echoed with his lips Mao's call for the impractical Great Leap Forward, and when it faltered he was among those behind the brutal Central Committee reports which disclosed that the fudged statistics for output during that period had been as spurious as the "Great Leap" itself.

Nevertheless, Mao and Chou do not contend with each other so much as complement each other. Mao is an ambitious dreamer, a chauvinistic revolutionary with aggressive ideas and a sharp pen. Chou En-lai is the suave product of a polite bourgeois background, an "internationalist" and a realist who leaves fantasy to others. Chou plays *Yin* to Mao's *Yang*. In terms of the two faces of China's traditional imperial policy of cowing and then placating outer barbarians, Mao awes, Chou soothes. But both are dedicated to the same causes – Communism and China. A party vice-chairman, and a member of the Politburo since 1927, Chou may be accommodating but he does not compromise on principle. Like Mao, he regarded Stalin as a great if imperfect revolutionary, and when Khrushchev attacked the dead dictator at the 22nd Congress of the Soviet Communist Party, Chou's reaction was to go and put a wreath on his grave.

Neither Mao nor Chou seeks head-on collisions or eyeball-to-eyeball confrontations. They believe in craft, deception, the stratagem, the outflanking movement. The end always justifies the means, and the end is always the same. Mao may be a tough, rude Hunanese with a head full of heroic ideals, and Chou a patient, shrewd, flexible and compliant mandarin from Chekiang, but they are both resolute in the defence of the same ideological principles. They may differ over method and pace, but they agree on their objectives, and these include not only a classless communist society in China, but world revolution.

Chou's love-all introduction of ping-pong diplomacy was greeted in some countries with almost hysterical expressions of relief and gratitude. But his "internationalism", like his capacity for tolerance, can be exaggerated. He has on occasion displayed a curious lack of understanding of the ways of men in the world outside – in 1964, for example, he won the distrust of well-disposed African government leaders by describing their continent as "ripe for revolution". Ping-pong diplomacy is also based on the premise that it is possible for the Chinese to befriend governments that they are simultaneously urging armed native rebels to overthrow. It would therefore be dangerous to see anything more than cool calculation in Chou's strategy. A computer could have come up with the same formula, had it been programmed to produce the results the Communists wanted.

The Maoist principle involved is that "one divides into two". The American people are given the impression that Chou is a soft-line man, that the Chinese have been much maligned, and that it is the American government that has been the dangerous bully. The people – exasperated by the Vietnam war, the colour problem, rising prices, lower productivity, unemployment – can thus be divided from their rulers.

Faced with the dangerous hostility of their nuclear neighbours just across the Soviet border, and the rearmament of a rapacious Japan just across the Yellow Sea, the Chinese leaders had logical (not to say cynical) reasons for courting the Americans. Nevertheless, when it was first revealed that President Nixon would go to Peking, Chou En-lai was careful to imply to the Chinese millions that their government had not taken the initiative by inviting him – Nixon had said he wanted to come and Mao had therefore signified his readiness to receive him. To the Chinese mind the inference was obvious. Nixon was like the early emissaries from foreign states who visited Imperial China and were described as "barbarian envoys bringing tribute to the Son of Heaven", for it was customary for vassal kings to send periodical embassies to Peking to prove their continued fealty in this way. The purpose of the visit was to increase the prestige and security of Communist China, not that of President Nixon.

Chou may smile when Mao frowns, but the smile should never be taken at face value. Behind his air of tolerant understanding, his reassuring common sense, Chou is perhaps the best communist of them all. The biggest hazard he faced during the Cultural Revolution was the possibility that once Liu Shao-ch'i and the "black gang" were eliminated, he, Chou, would no longer be the man-in-the-middle, but a man out on a limb and liable to be damned as a revisionist in his turn. His alliance with the recalcitrant military saved him from that fate. But the accusation would have been justified. If that sounds strange, it is only because the world has been brainwashed into thinking that Maoists are heroes and revisionists are faint-hearts who have betrayed the revolution. As a revisionist stripped of the emotional idealism that often afflicts the Maoist, the realistic Chou En-lai is a much more resilient revolutionary, and a more dangerous long-term enemy to capitalism than the Chairman himself.

Chou did not emerge from the upheaval without scars. His state apparatus suffered heavy losses and four of his trusted vice-premiers in the State Council were dropped from the Politburo in 1969,[9] although thanks to his protection they remained members of the Central Committee of the party. However, by 1971 many had faith in Chou En-lai at a time when China, ransacked by Red Guards, had to be tidied up again. He had the new powerholders among the military with him, and on the Politburo his able and influential henchman, Vice-Premier Li Hsien-nien, who controlled one element vital to the national metabolism – the money.

4

Li Hsien-nien: the Money God

Political power may grow out of the barrel of a gun, as Mao has said, but both guns and gunners have to be paid for, and this in part accounts for the influence of Li Hsien-nien, China's Minister for Finance, as in the past it has accounted for the influence of China's traditional God of Wealth. By 1972 Li was the only vice-premier who played a really active role in the political arena, and just as Premier Chou En-lai may emerge as the *de facto* master of China, so the somewhat younger, sixty-seven-year-old Li Hsien-nien may emerge in turn as a second Chou En-lai. The two men are firm allies but, thanks to his past military and present financial role, the Money God is in a sense even closer than the Prime Minister to army commanders in the regions and, given his outstanding ability as a fiscal manipulator, Mao Tsetung has found it profitable and prudent to handle him with care.

Li and Lin Piao both came from Hupeh, but they had little in common. Unlike Lin Piao, Li had no schooling and began his working life as a carpenter's apprentice. He joined the Kuomintang forces as they passed through his home province on the Northern Expedition, and when the Communists and the KMT split in 1927, he became a Red guerrilla. But while Lin Piao rallied to Mao, Li Hsien-nien's revolutionary career was to follow a different path. He was a native of Huangan county, and a member of the so-called "Ma Huang Group" associated with a local peasant insurrection in 1927 which a certain "Slow March" Hsu Hsiang-ch'ien exploited two years later. It was from this starting-point that Slow March was to create the Oyuwan Soviet* whose fighting forces became the Fourth Front Army, while Mao organised the Kiangsi Soviet whose forces became the First Front Army. There was to be more than comradely competition between them, however. For Slow

---

* Oyuwan—taken from the classical names of the provinces it partly covered: Hupeh–Honan–Anhwei.

March was always true to his name, a lean, sad, patient man with a small nervous face who moved cautiously and was quickly overshadowed within the Oyuwan Soviet by his political commissar Chang Kuo-t'ao. This man became Mao's detested rival and is now in exile in Canada.

After Kuomintang pressure had compelled the Communists to break out of the Oyuwan and Kiangsi Soviets, their two armies met in July 1935 at Maokung in Szechuan province. But a stormy conference ensued, for their leaders were violently opposed to each other. Mao Tsetung wanted them to march northward together to the three provinces of Shensi, Kansu and Ninghsia and, if necessary, to retreat further into Mongolia and make contact across the border with the Soviet Union. But Chang Kuo-t'ao urged that the army should stay in Szechuan and neighbouring Sikang and, if necessary, retreat further west into Sinkiang.

In the end, Chang yielded to the decision of the Central Committee and accepted the post of political commissar of the combined armies, which now set off north towards Kansu in two columns. But Mao and Chang quarrelled further at a place called Maoerkhai, and although they agreed to continue because the Nationalists were close on their heels, their columns were soon divided by a river swollen after heavy rainfall, and they split up. Mao moved on with Lin Piao and P'eng Te-huai, while other leaders went to Sikang with Chang Kuo-t'ao.

After many months in Sikang, Chang Kuo-t'ao was finally persuaded to march north again to Mao's new guerrilla base around Yenan, but before he arrived he ordered his main force to swing west and cross the Yellow River, for he still hankered after a stronghold of his own. In consequence the bulk of his Fourth Front Army, under command of Slow March, was trapped by the Kuomintang and almost totally wiped out – 25,000 men were killed or captured and fewer than two thousand survived.

Li Hsien-nien, now political commissar of a subordinate army, was cut off from Slow March and took the remnants of his column westwards into Sinkiang. They were attacked repeatedly by the troops of local warlords, and when they finally reached Urumchi, capital of that immense, sparsely-peopled Central Asian region, Li had only 700 men left. But there were friendly Soviet units from across the border in the area, and the Russians eventually arranged for him to be sent safely back to Mao in Yenan. There he was to find that of the rest of the troops engaged in that disastrous battle with the KMT, only about 500 had straggled into the new Communist stronghold.

The precipitous decline in the power and fortunes of the Fourth Front Army had been observed by Mao Tsetung without sympathy, and even with distinct pleasure. He was distrustful of this element of the Red forces that constituted the power-base of his arch-enemy, and now that the base had gone and Chang Kuo-t'ao stood discredited, he lost little time. In January 1937 the Central Committee formally tried Chang, and Mao branded him a "flightist" and an opportunist. After many recriminations and counter-charges, he was able to ruin and rid himself of this fellow founder-member of the communist movement. Chang was obliged to confess his faults publicly, and was then degraded and put under surveillance. In 1938 he fled to the Kuomintang and was drummed out of the party. But Mao was good enough to remark, however sourly: "Of all the cadres of the Fourth Front Army, only Hsu Hsiang-ch'ien and Li Hsien-nien were not influenced by the Chang Kuo-t'ao line." This meant that they would not be punished, but they were still regarded with doubt and disfavour.

Mao nonetheless appeared to repose more confidence in Li than in Slow March, and when hostilities opened between China and Japan, Li was able to show his real paces. Mao's main object was to expand his army and the population and territory it controlled without risking unnecessary losses at the hands of the Japanese. He wanted to conserve his strength for the struggle yet to come against the KMT. Li's tactics harmonised with this strategy, for while the fundamental principle of guerrilla warfare is "attack when you can win, run when you cannot", few could both attack as well as Li and run as fleetly. He proposed to "sit back and watch the tigers fight", as he put it, and he proceeded to do just that when he slipped into the old Oyuwan area again in 1939.

In the early stages Li did not threaten Japanese communications enough to tempt the enemy to try and annihilate him, but hid between fronts, leaving it to the Nationalists to face up to the invader, and to the invader to attack the Nationalists in the belief that they offered the only real resistance to the occupation. Meanwhile he set out to organise a strong Communist base and to win all within it over to his side. He coaxed local defence forces and KMT guerrilla groups into his own "patriotic" camp, using Japanese pressure as his goad, and where he could not join them, he beat them, disarming the smaller KMT units that refused to put themselves under his command and forcing them to work for him.

He formed the peasants into a static militia that was ready to fight and farm at the same time, and from the best of them he created a mobile militia exonerated from the chore of producing rice. His political cadres scoured the countryside for young men ready to join his growing guerrilla army, and while he taught these recruits the basic hit-and-run tactics of his trade, he trained older and less agile men to build defences.

The base was outstandingly successful, for the people were ready to defend their home provinces and Li instilled into them the spirit that had prevailed in the Fourth Front Army. This could only be done by officers and cadres who were ready to break down every barrier that stood between themselves and the poor, and to share the hardships of their own peasant-soldiers.

Chinese philosophers have always taught that it is not poverty that is the source of social unrest, but the gap between the rich and the poor, for as happiness and misery move towards their respective extremes, incomprehension and hatred grow between man and man. There can only be friendship when people have mutual respect and understanding and concern for one another. A Chinese communist authoress* who had worked in the countryside and lived with villagers wrote: "If a louse from the body of an old woman crawls on to my body, what ought I to do? I must let it go on crawling. If I get rid of it, that will show that there is a wall between us, and we cannot work closely together." As another Chinese put it: "If the dirty hand of one who has been picking up horse dung touches the face of your beautiful daughter, you must take it with a smile and ask her to call him 'uncle'. Otherwise you will see his sense of class struggle burning in his eyes."

In the spring, the villagers in the Oyuwan area would take off their clothes to search for lice, and with their nimble fingers would soon have squashed most of their tormentors, repaying their "blood debt" with shouts of triumph. But the officers and

* Ting Ling.

42

soldiers were equally verminous – including Chang Kuo-t'ao in the days of the old Fourth Front Army – and the peasants felt warmly towards these fellows who shared their hunger and poverty and sickness and bugs. Even lice helped the Communists to win their well-deserved victories.

By 1941 Li had a force of 60,000 men under him whose hard core was his own division in the New 4th Army commanded by Ch'en Yi (China's future Minister for Foreign Affairs until he died in 1972). The Japanese turned on this growing menace to their lines of communication in 1942, but Li slipped out of their closing ring of troops as he had slipped into the area three years before. In 1946, the Japanese gone, the enemy was the Kuomintang, and Li was again cutting river and rail communications from hideouts north of the Yangtse. The exasperated Nationalists surrounded him with 200,000 men, the Yangtse was in flood, and Li did not have the boats he needed to cross it and withdraw before these immeasurably superior forces. The only alternative was to disperse, following Mao's principle that the guerrilla army "comes from the people, goes back to the people". Li's forces simply dissolved into the population and he himself escaped. One year later he was back on the ground again in Hupeh, and by 1949 he was governor, military commander, and political commissar of the province.

However, in that year peace came, the People's Republic of China was proclaimed, and Li's life was to take a new turn. Five years later he was elected to the National Defence Council – but he was also appointed Minister of Finance.

Except for a course that he took in the Anti-Japanese Military and Political University in Yenan, Li never studied, and he is one of the genuine proletarians in the upper hierarchy of the Chinese Communist Party. In his guerrilla days, he was a tall stick of a man, thin of face, quick-witted, careless of his appearance, and lively as a deer in the mountains – they called him the Barefoot King. Now he was to display other, complementary talents. Today he is bespectacled, a little stout, particular about his clothes, and the image of a communist fat cat. He is plausible if crude of speech, argues convincingly, and has a flair for bringing others over to his side and filling them with enthusiasm which serves him well in his many international encounters. He is among the most travelled of Chinese leaders,

43

and also among the most experienced in dealing with visiting delegations, whether from Albania or Iraq, Tanzania or North Vietnam. He impresses foreigners, for he is a thoughtful negotiator.

However, if he sees something that he considers impractical or foolish, he will often be frank, regardless of the consequences. When the Chinese millions were encouraged to throw themselves into the study of the Thought of Mao almost with the blind faith that is born of religious exaltation, Li warned them repeatedly, "the directives of the Chairman lay down the basic doctrine on strategy and the solution of long-term problems. But if we ignore the necessity of analysing what he says carefully before we implement them, we can find ourselves in trouble."[1] At the time, this was near-heresy, but later Mao endorsed his view. For the Money God is a steady, careful planner himself, never impulsive, and known for his own minute analysis of all problems that present themselves. Furthermore, he has a keen appreciation of the value and importance of money. That could not possibly be said of Mao himself, but Mao must be thankful for this quality in Li.

In 1949 the Reds inherited the prostrate colossus of China, ravaged by years of invasion, alien occupation and civil war. Out of this, and with no more experience than they could have gained in their fugitive guerrilla bases, they proposed to create not only a prosperous, modern, independent power of the first magnitude, but a Utopian communist society. Even had their ambitions been far more modest, they would have been faced with acute problems and needs in the fields of currency, commerce, credits, revenue, and reserves.

It was Li* who, as Director of the "Finance and Trade Office" that controlled the Ministries of Finance, Commerce, Foreign Trade and Food, organised a unified fiscal system served by people's banks, peasants' banks, financial cooperatives and trusts, tax offices, exchange bureaux and Overseas Chinese investment companies, and a great network of other interlocking money-handling bodies. All were under his control, all well-managed, and all benefited the party. Almost miraculously, Li and his colleagues contrived to pay off China's foreign debts

---

* Together with men like Ch'en Yun, former Minister of Commerce and Chairman of the State Capital Construction Commission, and Li Fu-ch'un, former Chairman of the State Planning Commission.

and earned her a reputation for being a trustworthy partner in any banking, trading or other transaction. They rationalised the pattern of internal markets in China, suppressed inflation, and kept the currency remarkably stable and strong considering the convulsions the country experienced, culminating in the Cultural Revolution of the late sixties. Since his super-ministry controlled all movements of commodities and the management of all markets, Li was able to eliminate price-fluctuations and speculation in shortages to a creditable degree.

But although he had a firm and expert hand on the state budget, and on the financing of every sector of national life, including the armed forces, industry, agriculture, education and government, the Cultural Revolution nearly destroyed what he had built, and brought the country to the verge of an economic relapse. Moreover, Li Hsien-nien did not escape the witch-hunting of the Red Guards and "rebels", for all technocrats were suspect to the Maoists. He was cat-called "the faithful muscle-man of Liu Shao-ch'i," and for one month early in 1967 he was replaced by his deputy-minister. But only for one month, after which the deputy was detained by the PLA, and the Money God put back on his altar. "The rebels," his patron Chou En-lai had declared flatly, "may supervise the activities of the Ministries of Finance, Public Security and Foreign Affairs, but they cannot take them over."

Li had nonetheless sinned blatantly. He had branded the "rebel headquarters" a counter-revolutionary base, and at a rally of 100,000 Maoists in Peking he had warned the rebels themselves not to touch state property. He had then issued an emergency directive ordering the Red Guards to give back everything they had "confiscated". Li's was a blunt, down-to-earth reaction to the "seizure of power" by revolutionary mobs, however Maoist they might be. It was typical of a man who had also asked boldly in a land where people can be pilloried for thinking in terms of cash: "Is earning money a crime? To think that only profit counts is wrong, but to ignore profit completely is also wrong. If one does not make a reasonable profit, one has made a mistake."[1]

Li has concentrated on maintaining the stability of the state's finances and economy, on accumulating national treasure when others would throw it to the winds. Mao has had reason to appreciate his impartial, almost apolitical management of the country's revenue. Li held the purse when Mao brought eleven million Red Guards into the capital to inspire them to "seize power" from the well-ordered bureaucracy in which the Money God himself was so prominent. But he made no difficulties about providing the necessary funds. His tight control of foreign exchange, on the other hand, ensured that none of the "small handful who took the capitalist road" could salt away millions in a Swiss account or in neighbouring Hongkong. But Li worked closely with Chou En-lai – that other "Pu-tao-weng" (the doll that always bobs up again if pushed over) – when the Prime Minister set out to persuade Mao that the revolutionaries must be restrained if ruin was not to follow.

Li himself had no direct dealings with Mao, however, and he is among the more unobtrusive members of the Politburo. His record and references cannot afford the old Chairman unadulterated pleasure. He is a pragmatist, and he has little sympathy with Mao's impractical political campaigns and economic daydreams. In the early stages of the Great Leap Forward and the formation of people's communes he was still urging comrades to study the common-sense proposals of Liu Shao-ch'i before committing the country to Maoist "doctrinairism", and the follies of that vast and catastrophic experiment soured his belief in the leader to whom so far he had been consistently loyal. "The first emperor is always the most glorious," he told a junior colleague in 1962 when its consequences were fully appreciated, "but he is also the most fierce."

Mao showed his ferocity by denouncing one of the Money God's subordinate departments for helping the peasant to sell his private output on free markets at the expense of the collective, dubbing it the "Ministry of Destruction", and demanded why ministerial cadres were not spending more time in factories and communes "making revolution" with workers and peasants. "Damn it all," the exasperated Li is said to have commented, "we have not even accomplished our revolution here in Peking . . . Is weakening our organisation by sending cadres down to become ordinary people any way to increase production?"[2]

There are other entries in the dossier displeasing to the Maoists. Li is a man with both military and fiscal influence. He was a comrade-in-arms of powerful Red warlords like "Tiger" Ch'en Hsi-lien and "Ironsides" Hsu Shih-yu, the commanders of Shenyang and Nanking Military Regions who by 1971 were regarding Lin Piao without enthusiasm from their seats on the Politburo. Yet at the beginning of the following year the Money God was the only vice-premier out of the sixteen appointed in January 1965 who was still officially listed as working in that capacity. While it is always possible to change the man who holds the purse-strings, however, it would hardly be advisable in this case. The egregious Li is the protégé of Chou En-lai and the financial key to China's multifarious drive for greatness among nations in terms of her expanding diplomacy, her expanding trade – and, most significantly, her expanding nuclear programme.

5

The Nuclear Monk

Mao once remarked in the forties: "There was Lu Ta in the past and there is Nieh Jung-chen in the present." Lu Ta was one of the 108 bandit heroes of the marathon Chinese classical novel, *Men of the Marshes*, which in part inspired Mao's own guerrilla struggle against infamous government. He was referring to the fact that the hilarious adventures of this fugitive from justice had occurred in a part of North China in which Nieh had set up a Communist stronghold against the Japanese and the Kuomintang. Violent and quick-tempered, Lu Ta killed a man in a righteous cause and took refuge in a temple, where he was obliged to shave his head and become a monk but could not rid himself of an unholy craving for dog-meat and wine. Mao's comparison thereafter saddled Nieh with the nickname of his fictional forerunner, and this marshal who has been described as the "father of atomic energy" in China is therefore privately known as "The Profligate Monk".

Nieh Jung-chen is 73 now, an alert, proud, ruthless man, neat and methodical in all things, his wide mouth as sharply creased as his impeccable proletarian uniform. He was born into a family of wealthy land-owning peasants and was to prove a brilliant and tough guerrilla leader. Yet he acquired not only military but political and even some scientific know-how with that apparently effortless facility whose secret is hard work. When the Cultural Revolution erupted, Nieh was chairman of Peking's two scientific and technological commissions and responsible for everything in the field which that suggests, up to and including China's nuclear development programme.* Scientists and technical experts working under these commissions were automatically looked upon with suspicion by the young Maoist revolutionaries as men who were more "expert"

---

* The two Commissions were responsible respectively to the State Council (Government) under Premier Chou En-lai, and to the PLA through the party's Military Affairs Commission.

48

than "red", and almost certainly guilty of the heretical belief that practical work was more important than political education. At first they were spared the importunities of the Red Guards, as their contribution to the nation's defence was considered too vital to be interrupted, but in time the Profligate Monk, earlier so praised by Mao, came under dangerous crossfire from Chiang Ch'ing's rebels on the one hand and from Chiang Ch'ing's rival, Lin Piao, on the other. The past had made this paradox inevitable.

Nieh was from Szechuan and was a boyhood friend of Teng Hsiao-p'ing, the disgraced revisionist secretary-general of the party. As young men, he and Teng went to France together under the "work and study" programme and there met Chou En-lai and Ch'en Yi. Like them, Nieh joined the Communist Youth League, but unlike many others, he studied more than he plotted. He read engineering in France and natural sciences in Belgium, he worked at the Schneider-Creusot arms plant and at the Renault car factory, but his performance as an agitator nonetheless attracted favourable attention and he was invited to Moscow. After a course in military science at the Red Army University he returned to China and became an instructor at the Whampoa Military Academy in Canton – where Chou En-lai was his political chief and Lin Piao was one of his students.

Nieh later joined Chou En-lai, with whom his political life has since been closely intertwined, in organising the insurrections in Shanghai that opened the gates to the advancing Chiang Kai-shek. When Chiang turned on the Communists, Nieh took part in the Nanchang and Canton Uprisings against the Nationalists and, like Chou En-lai, was forced to flee to Hong-kong. Both men later made their way to Mao's mountain stronghold in Kiangsi, and when the party appointed Chou En-lai chief political commissar of the Red Army, Nieh was his deputy. This temporary blow to the authority of Mao was an affront to guerrilla commanders like Lin Piao, who was not only a rising star but one of his most loyal lieutenants. Seeing how the land lay, therefore, Chou En-lai made the Profligate Monk political commissar of Lin's corps so that he could keep an eye on him, and this sowed seeds of future animosity between them.

When China went to war with Japan in 1937 and Mao's

49

Communist forces in the north were reorganised into the Eighth Route Army, Lin Piao was given command of the 115th Division with Nieh as his deputy. But while Lin Piao advanced eastwards from their base with most of the fighting units, and soon trapped a Japanese brigade at the much-publicised battle of Pinghsingkuan, Nieh stayed in the mountains of Shansi, the scene of the original Profligate Monk's antics several centuries before, to build up a guerrilla stronghold.

The heroic Lin Piao was wounded and disappeared to the Soviet Union for treatment, while the less spectacular Nieh took advantage of the vacuum left as the KMT retreated, moving in and developing a large and highly successful Communist base in the Shansi–Chahar–Hopei border region which by 1944 controlled a population of 20,000,000. He set up a people's government, trained the local young men as army cadres, and was soon the soul of a new Soviet, with his photograph everywhere and his sayings painted in enormous characters on the walls of buildings. The party took his region as a model and instructed all units to learn from it, and when the Nationalists overran the Communist "capital" at Yenan two years after the end of the Sino-Japanese War, Mao took some members of the Central Committee into the hills of north Shensi, but others joined the Profligate Monk in his citadel. Among these was Liu Shao-ch'i, who was to become the principal villain and victim of the Cultural Revolution twenty years later.

Nieh's expanding forces were organised into the North China Liberation Army, and this in turn became the 5th of the five field armies into which all Communist forces were regrouped for the final drive against Chiang Kai-shek in 1949. Nieh's achievement owed nothing to either Mao or Lin Piao. But it had involved other loyalties. A certain Yang Ch'eng-wu commanded an independent regiment under Nieh, and its deputy commander was Huang Yung-sheng. Initially backed by the patronage of the Profligate Monk, both of these men rose to the rank of full general within ten years and later became successive chiefs of staff of the PLA.

Yet, within this design of loyalties and rivalries, trouble lay in wait for the haughty and meticulous Monk. In 1967 he was berated by Chiang Ch'ing's Red Guards for allegedly taking a "bourgeois line" in matters affecting defence and opposing the Cultural Revolution, and he was obliged to admit his responsibility for mistakes made by the state Scientific and Technological Commission. In April 1968 he was again denounced – this time for trying to create a personal kingdom for himself and for conspiring with Yang Ch'eng-wu, his former regimental commander, who had just been dismissed from his post as chief of staff.

What had happened? Mao's dictum *"Wen kung wu wei"* – "attack with words, defend with arms" – sums up China's entire international strategy, and he was faithful to it when he launched the Cultural Revolution. For the offensive, he relied on the tidal wave of propaganda set rolling by the controlling group under Chiang Ch'ing. For defence, he relied in Peking on the troops under Yang Ch'eng-wu, Acting Chief of Staff. And in the early stages Yang earned the confidence not only of Mao but of Lin Piao, for he quickly brought units from his loyal North China army into the capital, ostensibly to enable the Maoists to "seize power" with safety.

But their amicable relationship did not last long. Chiang Ch'ing began to make use of Yang's military authority to compel the soldiers to back the revolutionary rebels unquestioningly, even when they set out to destroy her opponents within the army itself, and in this way she engineered the downfall of several "Lin Piao men". Relations between Mao's wife and Mao's successor therefore cooled further towards zero, and Lin decided that Yang Ch'eng-wu must be stripped of power.

They had all miscalculated. Chiang Ch'ing – and possibly Mao himself – had underestimated Lin Piao's reaction, but Yang Ch'eng-wu's position was even more ironical. He was a long-term schemer and his friends were none of these people. They were Yang Ch'eng-wu primarily, and then Chou En-lai and the Nuclear Monk. He had acquiesced to all that Chiang Ch'ing had asked of him simply because he wanted to pre-empt any Maoist misgivings about his future actions. If he enjoyed the confidence of Mao and Chiang Ch'ing, his position would be stronger, his friends would be safer, and he would have a freer hand to do what he planned. And what he planned to do was to reorganise the general staff, to reshuffle commanders in the big military regions in the provinces, and to champion Nieh and his Commissions in order to establish as a dominant influence the clique whose ties of mutual loyalty had been forged in the Profligate Monk's Shansi–Chahar–Hopei Soviet.

"Mutual loyalty" in the Chinese context is not based purely on sentiment and a shared thick-and-thin past. Its real cement is an identity of ideas and interests. "Comrade", says the Concise Oxford Dictionary, is a "mate or fellow in work, play or fighting". It does not mention "ideals" or "will". But, very significantly, the Chinese communist equivalent of "comrade" is *t'ung-chih*, "same-will" or "same-ideal". In a society whose dissembling has prompted the West to call its members "inscrutable", words and even actions may deceive. Only thought – as Descartes would have agreed – is valid. Once men are *t'ung-chih* and have the same ideals and ambitions, firm friendships can take the form of a sacred Chinese bargain struck on the "I-know-you'll-back-*me*-up-and-you-know-I'll-back-*you*-up" basis.

Where they are not *t'ung-chih*, Chinese make and break expedient alliances with often bewildering facility and speed, for they have no common purpose and a threat that brought them together today may give way to a promise that divides them tomorrow. Mao and Chiang Kai-shek were not *t'ung-chih*, yet they ganged up temporarily against the Japanese. Conversely, Mao and Liu Shao-ch'i were not *t'ung-chih* and Mao therefore attacked even his old "comrade" without compunction. Mao and Richard Nixon are not *t'ung-chih*, and Washington would do well to remember it. For in these circumstances, opportunism is all and Chinese individuals will behave not like persons, but like states among whom friends and foes are interchangeable as history evolves and national interest dictates.

The game is fair, for everyone understands the rules. Chiang Ch'ing and Lin Piao and Yang Ch'eng-wu knew that they shared no common aims, and therefore shared no common loyalty, and each knew the other knew, yet it suited them to use each other for their own ends in a pragmatic conspiracy of distrust. It was enough for Chiang Ch'ing that while Yang's long-term strategy might be hostile, his short-term tactics for achieving his aims harmonised with her plans. Once the situation changed, and Yang was a liability rather than an asset, she was the first to cast a stone.

It was Lin Piao who did the hatchet work, however. Lin had two scores to settle with Yang, one for each of his false faces, and he did not waste time. He publicly accused the Chief of Staff of dishonourably dismissing good men, of undermining the unity of the PLA, and of dabbling in factionalism. But although he was pointing his finger at Yang and his North China army, his target was Nieh, its one-time chief. Having first found himself assailed by Chiang Ch'ing, Nieh now found himself assailed by her antagonist, Lin Piao. The Monk's star was beginning to pale. But he was not to disappear into oblivion, for Chou En-lai came to his rescue and persuaded him to submit a letter of self-criticism to Mao, which was accepted.

Chou owed Nieh his protection, for the attack on the Monk was also a veiled attack on the Premier himself. For years Chou had depended for support on two former marshals of the PLA – Nieh the Profligate Monk and Ch'en Yi the Bald. Both men had given up their army careers, one becoming head of the two Scientific and Technological Commissions, the other Foreign Minister, but both still enjoyed great prestige among soldiers. Nieh was admired for the model Soviet he had created out of a wild border region, and as commander of the 5th Field Army he had taken the surrender of Peking by the KMT. Ch'en Yi had led the 3rd Field Army in at least two brilliant campaigns. The Prime Minister's opponents knew that the authority of these men would have to be cut away before he himself could be toppled. If Nieh had been the target behind Yang Ch'eng-wu, therefore Chou En-lai was the target behind Nieh.

Yang had now been sacked, and Lin Piao had won the first round, but in China one side can be victorious without the other being totally defeated. Yang's successor was Huang Yung-sheng. He was picked for a number of reasons, among them that he was acceptable to all parties (if grudgingly, as far as Chiang Ch'ing was concerned), but it was Chou En-lai who did the picking. He had given way over Yang, and it was Mao's turn to give way over Huang. This is the kind of Chinese solution that often makes an inflexible Western concept like "power struggle" act as a distorting mirror in which China's affairs are not so much reflected as caricatured.

Lin Piao remained unhappy that Chou En-lai and Nieh should be so close, that between them they controlled China's nuclear effort, that they were associated with factions within the army that gave their loyalty to others and only lip-service to himself as Minister of Defence and Mao's heir; and although after 1968 technical experts working on the nuclear programme were listed as "responsible persons of the Liberation Army" instead of "responsible persons of the State Council", Lin Piao still could not put his hands on the warheads. Mao made Su Yu, one of Lin's vice-ministers, effective head of the Scientific and Technological Commission of the PLA and the senior commander "responsible" for China's nuclear development for military purposes. But Su Yu was not a Lin Piao man. His lineal loyalties went back to Chou En-lai's other marshal – Ch'en Yi the Bald.

By 1971 Ch'en Yi and Nieh Jung-chen had both been dropped from the Politburo and appeared to be in the same precarious position, yet neither was necessarily out in the cold for good. In 1972, Ch'en Yi died of cancer, but Nieh remained at least titular head of China's two leading scientific and technological commissions, and a simple twist of the wheel could carry him to the top again in terms of real authority if Chou En-lai's "line" prevailed in the future. However, "from ancient times, beauties and famous generals have been alike in that they could not allow this mortal world to see their white hairs". Nieh's problem is not his past, for he has made as many potential allies as he has made potential enemies. It is – as in the case of so many others – his age.

6
Cloak and Dagger

If the missile is among men's greatest fears, so is the midnight knock at the door, and the cadres who control the all-pervasive power of radioactive fall-out are matched by those who control the all-pervasive power of secret police. It is not surprising, therefore, that despite his enemies Chang Shao-ch'ing *alias* Chang Wen *alias* Chao Jung *alias* K'ang Sheng should still have been listed in 1971 as a member of the Standing Committee of the Politburo and the fifth man in all China.

This self-styled Chinese Beria is close to seventy now, a thin, balding chain-smoker with a disconcerting, hypnotic gaze that is partly concealed by steel-rimmed spectacles, a narrow, inconsequential moustache, and two rows of untidily-spaced and yellowing teeth stuck into a thoughtful, crafty, rather scholarly face. Born into the family of a rich landlord in the same Shantung village as Chiang Ch'ing, K'ang Sheng was a studious undergraduate at the University of Shanghai when he joined the Party in the twenties, a good calligrapher and a painter of flowers and landscapes. But while young he also learned to fight with sword, knife, iron staff, and his fists, and was known to be a formidable opponent, able to take on several men at once. He became an almost legendary hero in the clandestine struggle in Shanghai, where he led three uprisings and, although arrested but subsequently released, continued to organise the underground Communist movement in the city for four more years. He was a henchman of the unfortunate agent whose entire family Chou En-lai had exterminated after he had squealed to the Kuomintang, but he survived this betrayal to devote the forty years that have since elapsed to secret intelligence work.

He moved up fast in the early days, and in 1931 was elected a member of the Party, Politburo, which was at that time under the guidance of the Russians. He was then sent to the Soviet Union, where he spent most of the five years that followed.

He studied intelligence techniques in Moscow, worked for the Comintern as an assistant of a hated, pro-Russian rival of Mao named Wang Ming, and was later appointed secretary of the Manchuria Bureau of the Chinese Communist Party. In 1935 he recruited Chinese workers and students in Russia, and communists from Korea and other countries, for a 4,000-strong cavalry regiment that was despatched to Outer Mongolia to support Mao Tsetung if necessary during the final phases of the Long March.

Two years afterwards he joined Mao in Yenan on Stalin's orders, and set about reorganising the Chinese Communist secret service. He took over as director of the party school, where he lectured on the problems and techniques of clandestine work in the revolutionary struggle, according to a one-time comrade who adds: "Of all our leaders in Yenan, he was the most conspicuous, for he was fond of wearing leather boots, riding, and hunting to foreign hounds. When he went out, he was usually escorted by at least four guards, and he was far more pretentious than Mao Tsetung himself."

Mao did not seem to mind. In 1942 he launched a campaign to give party members a better political education and to remould those who slavishly echoed foreign ideologists. He was going to "sinify" Communism so that they echoed him instead, and at the same time eliminate the influence of sectarians like his "Bolshevik" rival, Wang Ming, who could only air Marx as interpreted in Moscow. It meant "rectifying" (in many cases "liquidating") an estimated ten thousand men and women over a period of three years, and it was the Moscow-trained K'ang Sheng who did the job for him. He had already been instrumental in bringing Mao and Chiang Ch'ing together.

The political fates of K'ang Sheng and Chiang Ch'ing continued to touch where they fitted, and when Mao launched the Red Guards on their mission of political destruction in 1966, both worked on the Cultural Revolution Group that subsequently directed the onslaught. Mao wanted to make sure of the loyalty of his secret-service chief, and from being only an alternate member of the Politburo at that particular moment in his fortunes, K'ang was soon pushed into fifth place in the party hierarchy. His organisation duly helped to undermine the revisionists led by President Liu Shao-ch'i, whose left-hand man he himself had been at many meetings with foreign delegations – Rumanian, Japanese, Belgian, British – in less controversial days.

K'ang was such an outstanding mixer that it was believed he also headed the party's International Liaison Department. But it has always been one of the duties of the T'e Wu – the Chinese "Special Service" – to "get alongside" other communist movements. The disarming cover-name of this organisation was – at least until recently – the Social Affairs Department of the Central Committee of the Chinese Communist Party, but it was originally modelled on the old Russian OGPU. Apart from fulfilling its internal secret-police role, it operates as an offensive intelligence service overseas, using a variety of means.*

According to available sources, Afro-Asian and Latin American countries to be penetrated by secret agents of the T'e Wu fall into three categories:

1 those with which China has diplomatic relations and where embassies can therefore be used as cover;
2 those with which China has as yet no diplomatic relations, but where spying can be conducted under cover provided by the local offices of the New China News Agency (Hsinhua) or of the Ministry of Foreign Trade;
3 those with whom relations have not reached this point, but where visits of cultural and artistic groups can break the ice.

In Europe, the Chinese often depend on native communist movements that are prepared to act as bases for their secret operations, and these may be repaid with "economic assistance". Communist organisations in Belgium, Switzerland and France were known to be working with K'ang Sheng in this way up to 1971.

Hongkong is the Chinese agent's gateway to the free world, and for years past the T'e Wu has been filtering well-trained men into the British Crown Colony as refugees. Once these

---

* This account of Chinese intelligence and secret police organisation is subject to changes made as a result of the Cultural Revolution. The Social Affairs Department may have been renamed, and it has been reported that espionage abroad is now the responsibility of a new Overseas Investigation Department. But these changes may prove almost as ephemeral as the Red Guards themselves.

men have obtained Hongkong identity cards, they lodge applications for visas to emigrate further, and in this way the organisation eventually plants its resident agents in other countries. A Chinese Communist intelligence cadre has also boasted that the immigration and coastguard services of Nationalist Formosa present no effective obstacle to his comrades.

What of the home front? In Peking the party dominates the government, and where they both have offices with parallel responsibilities it is in the party organ that one must look for the real boss. The Social Affairs Department of the Central Committee or its successor therefore controls the Ministry of Public Security. The ministry is divided into eight bureaux of which four are responsible for political, economic, military and frontier security, and it casts a fine net. It disposes of some 300,000 men in all, and a system of subordinate offices throughout the country whose lowest unit is a sub-station. This will be the headquarters of local "household police" who are responsible for keeping complete files on every family in the country, including details of the births, deaths and personal and political histories of all members, their jobs, income, friends and relatives at home and abroad, their overnight visitors, and their own movements.

K'ang Sheng has been the political planner and party brain behind this entire administrative empire of spying, informing, dossiers, interrogations, labour camps, and liquidations, but the man who executes – sometimes in more senses than one – is Mao's corpulent bodyguard, Wang Tung-hsing.

Little is known of the career of this obscure and sinister "Kiangsi Favourite"* before 1947, when the Kuomintang captured Mao's headquarters at Yenan and compelled the Chinese Communist leaders to withdraw. Wang commanded the guards responsible for the security of party chiefs and escorted the Chairman to safety. Mao was impressed. Two years later he took Wang to Moscow with him on his first trip outside China, and thereafter treated him as his private watchdog. But there was to be more to this than guarding Mao's person.

In 1955 Wang was appointed Vice-Minister for Public

* See Chapter 9.

Security and, except for one short break, he has held the post ever since. Mao has confided to him some of his most vital and secret requirements, and after years of turbid revolutionary history evidently trusts him implicitly. Wang accompanied Liu Shao-ch'i on his ill-timed visit to Pakistan, Afghanistan and Burma in the spring of 1966 in order to keep an eye on the doomed President's movements while Mao took advantage of his absence to return to Peking. It was Wang who later arranged for the arrest of the former Defence Minister and of the Chief of Staff* and placed under house-surveillance the luckless Liu and the Secretary-General of the Party, Teng Hsiao-p'ing. In addition to being Vice-Minister for Public Security, Wang is chief of the Security Department of the party's Military Affairs Commission, and by virtue of this post he has been able to bypass his minister and acquire increasing control of the public security apparatus.

Nicknamed "The Devil's Clutch" after his flair for catching anti-Maoists and flinging them into labour camps, Wang's immediate duty in Peking has been to protect the central organs of party and government, and to assure the safety of Mao and of other high-ranking Communists whom Mao nominates. In 1960 the Central Committee abandoned the system whereby party leaders carried guns for their personal defence, and responsibility for their lives has since fallen upon the Party guards (whom Wang commands) and the Public Security forces.

To this end, Peking is reportedly divided into protected areas. The environs of the Gate of Heavenly Peace and the Forbidden City behind it are heavily patrolled by police equipped not only with radio but radar. Chungnanhai, the nearby enclave in which Mao and top party leaders live and work, is riddled with underground bunkers and tunnels, and subterranean posts for about one thousand Public Security troops.

Ready for any eventuality, these troops are armed with everything they may need from fire-hoses to machine-guns, and their signals equipment is superior to the army's and comparable to that used by similar special forces in the USSR. They are supported by PLA units in barracks near by. Subways which lead into the complex are lit day and night and constantly patrolled by armoured cars, and the perimeter is defended not only by

---

* P'eng Te-huai, Lo Jui-ch'ing.

small arms, but by artillery. Shanghai, Mao's revolutionary base, is the headquarters of another powerful concentration of Public Security forces covering the whole of East China.

Wang Tung-hsing's fingers appear to stretch further afield, however, and although many aspects of civil security would not normally be the direct concern of his Department, he has shown a tendency to meddle everywhere on the principle that in Mao's China "politics commands all". The PLA is his main target. The normal Public Security cadres working with the army are responsible for counter-espionage against enemy intelligence services, propaganda to promote the study of the Thoughts of Mao among the soldiery, and the eradication of anti-Maoist tendencies. But they are indistinguishable from the special cadres among them who are acting under the direct orders of the T'e Wu, whose identities are secret, and whose business is political espionage.

These agents form a network for Wang Tung-hsing that extends throughout the thirty-odd armies into which the PLA is divided. For Wang is reputed to have been briefed by the Chairman himself to "control" the PLA, to watch for signs of anti-Maoist plotting or even of "dumb insolence" towards Mao's instructions among its powerful commanders, to know who is loyal to whom when he is not so loyal to Mao, how strong the opposition to Mao's military theories is, and what cliques are coalescing around that opposition.

The PLA is conscious of this alien, exploring hand of the T'e Wu, and some local military chiefs took advantage of the breakdown in communications and services during the Cultural Revolution to limit its activities in one field at least – they ordered local people's courts to report their cases to the provincial revolutionary committees which they themselves dominated, instead of to Peking. For what goes to Peking goes to the party, and all information affecting law and security that goes to the party goes to the T'e Wu.

But they could do little else. Wang's position is exceptional. He is under the general direction of K'ang Sheng, but some sources insist that he receives orders straight from Mao, whose shadow he is generally considered to be, and his duties appear to be without final demarcation. He is like the organisation he serves, for the Chinese say "where water goes, the T'e Wu can go". He is an alternate member of the Politburo, but he is also the eye, the ear, and the hatchet of the Maoists – Mao, Chiang Ch'ing, and the extremists of the old Cultural Revolution Group; and he has not a political thought in his head beyond what he hears from Mao the Great Helmsman.

When Mao dies, therefore, matters will doubtless be different, for if Wang is the Chairman's shadow, how, ask the Chinese, can the shadow continue to exist without the body? The men who succeed Mao may well earmark him for early elimination, if they cannot quickly bend him to their will.

Wang also has his successors, however. The most prominent of these is Yu Sang, who was responsible for the security arrangements when President Nixon visited China and among the senior Communist officials who met the American party at Peking airport. Yu Sang was appointed a vice-minister of Public Security in 1964 and a member of the Central Committee of the party five years later. He ranks immediately after the "Devil's Clutch" in China's secret hierarchy, and is believed to be the real work-horse of the organisation. It was he who assembled the evidence on the anti-Mao activities of the Chief of Staff in 1966 and carried out his arrest. While Yu Sang specialises in the security of people, his assistant Yang Te-chung specialises in the security of places. He has been a protégé of Wang Tung-hsing since their Yenan days, and if he is not axed with his master when Mao dies, he and Yu Sang may be the "Chinese Berias" of the future.

But although K'ang Sheng appeared to be seriously ill in 1972, he was not yet dead, and he could still in theory survive the passing of the Chairman himself. He was the country's outstanding intelligence expert, and a man who had built up a nation-wide system of secret agents, controls, and communications. That was his political capital. Whoever took over from Mao might be hard put to it to find a fully qualified replacement for him in a hurry. And unlike Wang, he was not ambitious.

On the other hand, he was a confidant of Mao and a friend of Chiang Ch'ing, and closely associated with the Red Guard movement that once tried to seize power from the unforgiving local military in the provinces. And it was not for nothing that Mao had briefed Wang Tung-hsing to watch the army above all, for when the unique figure of the Chairman was no longer there, the soldiers would be holding the ultimate argument in China – with the safety catch on but with a round in the breech.

PART TWO

THE SOLDIERS

7

The Barrel of the Gun

"Political power grows out of the barrel of a gun" is the most Chinese of all the sayings of Mao, the most quoted, and the most misunderstood. It is the most Chinese because the Chinese have always believed that whoever holds the gun wins the argument. He does not have to use it to do so, for a sensible adversary will acknowledge his superiority and come to terms – much as bridge-players will acknowledge a lay-down hand without insisting on seeing the game through. In any so-called "struggle for supremacy" in China there is as much compromise as conflict, for Chinese only fight if they think they can win, and for the rest will either surrender or bargain or try to entice those who hold superior power over to their side. But the basic rule of this game has always been: guns are trumps.

The quotation of Mao is also much misunderstood because it is frequently taken to indicate that Mao accepts this as an immutable political law, and that logically, therefore, he believes in military dictatorship. But Mao meant that the Communists must use the gun to capture power from their enemies when they were pitted against the ruling Kuomintang. He did not mean that the army should hold power once victory had been achieved. He has always preached that "the party must command the gun, not the gun the party". Political commissars of Chinese Communist armies in the field wielded more authority than their military commanders, and Mao laid down that when the soldiers took a city, the first item on the agenda must be the establishment of a party committee whose chief would concurrently hold the post of political commissar in the local armed forces.

By 1971 the boot was on the other foot, however, and throughout the provinces the army was master of the party. How did this come about?

Mao launched the Cultural Revolution in order to smash President Liu Shao-ch'i and all his works. A new China of communes, run by the masses, would then arise from the rubble of the old revisionist administration. The masses themselves – the Red Guards and militant "rebels" among the workers and peasants – would carry out the revolution. The People's Liberation Army would be their backstop.

But resistance to Maoism was too strong, and as we have seen, the revolutionaries got out of hand, the ordered Chinese state gave way to confusion and near-anarchy, and the army became increasingly restless as the chaos continued. Forced to fall back upon his second plan since his first had failed, Mao approved a series of directives in 1967 which the PLA interpreted as mandates to quell the mobs and keep the peace. By the spring of that year, the army was supervising the administration of the provinces. By October 1968 the entire country was being governed by revolutionary committees on which the soldiers made most of the decisions, the whitewashed cadres of the old order did most of the work, and representatives of the masses enjoyed only marginal influence. The rise of the military had produced a new group of powerholders who had far more in common with the moderates loyal to the down-to-earth Chou En-lai than with the revolutionaries inspired by Mao.

Nominally, Mao held everything in his hands as Chairman of the Chinese Communist Party, but the Ninth Party Congress in April 1969 revealed the political strength of the soldiers themselves. Nearly half of the members of the Presidium of the Congress were senior officers of the PLA and "battle heroes". On the other hand, many civilian party members of long standing had been dropped, and in their place sat representatives of workers, peasants, and youth – semi-literate pig-breeders, shepherds, and factory hands, almost none of whom had any real understanding of communist theory. These were Mao's counterbalance.

The Central Committee "elected" by the Party Congress – the first for eleven years – had 279 members, of whom 38 were workers and peasants and only two were Red Guards. But PLA representatives numbered 123 and accounted for 44 per cent of the total membership. They included the army chiefs of all the military regions into which China was divided with, in the majority of cases, their deputy commanders and political commissars, and sometimes the commanders of the military districts under them – eighty officers in all. Most of the remaining 43 were prominent military figures in Peking itself. And when the new Politburo was later announced, it was revealed that five out of its seven new members were generals* of the up-and-coming group within the army.

The Congress adopted a new draft constitution which enshrined the Thoughts of Mao as gospel, and nominated Lin Piao as his successor. It also said: "leading bodies of the party at all levels are elected through democratic consultation". "Democratic consultation" is the alternative to the hazardous business of open elections which Mao and Lin Piao had found to be such a disturbing aspect of the "Paris Commune" system. It provides for private bargaining instead of public balloting, it gets over the awkward problem that arises when the wrong side has the majority, and so for the Maoists it offset to some extent the strength of the new military powerholders in the provincial revolutionary committees. It is fair to conjecture that this give-and-take system enabled Mao to persuade their detractors to allow Chiang Ch'ing and Yao Wen-yuan, the "Trigger-Finger" of the Shanghai "January Revolution", to become high-ranking members of the new Politburo.

All is a question of *quid pro quo*. In his report to the Ninth Party Congress, Lin Piao urged that the cadres of the old order who had earlier been spat on and stamped into the ground were in the main good men after all. They had simply "made mistakes". They should be "re-educated", and, once politically cleansed, "promptly liberated and assigned suitable work". In order to restore China to economic health the masses should "grasp revolution and promote production", Lin Piao said, but added carefully, "this is not to replace production with revolution, but to use revolution to command production, promote it and lead it forward". Finally, he made a strong appeal for national unity "as the basic guarantee of the sure triumph of our cause". His report was in itself a gesture of reconciliation, of recognition that the PLA and the pragmatic cadres opposed to the Cultural Revolution held powerful

---

* Although ranks were abolished in the PLA in 1965, it may sometimes be convenient to continue to use them in this book.

cards, and that the country was as disunited as ever beneath all the slogans and the speechifying.

After the election of the Central Committee and the Politburo, the next task was to create party organs consisting of "old, middle-aged and young people" which would assume ultimate political authority in China's 29 provinces. But in nearly every province the soldiers already controlled the revolutionary committee which provided the starting-point for the selection of future members of the new party committee, and they had no intention of being robbed of local power if it shifted from one to the other. Although Mao had urged all organisations to "discard the stale, take on the new", few of the younger representatives of the masses found themselves accepted as candidates for the top jobs.

When in August 1971 the last of the 29 party committees had finally come into being, it was clear that all but two (Peking and Shanghai) were run by the generals and the "professional" cadres of the old regime, and less than 5 per cent of the available places on them were held by "revolutionaries". For it had been laid down that when the delegates from the different streams of the "three-way alliance" – the army, the cadres, and the masses – disagreed over candidatures, the dispute would always be referred to the PLA.[1]

In theory, the party commanded the PLA, but in practice the soldiers controlled the party. This was the price that Mao had paid for knocking out Liu Shao-ch'i and the "small handful that took the capitalist road". Moreover, the argument that there could be no real conflict of interests because army and party were inextricably interwoven is untenable. The army was and is packed with commanders who believe that soldiers should be "expert" rather than "red", and who quarrel with Mao because he thinks it more important to arm troops with Maoism than with modern weapons and techniques (he is, of course, in favour of both – he is not *opposed* to modernisation). It is also full of senior cadres who originally joined up to fight the Japanese, not to become Marxists, of brothers-in-arms bound by local allegiances, and of generals anxious above all to preserve their own regional authority. It would be absurd, therefore, to try to determine what will happen when Mao dies without studying China's heirs apparent in military uniform against the patchwork of warring loyalties that is the People's

Liberation Army.* For whether Mao intended it or not,
political power still grows out of the barrel of a gun.

---

* The PLA (including the Chinese army, navy and air force)
numbers nearly 2,900,000 men. After the Cultural Revolution the
country was reduced from thirteen to eleven military regions, each
subdivided into two or three military districts corresponding to the
Chinese provinces. Each military district is assigned one "army" (it
is believed), usually of three divisions and therefore equivalent to a
large Western army corps.[2] Before the Communists declared the
People's Republic of China in 1949 and the PLA was reorganised,
however, the term "army" was extremely flexible.

8

The Mountain-Tops

The Chinese may seem strange in temperament and outlook to Europeans, but the difference is a matter of the mixture, not of the ingredients, for these are basically the same. It is common to find that what is taken to be a peculiarly Chinese social characteristic is simply a universal human trait in exaggerated form. Clannishness is a case in point, and their loyalties to family, clan, blood-brotherhood, home village and province weave a fabric which to the West may appear exotic or distorted, although the threads are just as familiar in Wales or Wichita. Local loyalties are fiercer, because for nearly three thousand years life has too often been cruel and emperors ruthless and despotic, and men who trusted each other have banded together for protection – even against society itself.

The Chinese Communist revolution was a patchwork affair, for individual leaders in different provinces and regions established their own guerrilla bases as and where and with whom they could in order to resist suppression by the Kuomintang armies of Generalissimo Chiang Kai-shek, and it was only when the KMT was on the run in 1949 that they could finally coalesce until all China was red. These earlier Soviets were often isolated, territorial commands, within which the revolutionaries organised the local peasants and relied upon captured weapons to hold off the enemy around them. Although owing political obedience to the Central Committee of the party, each Red chieftain was in fact king of his own castle, master of his own "mountain-top", as Maoist jargon has it. And when, like Montgomery's Eighth Army or Patton's Third Army, the mountain-top physically disappeared, its shadow nonetheless remained in the peace that followed, outlined by the loyalties of the units and the men and the ideas which had given it shape.

There is a modern tendency among foreign observers to scoff at those who say that important clues to the outcome of any power struggle in China may still lie in a line-up dictated by past or provincial military allegiances, but Mao himself and other Chinese Communists choose to ignore this fashion, and "mountain-top-ism" was repeatedly denounced by Peking as a cardinal sin committed by local leaders during the Cultural Revolution. Old loyalties must obviously be overlaid by new considerations in many cases, and the interplay among men can be deceptive, for the Chinese apply guerrilla tactics to political rivalry, and, rather than go down with a comrade when he falls into disgrace, will often run away to fight for him another day. But the jostling for position among generals and their followers from different revolutionary armies and provinces is as determined as ever.

This almost infinitely complicated subject can be simplified without dangerous distortion by reducing the development of the mountain-tops into three phases:

1 the Soviets and the Front Armies (the early thirties)
2 the Divisions and the Route Armies (1937–1938)
3 the Field Armies (1948–1949)

THE SOVIETS AND THE FRONT ARMIES

1 The Kiangsi Soviet and the First Front Army of Mao Tsetung

When Mao Tsetung withdrew to the mountain fastness of Chingkangshan after the abortive Autumn Harvest Uprising had cost him dear in dead and deserters, he disposed of only a few hundred men whom he organised into one regiment. But he was later joined by the veteran Chu Te, by the ex-Nationalist brigade commander P'eng Te-huai who brought a thousand soldiers with him, and by Lin Piao. After being besieged and dispersed, these comrades reassembled in Kiangsi, set up a Soviet, and later organised their troops into the First Front Army. Chu Te was Commander-in-Chief, P'eng Te-huai and Lin Piao commanded subordinate corps, and although in 1931 Chou En-lai may have succeeded Mao as political commissar, the Kiangsi Soviet and the First Front Army were nonetheless the mountain-top of the man who wielded the effective power, Mao Tsetung.

2   The Ohsiang* Soviet and the Second Front Army of Ho Lung

Ho Lung, nicknamed "The Moustache", came from a family of bandits who belonged to the Ko Lao Hui, a secret brotherhood of heroes who were ever ready to help the poor and attack and rob unscrupulous, rich and corrupt officials (but prudently depended for their regular income on salt-smuggling). He was born in 1896 in a poverty-stricken village in Hunan, where life verged on the barbarous and there were constant outbreaks of violence. As a young man The Moustache beat up his teacher, stole horses, sold opium, and when he was 19 he lost his temper one day with an officer who had exacted an exorbitant tax from him on "goods" he was transporting during a "business" trip. Bent on revenge, he gathered together twenty fine fellows and, armed with two choppers, led them into the local army post after dark. He then killed the offending detachment-commander, seized ten guns from his men, and fled into the mountains to begin his own independent career as a brigand.

Within five years he had collected around him a force of several thousand men and, like many bandits who made good in those days, he finally went "legitimate" by taking them into the Nationalist army of Chiang Kai-shek, where they were organised as a mixed brigade. He next joined the Communist Party, and with other Red commanders within the KMT (with whom the Communists were still officially cooperating) participated in the left-wing uprising in 1927 whose ultimate failure sent Chu Te and P'eng Te-huai to Mao in Kiangsi, but Ho Lung back to his home village. There The Moustache took over a group of bandits led by his sister, and from this built up what was to become the nucleus of the Second Front Army, once he had established the Ohsiang Soviet as his mountain-top.

The Moustache was known as a dashing philanderer among the girls of this area, who have a reputation for being passionate anyway, and was admired as a handsome, flamboyant swashbuckler as imaginative in war as he was in love. Operating around the shores of the Tungting lake, he captured not only arms and ammunition but horses and field pieces from the KMT, mobilised a motley collection of armed vessels, and was

---

* Ohsiang—taken from the classical names of the provinces it partly covered: Hunan and Hupeh.

soon running the only Soviet with its own cavalry, artillery and navy. A figure who magnetically attracted loyalty, he was denounced in 1967 as a member of the revisionist "black gang" of President Liu Shao-ch'i. Mao and Lin Piao knew they must still reckon with this man who, among all the Communist leaders, personified the "Robin Hood" spirit and style the Chinese so admire, and whose guns in the past had owed allegiance only to him personally.

3 The Oyuwan Soviet and the Fourth Front Army of "Slow March" Hsu Hsiang-ch'ien

As already noted, the political chief of this mountain-top was Chang Kuo-T'ao, whose quarrel with Mao so bedevilled the Long March.

These three Soviets were the frames on which Chinese Communist military loyalties were first woven, and the pattern is far more vivid than anything a Montgomery or a Mark Clark could achieve. For in Chinese armies generals often look upon their trusted subordinates as their own personal followers, and afford them protection and patronage to a degree unknown in the West. Chinese are accustomed to identifying officers as "Lin Piao's man", or "Ho Lung's man", or "Su Yu's man", for even in Mao's China a commander may still be a warlord in modern dress.

THE EIGHTH ROUTE ARMY AND THE NEW MOUNTAIN-TOPS

Between 1932 and 1934 Chiang Kai-shek, having earlier signed a truce with the invading Japanese which left him free to launch his successive "extermination campaigns" against the Communists, forced the First and Fourth Front Armies (comprising some 85,000 and 60,000 troops respectively) out of their beleaguered Soviets, and Ho Lung's Second Front Army, which was about 40,000 strong, followed in 1935. The Communist forces, therefore, made three "Long Marches" westwards to Szechuan and then northwards until they were united at their new main base around Yenan in 1936. The three mountain-tops had been left to guerrilla rearguards to hold where they could. But the cliques remained.

In the following year war broke out with Japan and the Communists agreed to fight as allies of the Nationalists. Their forces were organised into the Eighth Route Army, which was commanded by Chu Te "The Cook" (so named after he had escaped from the KMT years before disguised as one), and they were divided into three divisions. But it is not difficult to see how the loyalty system survived.

The three divisions were:

1 115th Division. This absorbed the First Front Army and was logically commanded by Mao's comrade from the Kiangsi Soviet, Lin Piao.*

2 120th Division. This absorbed the Second Front Army and was logically commanded by Ho Lung The Moustache.†

3 129th Division. This absorbed the convalescent Fourth Front Army, and should logically have been commanded by Slow March. But he was only second-in-command. The division was given to Liu Po-ch'eng (of whom more later), because Slow March had been close to Mao's enemy, Chang Kuo-t'ao.

The Communists then set about establishing new guerrilla bases in the north, and in consequence, new mountain-tops appeared. These were:

1 The North-West Border Region, Mao's base of resistance against Japan (and the KMT), with its capital at Yenan. This was defended by 60,000 men under the command of his other close lieutenant from the First Front Army in the Kiangsi Soviet, P'eng Te-huai.

2 The Shansi–Chahar–Hopei Soviet, the mountain-top of the Profligate Monk Nieh Jung-chen, second-in-command of the 115th Division.

3 The Shansi–Suiyuan Border Region, the new mountain-top of Ho Lung and his 120th Division.

4 The Shansi–Hopei–Shantung–Honan Soviet, the mountain-top of Liu Po-ch'eng with his 129th Division, and headquarters of the Eighth Route Army.

5 The North-East Democratic United Army, the basis of

---

* The 115th Division also had some detachments from the Fourth Front Army.

† Mao put two regimental commanders he trusted under Ho Lung's command to dilute his power within the 120th Division.

Lin Piao's mountain-top in **Manchuria**. This consisted of the forward units of his 115th Division plus elements drawn from other formations and Soviets.

6 The New 4th Army of Ch'en Yi, on the Yangtse River. The New 4th Army was assembled in 1938 from the forces left in the Red pockets still remaining in the south, and Ch'en Yi became its commander in 1941.

THE FIELD ARMIES

After the Sino-Japanese war, the Communists again regrouped to fight the Kuomintang, and in 1948 they organised their forces into five field armies. At this point the threads of allegiance ran as follows:

1st Field Army: from the Border Region defence force or "Yenan Army" of P'eng Te-huai and the 120th Division of Ho Lung The Moustache.

2nd Field Army: from the 129th Division under Liu Po-ch'eng.

3rd Field Army: from the New 4th Army of Ch'en Yi.

4th Field Army: the product of the 115th Division (forward units) and units from other formations in Manchuria sent by Mao to reinforce Lin Piao, and under his command.

5th Field Army: based on the forces of the Profligate Monk Nieh Jung-chen in his Shansi–Chahar–Hopei Soviet, where he commanded the rear of the 115th Division.

The chart overleaf shows the successive changes in the Red Army and its mountain-tops. From this it can be seen that most of the hard-core veterans in any given formation had made the same "Long March" together across twenty years from the same front army to the same field army. And what must be stressed is that after another twenty years most of them were still together, some in mountain-tops that can only be measured in terms of loyalty, others in mountain-tops that can actually be measured in terms of land.

When the Communists came out of their corners against the KMT for the knock-out in 1949, the main forces of 1st and 2nd Field Armies marched into west and south-west China, the 3rd Field Army occupied east China, and the 4th Field Army of Lin Piao, which had overrun Manchuria, drove down

THE CHINESE FIELD ARMY SYSTEM

The Soviets (1927–1930)	Front Armies (1931–1936)	8th Route Army (1937–1945)	Liberation Armies (1946–1948)	Field Armies (1949–1954)	Military Regions (Post-Liberation)
Ohsiang Soviet →	Second Front Army →	120th Division Shansi-Suiyuan Border Region (Ho Lung) →	Shansi-Suiyuan Army	1st Field Army (North-West China) →	Chengtu Lanchow Sinkiang
Kiangsi Soviet →	First Front Army →	North-west Border Region (P'eng Te-huai) →	Yenan Army		
		115th Division: – Advance Forces (Lin Piao) →	North-East Democratic United Army – North-East Liberation Army →	4th Field Army (Manchuria) →	Shenyang Canton
		– Shansi-Chahar Hopei Soviet (Nieh Jung-chen) →	North China Liberation Army →	5th Field Army (North China) →	Peking Inner Mongolia
	Southern Soviet stay-behind forces →	New 4th Army (Ch'en Yi) →	East China Liberation Army →	3rd Field Army (East China) →	Tsinan Nanking Foochow
Oyuwan Soviet →	Fourth Front Army →	129th Division Shansi-Hopei-Shantung–Honan Soviet (Liu Po-ch'eng) →	Central Plains Liberation Army →	2nd Field Army (Central China) →	Wuhan Kunming (Tibet)

(Note: at this stage the Communist forces were organised into "Red corps" and "Red armies" of varying strengths) to the southern provinces of Kwangtung and Kwangsi. The 5th Field Army of Nieh the Profligate Monk consolidated the Communist hold on North China, including Peking itself. Generals who had commanded mobile forces in the field now became governors administering static territorial domains. War broke out, and subsequently two-thirds of their veteran troops were despatched to Korea. When it was over, however, these men "returned to their units" – *Kuei Tui*, as the Chinese say, reading into it almost the sense of "returning home".

The field armies disappeared as commands, and Chinese forces were divided among thirteen (later eleven) territorial military regions. But new names do not alter geography, and even the physical pattern of allegiances was still clearly visible through the overlay of years and organisational change. The majority of the veterans and fighting units in the three western military regions were still from the 1st Field Army tradition, while in the south-west they were from the 2nd Field Army, in the three East China commands they were from the 3rd Field Army, in Shenyang and Canton (headquarters for Manchuria and South China respectively) they were from the 4th Field Army. And the former 5th Field Army – Nieh's one-time "North China Liberation Army" – was still in North China.

China is not a single unit, but the sum of its semi-autonomous parts. Among the Chinese, who know their country for a continent of diverse regions which give political fealty to one centre but largely run their own local affairs, this polarisation of military forces raises no eyebrows. It demands, however, that a careful balance be preserved between Peking and the provinces and between region and region if the nation is to hold together. A military district that has become the zone of influence of one field army, therefore, will always be dosed with a minority of commanders and units from another, and provincial "warlords" accept this exchange of monitors – within reason. Carried to excess, however, the system defeats itself. When Lin Piao pulled rank and imposed too many 4th Field Army officers of his own on a region that owed loyalty to another of China's revolutionary commanders, they were liable to find themselves isolated at the top of a pyramid of local distrust.

How have the other prestigious marshals who commanded the field armies and wrested China from the Nationalists in 1949 fared in the years that have followed?

P'eng Te-huai, the brilliant, hard-working ex-Nationalist general who came to command the 1st Field Army, was from the same county in Hunan as Mao Tsetung, and known as "Hades" because he was a devil for duty and seldom had time to smile. Although he was second-in-command of the Eighth Route Army, he was in fact more important than Chu Te, his older C-in-C, for he had been entrusted with the defence of Yenan, the holy city of Chinese Communism itself. But in 1959, as already remarked, he was nonetheless dismissed with ignominy from his post as Defence Minister after he had criticised Mao's Great Leap Forward. He was later arrested, and has since fallen from sight.

The other great commander in the 1st Field Army was Ho Lung The Moustache, who brought to it the traditions of his original Second Front Army. When the Communists were chasing the KMT out of China in 1949, Ho Lung led part of the 1st Field Army into Szechuan, and for five years occupied military and party posts which enhanced his influence in that province and the adjoining regions of Tibet and Sinkiang, the scene of China's current nuclear build-up. In the early sixties Mao looked on askance as ex-President Liu Shao-ch'i and the now discredited party secretary-general, Teng Hsiao-p'ing, gave The Moustache the necessary support to enable him to take over the day-to-day direction of the powerful Military Affairs Commission of the party from Lin Piao, the Defence Minister. It was later claimed that they then tried to use him to detonate a revolt against the Maoists in south-west China during the Cultural Revolution.

The upshot of this was that a large number of senior cadres of the 1st Field Army were branded as members of the revisionist "black gang". The Red Guards characteristically accused Ho Lung himself of being a terrorist, of leading a corrupt life, of keeping both Chinese and Western chefs and ten sedan-chair carriers, of gourmandising and boozing and extravagance. The Moustache was eliminated and his whereabouts are not known. The 1st Field Army man who commanded Chengtu Military Region was replaced by one from the 4th Field Army.* So was Wang En-mao, the former commander in Sinkiang and a veteran of the Ho Lung line from the days of the Second Front Army.

---

* Liang Hsing-ch'u (p. 135 ff).

Liu Po-ch'eng of the 2nd Field Army is also from Szechuan, and he linked up with Ho Lung when The Moustache marched his forces into the province in 1949. Blind in one eye, this "One-Eyed Dragon" quickly earned a name for ferocity among the Communists when young. Yet as a boy he studied literature and wanted to write, and was only kept down by the lowliness of his background – his father belonged to the despised calling of the hired bandsmen who still play excruciatingly at Chinese marriages and funerals outside China itself. The Dragon therefore turned to the martial arts and became a brigade commander under a Szechuan warlord, crossing to the Communists when he was robbed of his job, primarily because he was out for revenge. The party sent him to the Soviet Union for higher military training, and subsequently he wrote treatises on modern military theory and the lessons to be drawn from the Russian Army. He was with Mao in Kiangsi, and Chief of Staff on the Long March, but he turned back into Szechuan again with Chang Kuo-t'ao when the Red armies separated north of Maoerhkai. It is said that Mao deliberately attached him to Chang's Fourth Front Army as his watchdog, and that was why the One-Eyed Dragon came to be given command of the 129th Division, instead of Slow March.

His second wife was a tough campaigner who followed the army everywhere, and whose durability earned her the sobriquet of The Donkey. It was while they were arduously establishing his mountain-top in the Shansi–Hopei–Honan Soviet in the north that she first bore him a son which he humorously named after the great range that provided him with his stronghold in the area, Taihang. In time this became the largest base of the Communists, and the Dragon was the overlord of many million people by the time the Japanese surrendered. But his political commissar was Teng Hsiao-p'ing, the main target of the Red Guards during the Cultural Revolution after President Liu himself, and this was chalked up against him and his 2nd Field Army, despite – or in addition to – their successes.

The 2nd Field Army had taken more than 20,000 Japanese prisoners, and when it then turned upon the Kuomintang and started to move south, Liu Po-ch'eng's brilliant tactical sense and talent for surprise attack came to the fore. The 2nd and 3rd Field Armies (the latter under Ch'en Yi) won the model but merciless Suchow campaign which cost the KMT half a million men in 65 days, broke the heart of Nationalist resistance, and opened the way for the Communists to drive the enemy into the sea a thousand miles to the south. These were also the armies, 600,000 strong, that forced the crossing of the principal obstacle that remained, the two-mile-wide Yangtse River.

The indefatigable One-Eyed Dragon engineered the surrender of the last of the enemy in front of him when he reached Szechuan, but at the beginning of the fifties Mao, fearing that he wanted to turn that rich and remote province into a new mountain-top, had part of his army ordered to Tibet and another part to Korea, and Liu Po-ch'eng himself was transferred to Nanking as President of the Military Academy. Honours continued to be heaped upon him, but he was through as far as Mao was concerned.

The Dragon was nonetheless highly respected as a commander and military theorist, and is a proud man to boot. In his famous treatise "Our Red Army's Comprehension of Modern Strategy and Tactics",[1] he sharply reflected the dissatisfaction felt by many senior Chinese officers with Mao's military concepts, which he criticised as out of date and incapable of serving the needs of modern warfare. At the same time he again stressed Russian military theory, and urged that China should have a "professional" army.

In the days of their guerrilla struggle against the KMT, the Chinese Communists – hardened in the furnace of experience – paid greater attention to political training than to military knowledge, for they depended on their ability to rouse and organise the masses against a corrupt adversary. But when the Russians began to supply the PLA with better weapons in the fifties, ideology gave way to professional skill, men became less "red" and more "expert", and this in turn vitiated personal worship of Mao himself. So like Hades P'eng Te-huai, the One-Eyed Dragon had to be curbed.

The same, it appeared, applied to Ch'en Yi, and others loyal to the traditions of the 3rd Field Army were also to feel the chill. There was a tendency not to take Ch'en Yi quite seriously as a Communist fighter. He came from a relatively genteel background, being the son of a magistrate serving in Hunan, and as a young man liked tea and talk and soccer and poetry, studied in France, edited a newspaper in his native Szechuan, translated Guy de Maupassant. He grew into a stout, bald, jowly man, fussy about food and his clothes. He had a reputation as a woman-chaser and a lover of the theatre, and once remarked "The women in the army cultural troupe – together with the radio and medicine – are what make war livable. Without women, guerrillas would have no souls." When Mao Tsetung's younger brother* was killed in the Kiangsi Soviet, he promptly married the widow (and when she died, he married an actress).

After the taking of Shanghai, Ch'en the Bald became city mayor, fell in love with a beautiful opera-singer, and even took her to a political conference in Peking to introduce a little sunshine into it. He regarded love as an art, and composed songs to express it, and his next passion was a dancer.[2] "Bald men are great lovers," it is said in China. "No palace eunuch was ever bald." Ch'en Yi, many suggest slyly, proved the old saying to be true.

But he was thrown out of France for assaulting the Nationalist Chinese ambassador, served as the adjutant of a Szechuan warlord once back in China, took part in the Nanchang Uprising in 1927, and joined Mao on Chingkangshan. It was Ch'en Yi who commanded with notable savagery the rearguard that held the Kiangsi Soviet for several months after Mao had left on the Long March. He again showed considerable military skill in adversity when leading the New 4th Army, and together with his political commissar, Liu Shao-ch'i, and his able deputy commander, Su Yu, he strengthened and expanded his forces progressively until they were reorganised as the 3rd Field Army. But just as 2nd Field Army officers are associated in unfriendly minds with Teng Hsiao-p'ing, their political commissar, so 3rd Field Army officers are associated with Liu Shao-ch'i. Like the cadres of the 2nd Field Army, moreover, those of the 3rd Field Army were to develop strong prejudices about the crying need for more professionalism and modernisation in the PLA. For both sent "volunteers" to Korea.

The official propaganda assured any fainthearts that there might be among them: "The American is a paper tiger, a playboy soldier unable to endure hardship and afraid of fighting. A wooden pole can kill more than ten Americans carrying submachine guns, a grenade can destroy three or four tanks, and a bullet from a rifle can shoot down an American plane. When

---

* Mao Tse-tan.

81

the American soldiers meet the Chinese People's Volunteer Army, they immediately throw down their guns, kneel, and surrender." Armed with outdated weapons in which they had thus been tricked into putting full confidence, the Chinese learned the difference between rodomontade and reality on the Korean battlefield, and awoke from their dreams. The paper tiger, it was discovered, was capable of swallowing men by the thousand, given his tremendous firepower. Commanders returned to China convinced that the army must be revolutionised.

Ch'en the Bald, tough and unscrupulous behind all the bonhomie and the dark glasses, was not a man to keep his mouth shut on a subject like this. "If a pilot is more expert than red," he is reported to have said, "he may defect. But if he is more red than expert, he'll be shot down." In 1961 he was still putting technical knowledge before political doctrine. "A student's first duty is to study," he urged undergraduates. "Knowing his subject is his contribution to society." It was inevitable, therefore, that during the Cultural Revolution he should have fallen foul of the Red Guards, who at one point invaded his ministry, put in their own "four-day Foreign Minister", and aired secrets from the archives on "big-character" wall-posters in a sort of Chinese version of the Pentagon Papers affair.

Ch'en Yi was obliged to make a public self-criticism, but emerged as blunt and acerbic as ever, it seems, claiming that he had only done so under duress. He was smeared by Red Guard bulletins and revolutionary mosquito-papers, which accused him of mouthing such heresies as: "If you are talking about strait-jackets, then Mao Tsetung's Thought is the biggest strait-jacket of all . . . Speaking of fixed notions, the Thought of Mao is just one big fixed notion . . . The Central Committee of the party is now letting the students go mental . . . More and more big-character posters have appeared, and as the characters have become bigger and bigger, the level has become lower and lower . . . The dancers in one country always dance topless. Does this mean that if you dance topless you are watering down the revolution? It is a question of custom."

Chou En-lai sprang to Ch'en Yi's defence, but he lost effective control of his ministry as well as nearly thirty pounds in weight, his wife was dragged around the streets to be jeered at, and his son was given a suspended sentence of death for alleged anti-Maoist activities. "Ho Lung is a Politburo member and a marshal, how can you suddenly call him a bandit?" cried Ch'en Yi. He might almost have been speaking about himself – but not quite. He dropped from public view altogether, and his next official appearance was at his own funeral.

What of the 4th Field Army of Lin Piao? Its cadres have boasted: "Having liberated the whole of the north-east, the 4th Field Army occupied Peking and Tientsin, effortlessly seized control of Wuhan and Changsha, and marched triumphantly southward to Kwangtung and Kwangsi, crossing the sea in junks to liberate even the island of Hainan after a one-thousand-mile expedition that included overcoming such obstacles as the Yellow River and the Yangtse Kiang." This propaganda version of the achievements of the 4th Field Army completely ignores the fact that the 2nd and 3rd Field Armies won the vital battles that opened the way for it to advance so "effortlessly" and march so "triumphantly".

After the Cultural Revolution Lin Piao was not only Vice-Chairman of the Communist Party and Minister of Defence, but the official heir-designate of Mao himself. In Peking 4th Field Army ex-generals held four out of five key posts in the Chinese military machine and were members of the Politburo (see Chapter 11). But while it is evident that Mao and Lin tried to use this particular net of military loyalties to enable them to hold power, however elusive, firmly in their hands, it would be dangerous to oversimplify on this basis or to imagine that the label "4th Field Army" was an automatic passport to promotion, for two reasons.

First, the 4th Field Army was created out of Lin Piao's force in Manchuria, and this comprised not only the heirs to the First Front Army–115th Division system, but other units, including some from Ch'en the Bald's 3rd Field Army. Not all "4th Field men", therefore, were automatically trusted, long-standing comrades-in-arms as far as Mao and Lin were concerned.

Secondly, Lin Piao never enjoyed such overwhelming and universal respect as a soldier or a communist that the "mountains" were ready to bow down to him. In consequence, Mao and Lin were obliged to woo other military cliques, and horse-trade where wooing failed. This explains why a post of importance would sometimes go to a cadre from a different tradition of allegiances who might otherwise be troublesome, instead of to a 4th Field man whose compliance Lin did not have to buy.

It is because it persists that the concept of the mountain-top and the independent kingdom must be vigorously attacked. The One-Eyed Dragon may be eighty and half-blind, Ho Lung seventy-six and fallen from sight, but mountain-tops also have their heirs and successors in such men as the powerful commanders of the Nanking and Shenyang Military Regions, who dispose of more than half a million men between them, and the PLA is permeated with cadres who believe that the teachings of the One-Eyed Dragon must prevail, if only after Mao dies.[3]

The military, not the masses, were the masters of the provinces in 1972, and their autonomous powers had been enhanced by Peking's campaign to promote decentralised local industry. The territorial divisions of China do not fade but deepen, and it is probable that the mountain-tops themselves will not decrease, but multiply.

9

Three "Comrades"

PART ONE: "IRONSIDES" HSU SHIH-YU

In April 1969 the Ninth Congress of the Chinese Communist Party gave birth to a new Politburo, about half of whose 25* members were soldiers. Of these, three men could be said, broadly speaking, to represent three major attitudes towards Mao and Lin Piao within the People's Liberation Army. They are:

"Ironsides" Hsu Shih-yu, a Red warlord and a "new powerholder" who had risen from anti-Maoist roots in the Chinese revolution;

Li Te-sheng, "The Bayonet", superficially loyal to the Mao–Lin group, but in reality a fence-sitter, poised between Mao and the new powerholders;

Wu Fa-hsien, "Kiangsi Favourite" and trusted comrade of Lin Piao.

Commonly referred to as one of the Three Heavenly Guardians of the Chinese Communist Party,[1] Hsu Shih-yu is not only Commander of the Nanking Military Region, but was elected First Secretary of the Kiangsu Provincial Party Committee in December 1970. Of all 25 members of the Politburo, he has in some respects the most complicated history.

"Ironsides" was born in 1906 to a poor family in Hupeh,† but he dropped out of school at an early age, became a vagabond, and wandered footloose into Honan, where he entered the Shao Lin Monastery to learn boxing. The brothers of Shao Lin are well-known throughout the country as expert fighters. Early in the T'ang Dynasty an abbot of this monastery, aided by thirteen pugnacious monks, helped the Emperor T'ai

---

* Including four alternate members.
† Not Honan, as sometimes stated.

Tsung to suppress a rebellion. The Imperial Court offered them all rewards and the abbot accepted the title of "Great General". The others, however, insisted on observing Buddhist rules more strictly and refused to become imperial officers. Shunning worldly reputation, each accepted a purple silk robe from the Emperor, but retired again to the monastery to resume his secluded life.

It then became a tradition for the monks to learn the martial arts for, especially during the Ch'ing Dynasty, the neighbourhood was infested with bandits. The monastery was rich and stood by itself on a hill, and the monks practised constantly, until they had earned a reputation for winning all their battles, and the bandits left them severely alone. But at Shao Lin it was not customary to restrict instruction in mayhem to monks, and many ambitious young men, vagrants, fugitives and travellers were accepted as pupils.

When Hsu Shih-yu arrived at the monastery he was a poverty-stricken but hot-blooded young man, stocky and strong as a cedarwood rice-pestle. He had a broad head and a pleasant-looking face and, although quick-tempered, possessed a ready smile, which, together with a pair of child-like eyes, gave others a favourable impression. At Shao Lin, emphasis was placed not only on fighting skill but on the importance of cultivating courage and the heroic spirit in students, on instilling into them a readiness to "draw the sword to help all who suffer from injustice". With the passage of time, Hsu became tougher, more agile, intoxicated by his own hard-earned ability, and he made up his mind to fight for an "empire" for himself.

Having little education, he knew nothing about the situation in China and was quite unfamiliar with politics. So on leaving the monastery, he became a soldier in the army of a well-known warlord* who enjoyed British support. Training was strict, but Hsu enjoyed it, and his prowess at shooting, close combat, scouting, swimming, and mountain-climbing quickly won him the esteem of his officers. But not long afterwards the Nationalists launched the Northern Expedition, the warlord was defeated and fled, and Hsu returned to his native Hupeh.

He arrived home in time to take part in the same Communist insurrection as Li Hsien-nien and other comrades of the "Ma

---

* Wu P'ei-fu.

Huang Group" who by 1971 were of considerable significance: "Slow March" Hsu Hsiang-ch'ien, ex-marshal and a vice-chairman of the National Defence Council; Ch'en Hsi-lien, Commander of Shenyang Military Region; Li Hsien-nien, Minister of Finance; Le Te-sheng, Director of the General Political Department of the PLA; Cheng Wei-san, Acting Commander of Peking Military Region; Wang Shu-sheng, Deputy Minister of National Defence; and Wang Hung-k'un, Second Political Commissar of the navy. History bound these men together, and they played an important role in the rise of Ironsides both before and after the Cultural Revolution. When the Oyuwan Soviet that grew out of their revolt was besieged by the KMT in 1932, and the badly-mauled Fourth Front Army broke out of the ring to begin its own "Long March", Hsu Shih-yu led the vanguard. After months of struggling through treacherous mountains and crossing fast-flowing rivers the army penetrated the territory of the Szechuan warlords in western China. By then only about sixteen thousand men remained, according to some estimates, but fortunately for them, the Szechuanese were split by factional strife and, making use of this chaotic situation, the Reds rapidly overran several counties. As their political leader, Chang Kuo-t'ao then called for a grand meeting of workers, peasants, and soldiers, and founded a Szechuan–Shensi Soviet. To deal with this intrusion, however, the local warlords quickly shelved their disputes and attacked. The Fourth Front Army shortened its lines and with Hsu Shih-yu leading its best troops retired to Tapa Shan, a mountain range rising to 6,000 feet above sea level in northern Szechuan. The heterogeneous enemy mounted repeated assaults against them, but was repelled each time.

Ironsides was already proving a very capable officer, especially powerful in attack and counter-attack. He was much respected by Chang Kuo-t'ao, and by 1933 had been promoted to command the Ninth Corps although he was only 27 years old. His deputy was the present Commander of Shenyang Military Region, Ch'en Hsi-lien. He treated every aspect of soldiering seriously. He was hard on his officers, and always delivered his orders sharply. Thanks to his own extraordinary courage in battle, his forces often suffered heavy casualties, which provoked discontent in the lower ranks. Yet, because he had a strong, overbearing nature, his subordinates did not dare to give vent to their anger. It was for this reason that they called him Ironsides.

In August 1934, the Reds on Tapa Shan launched a series of sudden attacks on the Szechuanese anti-Communists and defeated the six armies surrounding them. Their territory expanded until it took in 26 counties and gave them control over a large population which they proceeded to organise very thoroughly. Adults were conscripted, the aged were pressed into making shoes for the soldiers, children were responsible for standing guard, women were detailed to wash and mend the clothes of the fighting men, and there were soon more than fifty thousand under arms. But it was just as they were consolidating this success that the Central Committee was forced to break out of the Kiangsi Soviet under overwhelming pressure from the Kuomintang. Mao's Long March had begun.

When Mao Tsetung regained official control of the army from Chou En-lai at the Tsunyi Conference in January of the following year, he inherited a precarious situation, for the Reds were everywhere harassed by the Nationalists. In the name of the Central Committee, therefore, he instructed the Fourth Front Army to move south to meet his weakened First Front Army. The union did not last long, as we know, but by the time Mao and Chang Kuo-t'ao had quarrelled and separated at Maoerhkai and Chang had turned back, the situation was much changed. The local Szechuanese armies had been combined under Kuomintang leadership and were now commanded by Hsueh Yueh, the redoubtable Nationalist general who had pursued Mao untiringly from Kiangsi.[2] His way blocked by strong forces, Ironsides could not break through with his vanguard and the Communists were compelled to change their tactics and retire to the T'ienchuan–Lu Shan region (from ancient times a favourite battle-ground, the encircling, close-packed mountains providing suitable camp-sites for the warring troops on their flat summits).

The weather was very bad. Rain fell continuously, and when at last it ceased, there was thick fog and a heavy snowfall. The Kuomintang could not use the air force for either reconnaissance or attack, and the roads up the hills were without cover. Hsueh Yueh felt that the landscape itself was against the Nationalists, and realised that an advance in broad daylight would exact great sacrifices. He therefore laid plans for an indirect assault.

Some Nationalist units were despatched to harass Ironsides, and at the same time Hsueh Yueh ordered his crack 92nd Division to launch a surprise attack. The infantry put on white cotton uniforms and, taking advantage of the falling snow, struck in the dark against the right wing of the communists, forced their way through the enemy lines, and seized a strong-point behind them. When the weather cleared, the Nationalist army mounted its main onslaught against the enemy's fissured defences, and the KMT air force carried out carpet-bombing. The Red army could not withstand the pressure and was finally overrun. Hsueh Yueh's troops charged right into the heart of Hsu Shih-yu's base and fierce close-quarter fighting followed. The Fourth Front Army was totally defeated and Ironsides fled hastily into Sikang with the remnants of his force.

"To close in on them tightly and hit them hard so that they could not counter-attack: that was the general principle of the Nationalist army," Hsueh Yueh told us years afterwards, explaining the ferocity of his assault. "Yet too often, on gaining ground, we concentrated on consolidating our position instead of pursuing the enemy to the end. He would then escape, and like rekindled embers, come back again. By that time, our opportunity had been lost. That was our greatest error." The shaken Reds spent several months recuperating in the fastnesses of Sikang, but when they marched north again, it was only to suffer the crushing defeat at the hands of the KMT from which the Money God Li Hsien-nien escaped into Sinkiang with only a fragment of his force.

Hsu Shih-yu did not participate in this fiasco, for he had temporarily remained behind in Sikang. When he did reach Yenan, however, Mao was in full cry against the "flightist" Chang Kuo-t'ao. He stripped Ironsides of all military authority and allegedly had other senior subordinates of Chang quietly executed.[3] Hsu was too fearless and impetuous to stand for this ill-treatment, and refused to bow to reality. He rallied members of the Ma Huang Group in the Fourth Front Army and incited 400 students of the Anti-Japanese Military and Political University in Yenan to rebel against Mao. This move failed, and he tried to escape with ten other members of the group but was caught. At first they were to be thrown into prison, but the news provoked a dangerous agitation in army circles, so Mao switched to softer tactics and sent Hsu to the Anti-Japanese

University himself for training. This, however, amounted to house arrest and was merely cover for a period of detention and "self-examination".

When the Sino-Japanese War broke out in September 1937 Hsu received a magnanimous pardon. He was posted to the 129th Division and in 1940 became commander of one of its brigades. The deputy divisional commander was Slow March, and the division was full of old comrades from the Ma Huang group. Its commander was the "One-Eyed Dragon", Liu Po-ch'eng, famous in the Communist world for his savagery. With many friends around him, therefore, Ironsides Hsu Shih-yu moved with the division into Shantung.

After the war ended in 1945, some of the divisional units were despatched piecemeal to Manchuria, but Hsu Shih-yu stayed behind to guard Shantung and to dominate the coast around the Gulf of Chihli with his own army. By mid-1946 relations between the Nationalists and the Communists were at breaking-point, and their struggle for the mastery of China developed rapidly. But the Red army was poorly equipped, and Ironsides' troops lay hidden in the mountains most of the time, making unpredictable appearances when they dared. They had no fixed camp and were like a band of guerrillas, their head-quarters usually perched on top of some steep cliff with a commanding view so that Hsu could place himself halfway between the sea and the sky. With these tactics he was nevertheless able to block the entrance of the Gulf of Chihli along the north-east coast of China despite the adverse conditions, and the Shantung peninsula became a big encampment for the Reds with direct communications to Manchuria.

It had hitherto been Communist strategy to avoid pitched battles with the Nationalist army, and his defeat at T'ench'uan and Lu Shan had taught Ironsides a sharp lesson. He seldom fought now, and his slogan while guarding Shantung was: "When the enemy comes, we go; when the enemy goes, we come, from nothing becoming the whole, and from the whole becoming nothing" (i.e. changing the civilians into an army, and the army back into civilians as the situation demands). When Hsu found a small Nationalist force intruding into his territory, he would implement the "big eats little" principle and devour his enemy. When the Nationalists occupied the cities, Ironsides made use of the sprawling, mountainous countryside to creep behind the KMT army and to spy out vulnerable points for attack, always with the intention of seizing more guns and ammunition. The Communist forces in Hsu's military zone grew steadily in strength under his leadership and were finally included in the 3rd Field Army commanded by Ch'en Yi, who treated him as one of his most trusted subordinates.

During this period, Liu Shao-ch'i was frequently on the move in southern Shantung, and had many opportunities to make contact with Hsu, and Ironsides was already in the confidence of the future President of China whom Mao was to hound from office. In 1954 Hsu was appointed Commander of Nanking, today one of the most important of the eleven military regions of Communist China.[4] He controlled the three military districts of Kiangsu, Anhwei and Chekiang provinces, was master of more than 200,000 men of the PLA (including air force and navy), and in the following year he was made a colonel-general.

In 1958, an anti-rightist campaign was launched within the PLA, and on Mao's orders Ironsides was reduced to the ranks for one month. This temporary demotion of party cadres and senior officers, who had to become manual workers and ordinary soldiers respectively, was designed to remould their thoughts but aroused widespread dissatisfaction among high officials and generals. The PLA was a classless army already, it was argued. A commander was not necessarily higher in status than a soldier, but their duties differed. Soldiers were young men in good health whose main purpose was to engage in combat, while an officer was responsible for their training and should have a rich knowledge of military affairs in general as well as practical experience in the field. It was totally unreasonable to make a fifty-year-old commander fight as an infantryman and by the same token it was demeaning for officers to be demoted, even temporarily, to the rank of private.

However, Mao Tsetung's order had to be obeyed. So when Ironsides became a soldier, he behaved as if he had taken off his armour: he felt light and free, since he was without responsibilities and, in sharp contrast to his usual solemnity, he started to sing popular folk-songs and joke noisily with the other men. His conduct was meant to be a not-so-silent protest against the instructions of the Military Affairs Commission of the party that officers be stripped of their rank to meet Mao's demand for "thought re-education".

In September of the following year Lin Piao succeeded the disgraced P'eng Te-huai as Minister of National Defence. Despite this move against professional officers critical of Mao's policies, however, Hsu not only escaped being purged, but was appointed a vice-minister, while remaining Commander of the Nanking Military Region. This appeared to indicate that he had special backing from Liu Shao-ch'i, and in 1967 a Japanese expert in Chinese Communist affairs published this curious report[5]:

"In 1965, the Central Committee of the Chinese Communist Party held a conference at which Mao Tsetung denounced Liu Shao-ch'i bitterly to his face. The burden of his outburst was that the 'Three Red Flag' campaign* inaugurated in 1958 had not been executed in accordance with his own directions. During his attack on Liu, Mao became very excited, like a man seized with apoplexy, and at one point fainted. After that he stood alone within the party, only Ch'en Po-ta and Chiang Ch'ing remaining loyal to him, and he was even put under house arrest. Feeling that his situation was not too favourable, Mao decided to leave Peking. Chiang Ch'ing told Wang Kuang-mei (Liu Shao-ch'i's wife) that Mao intended to go to Hangchow for a rest, but Liu did not approve . . . and once Mao was in Hangchow, he sent a secret order to the Commander of the Nanking Military Region, Hsu Shih-yu, instructing him to have someone keep an eye on the Chairman. Through Chiang Ch'ing's efforts, Mao managed to get into touch with Lin Piao, who was in Shanghai, and from Lin's investigations discovered that the officer in charge of this surveillance operation had been a pupil of K'ang Sheng, head of the Chinese Special Service. Mao then contrived to have K'ang come to Hangchow . . ."

The surveillance ended, but the fact that Ironsides should have anything at all to do with watching Mao in Hangchow shows how far he was now prepared to move against the Chairman. In 1966 the tables were turned, Mao and Lin were openly confronting Liu Shao-ch'i in Peking, and Liu was soon to be put under house arrest. Yet despite this drastic change in the situation, Ironsides started a campaign for the study of *How To Be A Good Communist.*

---

* Embracing the Great Leap Forward, the people's communes, and the general revolutionary line of Mao Tsetung.

How To Be A Good Communist was written by Liu Shao-ch'i when he was at the party school in Yenan. It was a draft for a series of addresses, and in all it ran to about 48,000 words. It condemned the idolisation of individuals, opposed struggles waged without any apparent reason, and encouraged solidarity with the Soviet Union. In essence, it was a practical Communist guide that in earlier years every Party member had to read. But by 1966 it was heresy – especially as Mao Tsetung himself was being inexorably deified.

Communist China was now bestowing more and more adulatory titles upon the Chairman – The Great Teacher, The Great Helmsman, The Red Sun in Our Hearts. In the early fifties already, a "Mao Tsetung Mass' was celebrated every Saturday at the reform-through-labour camp established at Yenan for members of religious sects, at which Communist cadres responsible for "liberation from religion" would repeatedly tell the devout: "With all your superstition and worship, your calling 'Amitabha Buddha' ten thousand times, saying 'Amen' a hundred times, or reciting 'Faith brings Salvation' a thousand times, does bread drop down from the sky for you? But all you have to do is to say just once 'Salvation lies in believing in Mao Tsetung' or 'Follow Mao Tsetung to salvation', and you will immediately receive your 'Mao Tsetung Mass meal '."

The "Mao Tsetung Mass meal" was the portion of food that the Communists distributed to all those who attended the Mass. It included four taels of steam-bread,* two taels of cooked pork, and four taels of sugar per person. The political cadres stressed that religion was the product of a feudal society, but told the Christians: "Jesus was an illegitimate child of Mary and the son of the carpenter, Joseph. Hence, Jesus and his whole family were members of the proletariat, and later he was crucified for leading the proletarian class against the despotic ruling class."

The last ceremony in the "Mao Tsetung Mass" was a prayer session led by the cadres. The prayer ran: "Under the banner of Mao Tsetung, I love my country, I love my people, I love the property of my people. I hold firm to my stand as a member of the proletariat. I accept labour reform and thought-reform. I will examine myself and continuously reform myself. Long live Chairman Mao."[6]

---

* The tael is the Chinese ounce.

Mao had become a God in China. There was always someone responsible for starting to clap the moment he entered a room, so that all those present would know that he had arrived and would stand up and give him an ovation. During the Cultural Revolution, clapping was not enough. Slogans had to be shouted too, for Lin Piao had declared: "It takes the world a few hundred years, and China a few thousand years, to produce a man of the talents of Chairman Mao. Chairman Mao is the greatest genius in the world. Therefore, without Chairman Mao, we would be without this great party of ours, without this great army of ours, without this great China of ours, without all that belongs to the people of China, and without the liberation of peoples throughout the world."[7]

Liu Shao-ch'i's condemnation of the cult of the personality inevitably came under fire. *How To Be A Good Communist* was branded "anti-Maoist" and a "poisonous weed" that betrayed the dictatorship of the proletariat. Yet Ironsides dared to start a campaign within the army to study this book, undoubtedly in order to give Liu Shao-ch'i moral support and to strengthen his following at a difficult moment. This display of opposition to Mao by Hsu, coupled with his loyalty to Chang Kuo-t'ao back in the Yenan days, faithfully reflects his uncompromising nature and his firm hold upon his own convictions and purpose. There are people who criticise him as rough-spoken, uncouth, and without restraint. But such men are often rich in human emotions, and perhaps Hsu is a true heir of the dying ideals of Shao Lin Monastery.

Inevitably, Ironsides had little sympathy with the Cultural Revolution, which increasingly threatened the stability of Nanking. Already filled with a sense of frustration for which there was no outlet, he had to stand by in 1967 and witness bloody clashes between the Red Guards and innocent villagers visiting the city which lasted for five consecutive days, since it was supposedly the army's duty to "Support the Left". Finally, however, he called out the troops and arrested more than 2,000 Maoist Red Guards and "revolutionary rebels". This dealt a body-blow to the Cultural Revolution in Nanking and for a while it seemed as if it might collapse. Pro-Mao factions accused Hsu of being a "king-protector" and a crony of Liu Shao-ch'i. The Military Affairs Commission of the party summoned him to Peking for an explanation, but he turned a deaf ear. He had already flouted Mao himself, so there was no one to whom he need kow-tow.

It was only about half a year later that K'ang Sheng was finally able to placate and reassure Ironsides enough to persuade him to go to the capital (they had worked together in Shantung after the Korean war – Ironsides as military commander and K'ang as political commissar – and they were on good terms). Once he was there, Chiang Ch'ing personally attempted to win Hsu over. She appeared to succeed – at least superficially – and before he returned to Nanking he attended Mao Tsetung Thought study classes for a few months. But his compliance subsequently proved to be simply a matter of sound strategy – his official authority was not in any way diminished and he was later elected first secretary of the new provincial party committee of Kiangsu.

It is more than 18 years since Ironsides Hsu Shih-yu became the boss of Nanking, and this is the longest term of office of any commander of a big military region. His influence is evidently very deep-rooted and he cannot easily be dislodged. He is, therefore, a tower of strength among the new power-holders in Communist China. Not only is he by nature thrifty, he is even miserly. He will risk his life to hold on to whatever he owns. For this very reason, most probably, only Hsu of all the senior officers in the former 3rd Field Army still holds a great regional command. Since he is jealous of what he has, and what he has is provincial power backed by nearly a quarter of a million armed men, Hsu will remain a major piece on the board, even if "covered" or cornered.

PART TWO: THE TWO-EDGED BAYONET

During the confused and tumultuous year of 1967 Hsu Shih-yu found himself not only stamping on the Red Guard movement on his own doorstep at Nanking, but rushing reinforcements to other parts of his disturbed fief like the province of Anhwei, where soldiers dutifully obeying Mao's instructions to "Support the Left" were attacked by undiscriminating left-wing rebels on the rampage. These Maoist rowdies were bent on seizing weapons from local troops of the 12th Army under Li Te-sheng in order to "make revolution". Li had moved adroitly, however, and they soon found themselves facing not only the soldiers of the anti-Maoist Ironsides, but the censure of their own champion, Chiang Ch'ing herself.

This was the beginning of a delicate, mutually advantageous understanding between mutually distrustful camps. Li threw himself into the task of suppressing the more obstreperous hotheads, but at the same time he allowed local radio stations to disseminate the Thoughts of Mao and to broadcast the inflammatory slogans of Chiang Ch'ing, urging all to complete the Cultural Revolution. In the course of this "culturally offensive yet militarily defensive" programme, the old bureaucratic party administration was duly overthrown and Li reaped long-term rewards. He was promoted to be Commander of Anhwei Military District, and when the Anhwei Revolutionary Committee was created in April 1968, he inevitably emerged as its chairman. Speaking at its inauguration, he solemnly declared: "After the formation of this Revolutionary Committee, the most important and fundamental task is to hold high the Great Red Flag of the Thoughts of Mao Tsetung and to follow the glorious example of Vice-Chairman Lin Piao. In our hearts there is only loyalty for Chairman Mao, Great Leader of the Proletariat. Towards the invincible Thoughts of Mao Tsetung, we have only one intention – to put them into practice. With class struggle as our platform, we shall spare no effort to revolutionise the ideology of the people and turn our Anhwei Province into a fiery red university of the Thoughts of Mao."

Li was learning. He came from Hupeh, like Lin Piao and Huang Yung-sheng, the Chief of Staff, but until a year before he had simply been one of thirty younger professional generals who had played little part in politics. By 1970, however, he was not only first secretary of the new party committee of Anhwei as well as the provincial army commander, but he had soared to the top in Peking itself. In 1969 the Ninth Party Congress elected him to be an alternate member of the Politburo, and in the following year he was appointed Director of the General Political Department of the PLA – in short, he was now chief commissar of the Chinese army.

His rise was so spectacular that many had come to regard him as a genuine Maoist. They felt that his appointment as Director of the PLA's Political Department reflected the mounting influence of the Chiang Ch'ing faction. However, there were others who held that, on the contrary, it reflected the mounting influence of the army. It is difficult to judge how far either reading is correct, but his promotion certainly owed something to the "barrel of the gun" he carried, as will be seen.

Li Te-sheng, now about 58, is stout, a little clumsy, but not obese. His fleshy yet somewhat childish face often wears an expression of doubt or tension, and his eyebrows seem to have been knit permanently into a frown, as if he had been beaten or censured by others and was close to tears. Sometimes he appears to have drawn all his energy up into his face in his determination to overcome his enemies, and it lacks any sign of serenity.

Though headstrong and vainglorious, he was always regarded as frank, trustworthy, and basically good-natured when younger. During the Cultural Revolution, however, he hugged his military power to himself and looked upward. He became sly and wily, yet at the same time unsure and perplexed. His aims and loyalties grew indistinct, and he appeared to have two different faces.

Li was involved in the Hupeh uprising of the Ma Huang Group, and was a company commander in the Fourth Front Army during the Long March. From this point onwards he followed, like so many others, his predetermined thread through the military tapestry of the PLA – he fought the Japanese with the 129th Division, and he fought the Chinese Nationalists with the 2nd Field Army that grew out of it. He rose from battalion to divisional commander and his patrons and teachers were Liu Po-ch'eng, the One-Eyed Dragon, and Ch'en Hsi-lien, "The Ferocious Tiger", today chief of the Shenyang Military Region that takes in all Manchuria.

For his courage in action, Li Te-sheng earned the nickname "Bayonet Commander", and became something of an idol among the troops. The sobriquet fitted him, men joked, for he himself was "brave but blunt". Ch'en Hsi-lien was different. The Ferocious Tiger had mastered the One-Eyed Dragon's trickery in military manoeuvre, knew his enemy, and fought with a mixture of flexibility and ruthlessness that made him an outstanding general. He would accept temporary setbacks and the loss of his supply lines, big towns or great stretches of terrain in order to conceal his corps in the rural areas and tempt the enemy to over-extend until he was burdened and weakened and his vulnerable points were exposed. Then he would attack savagely with all available forces and exterminate him. He had tremendous staying-power and the best equipment for his troops, and although Li The Bayonet did not share his talent, he nonetheless won battles under the guidance and command of the One-Eyed Dragon and this intimidating Tiger.

As the Communist struggle against Chiang Kai-shek's KMT armies developed, Li Te-sheng followed Liu Po-ch'eng back into his native Hupeh. Now, lying between the Tungpai mountains and the Tahung range in the north is a small plain known as the "Neck of Hupeh". By January 1948 the Neck had been much fought over by different armies, and at that moment it was under the control of the forces of Li Hsien-nien. To the west was a hillock named Yellow Dragon Stand with about one hundred houses on it. This was the homeland of Money God Li, and it lay at the boundary of the Neck and the neighbouring county of Hsiang Yang.

The One-Eyed Dragon now set out to overrun Hsiang Yang, hoping to join forces with the troops of the Money God and then march south to lay siege to Wuhan on the Yangtse River. Hsiang Yang was a stronghold of the Kuomintang Army. Its commander, K'ang Tse, had earlier created an efficient Nationalist secret-service organisation inside the Red area and he was an expert in guerrilla infiltration. But he had no experience of large-scale battles, so the task of defending Hsiang Yang, and particularly the county town of the same name, fell to his deputy. The town was strategically placed and well-fortified, and the defenders were armed with modern artillery that fired chemical shells capable of spreading fire, smoke and poison gas up to a range of nearly four miles. The KMT had also fortified the peak of Five-Mile Ridge, a natural keep to the west of Hsiang Yang covering the town itself.

Liu Po-ch'eng pitched camp at the foot of this ridge, and his troops dug trenches for a siege. Li Te-sheng was then ordered to use "human wave" tactics in an attempt to take the peak by night assault, but as they advanced, the Communists came under heavy fire from the guns in Hsiang Yang. The lower slopes were soon a sea of flames, and shadows could be seen moving grotesquely in the conflagration like paper figures, burning and then vanishing without trace. Suddenly flares were fired – three red and one green. This was the Red army's signal to retreat, and the heavily battered Communist forces withdrew. The flares expired. The earth returned to darkness.

However, the Bayonet's fighting spirits remained high and he directed the Communists in yet another violent attack, the soldiers yelling "Chinese do not fight Chinese" as they charged through the flames and shellbursts. In Hsiang Yang, K'ang Tse began to panic, and his deputy ordered the forward defence troops to abandon the ridge to Li and to fall back on the town under cover provided by the KMT air force. But the Money God now led 3,000 men in an assault on Hsiang Yang itself from the Tahung range, the demoralised defenders rebelled, blowing a big hole in the wall with land-mines, and the Communists poured into the surrendered town like flood-waters.

K'ang Tse tried to commit suicide, and was carried away like a wounded animal under an escort of a hundred men. But the leader of this column, proudly riding a fine white horse, was none other than his deputy commander who was a Communist agent planted in the Kuomintang forces.[1] The proverb says "Those who swim well will drown", and this aptly applied to K'ang Tse, who specialised in espionage and infiltration but fell victim to a penetration operation mounted by his adversary. K'ang Tse was well treated by the Chinese Communists after his capture, and is said to have given them valuable assistance in their intelligence war against the KMT. This further enhanced the reputation of Li Te-sheng, who became known as "The Hero of Hsiang Yang".

Early in 1949, the One-Eyed Dragon and Ch'en Yi the Bald fought their way to the Yangtse, where crack Nationalist forces were assembled to defend Nanking, the political centre of the KMT, and Shanghai, its economic life-line. Li Te-sheng was in the van throughout, and once over the river spearheaded the assault on Hwei Chow. In his war memoirs Li Te-sheng, somewhat pleased with himself, reports characteristically:

"The distance to Hwei Chow was more than fifty miles and it would normally have required two to three days for an army to reach it. But as we were then fighting for time against the enemy, we had all agreed to cover the whole distance in one day instead of three. We found on the map that there was a short-cut across a big mountain which would reduce the distance by several dozen miles . . . We therefore ordered a reconnaissance party to proceed along the orthodox route to confuse the enemy, while the main force crossed the mountain.

"After the sun had risen, the soldiers laboriously climbed the meandering hill-path, their uniforms soaked in sweat. But no one dropped out, and to keep the mortars and bombs safe, as well as not to block the path, our men took them off the horses and carried them up the mountain themselves. On account of our unexpectedly swift move, and the severe clamp we applied to news as soon as we occupied a place, the enemy in Hwei Chow was still sleeping when our troops arrived." In Hwei Chow, the division seized great quantities of arms and ammunition. The Bayonet, "Hero of Hsiang Yang", had once again surmounted all difficulties and opened a way for the Communist armies to march onwards. And in all the arduous and bloody battles that followed, the Bayonet was always to the fore.

Two years later Li Te-sheng took his division into Korea, but after an early success against the 2nd US Infantry division, won with his usual daring and panache, his force was shattered by the terrible firepower of the enemy. He fought on for two more years before he brought his defeated division – and his own nagging doubts about Communist guerrilla tactics – back to China. Once home, he was sent to military college for a refresher course. The director was none other than the One-Eyed Dragon Liu Po-ch'eng, his former superior. After his Korean experience, Li Te-sheng ardently supported Liu's proposals for the modernisation of the armed forces, and threw himself into studying the strategy and tactics of Soviet and Western armies.

Nevertheless, when Lin Piao became Defence Minister in 1959 and soon afterwards called for intensive close-quarter combat training at company level in the guerrilla tradition, Li made sure that he responded enthusiastically. He had been appointed Commander of the 12th Army the previous year, and it was in his own "Bayonet" division that was now evolved a method of teaching night-tactics, ambushes, "fighting at 200 metres" and hand-to-hand combat that the entire PLA was ultimately ordered to emulate. Two years later, however, Lin Piao fell sick, and Ho Lung The Moustache took over responsibility for the country's defences. Ho Lung and the Chief of Staff, Lo Jui-ch'ing, then converted Lin Piao's training programme into a nationwide "Big Military Contest" for all units. The Bayonet again responded enthusiastically, his troops put up outstanding performances, and he became a popular figure.

The contest was still based on the principles of "fighting at 200 metres" which presupposed a Chinese citizen army of massed infantry rather than a modernised and sophisticated jet-age force. But it was a classic example of "waving the Red Flag to beat the Red Flag". The Moustache and Lo Jui-ch'ing were no slavish admirers of Lin Piao or the military theories of the ageing Chairman, and they were using the company-level competition as an acceptably Maoist means of ensuring something else – that soldiers at least devoted their time to training for war, and were not distracted by too much ideological indoctrination or overburdened with civilian construction duties.

This became evident when Lin Piao resumed office and began energetically circulating the *Quotations of Mao Tsetung* to all units, emphasising the overriding need for a "political breakthrough" in army mentality and ideological education at all levels. The troops were still heavily occupied with their competitive training, and had no time to recite the Thoughts of Mao. Both Mao and Lin Piao became incensed, and at the outset of the Cultural Revolution, Lo Jui-ch'ing was dismissed. The Red Guards later accused him of exaggerating the importance of the martial arts, of disobeying Lin's instructions, and of belittling the sacrosanct Thoughts.

The Bayonet was not slow to act. His 12th Army was then deployed in the provinces of Chekiang and Kiangsi to back up the "front line" forces in Fukien, opposite the Nationalist-held island of Formosa. So he now withdrew from the limelight and suddenly became very busy moving troops into new positions and consolidating defences along the Chekiang coast, thus extricating himself from the "contest" and any embarrassing association with the Moustache and the unfortunate Chief of Staff.

It was after this that the Bayonet won the approval of Chiang Ch'ing by taking part of the 12th Army into Anhwei to "Support the Left". That was not difficult for him, however. Mao Tsetung was sparing no effort to win over key officers who were *not* old comrades or loyal lieutenants of Lin Piao, in order to broaden his overall control of the army. On the pretext of "discarding the stale, accepting the new" he also saw that younger commanders ready to "Support the Left" were promoted to more important posts in the Central Committee of the party and encouraged to strive for higher positions, in order to weaken the power of older commanders of doubtful allegiance whose local armies dominated the provinces. Bayonet Li was ideal for Mao's purpose. He had never been close to Lin Piao or under his command. And that explains the jump that enabled him to emerge suddenly as the Director of the resuscitated General Political Department of the PLA in 1970. It was not Lin Piao who gave the Bayonet his thrust. The "Red Sun" himself had bought his allegiance with three quick promotions, making of him what the Chinese sardonically call a "highly-paid hero" – in other words, a million-dollar mercenary.

This was not the beginning of a beautiful friendship, however. The Bayonet was among those who received instructions from Peking to persuade Hsu Shih-yu to cooperate more closely with the Chairman, and he did as he was told. But the outcome of the subtle test of strength between the Mao–Lin group and the new powerholders in the major military regions was yet to be decided, and it was hard to believe that Li Te-sheng was in conflict with these Red warlords, for he was the protégé of the One-Eyed Dragon, and had been trained by Tiger Ch'en Hsi-lien. One could not tell, therefore, in which direction the Bayonet would be pointing as the situation developed.

Although he had won the support of Mao, Lin and Chou En-lai, and his key appointment as chief commissar of the PLA obliged him to be in Peking most of the time, he remained party secretary of Anhwei and continued to exert authority over the local military. He was therefore a provincial powerholder in his own right. The up-and-coming army strong men in China were not only declining to renounce their hold on the provinces, but were tightening it, and this tendency was matched by the gradual weakening of the central authority in Peking. The trend persists at the time of writing, and whatever he does for tactical reasons, The Bayonet's long-term interests therefore demand that he does not give up his stake in the sticks for the sake of a seat on the Maoist bandwagon in the capital.

PART THREE: THE KIANGSI FAVOURITES

Appointments in the PLA are influenced not only by the rise and fall of this or that mountain-top of military power, but often by where a man comes from, and by 1970 Chinese geomancers (for whom destiny depends on the movements of dragons under the ground) were saying "The geomantic system of the Mao era has changed, the Red Guards of the Cultural Revolution have chased the dragon from Hunan to Kiangsi." For whereas formerly the "Hunan clique" from Mao Tsetung's home province dominated the Chinese leadership, Mao and Lin Piao had now begun to favour men from Kiangsi when choosing candidates for promotion. But these fortunate fellows did not enjoy the approval of all those at the top, and although Wu Fa-hsien, the most prominent among them, had endeared himself to Lin Piao, he was distrusted by Madame Chiang Ch'ing.

In 1970 Wu was fifty-six, Commander of the Chinese Air Force and a power among the "younger" military. He did not look it. He had a round, plump face with sagging cheeks and a double chin. His head was like a large melon, and his short, inflated body seemed to be bursting with energy. He had the stomach of a capitalist and a butcher, out of place in his shapeless Communist uniform, and the Red Guards had maliciously claimed that this airman not only knew nothing about flying, but was too fat to climb into a cockpit. The technical administration of the Chinese Air Force was in fact undertaken by the deputy commander, but Wu himself looked after planning and strategy.

He was a veteran comrade-in-arms of Lin Piao, and had served with all the right formations – notably the 115th Division and the 4th Field Army. He was with Lin at the battle of Pinghsingkuan, he accompanied him on his three offensives across the Sungari River in Manchuria, and he took part in the victorious campaign against the KMT that carried them both from north to south China, where Wu's savage liquidation of anti-Communists was later called "The Bloodbath of Kwangsi". Wu was also humble and amicable of manner, and copied Mao in despising theoretical education. Moreover, when Huang Yung-sheng, the Chief of Staff, commanded a regiment, Wu was his political commissar. All this enabled him to climb very close to the top of the tree.

After the outbreak of the Korean War, Wu was transferred from the army to the fledgling Chinese air force as deputy political commissar. Lin Piao had founded this arm of the PLA when he acquired 45 Japanese planes from the Russians in Manchuria at the end of the Second World War, and an air force school had been set up not far from China's border with the Soviet Far East and staffed entirely with Russian instructors. Soviet example was followed in everything, even the diet – Chinese trainees were given "the food of the high air" which included generous quantities of meat, fish, butter and milk. Uniforms, medical care, and accommodation were as close as possible to their Russian equivalents.

Apart from their exposure to this strong foreign influence, air-force trainees were not one hundred per cent Communist, for most of them were intellectuals drawn from the middle class. They might be Party members, but their outlook was unstable. At one point eighty of them were arrested for political deviations, and this provoked an ideological struggle which for a time broke the morale of many others, so that it became impossible to cultivate the aggressive spirit needed for war in the air. Wu Fa-hsien pin-pointed the weakness and eliminated the intellectuals by transferring them wholesale to ground duties. He then recruited the future pilots of the air force from the proletariat or the army. During the Cultural Revolution, Wu often made use of this incident to prove the validity of Mao's theories on education, for Mao had said:

"In all history, no leading scholar was ever exceptional. On the other hand, the great poets Li Po and Tu Fu did not take the imperial examinations. In the Ming Dynasty, those who did well were the Emperors Ming T'ai Tsu and Ming Ch'eng Tsu. One of them was illiterate, the other only half-literate. When intellectuals came to power after them, the country was badly governed. Too much study makes a bad king, and this is harmful to the people. Maxim Gorky studied for only two years, and was otherwise self-taught. Benjamin Franklin started life as a newspaper boy. Watt, who invented the steam-engine, was a labourer. Books must not be studied too much. Even books on Marxism must not be studied too much. A few books will do. One who studies too much will go astray and become doctrinaire or revisionist."[1]

Wu Fa-hsien was therefore an early exponent of Mao's

Thought on this subject, but it did not solve the problems of the air force. Its MiG jets were shot out of the air when they challenged the KMT over the Straits of Formosa in 1958, and expansion of the service remained slow. For its cadres were still suspected of half-hearted loyalty towards Mao's teachings – the principle that in combat politics is at least as important as technical training can be repellent to men who risk their lives in a highly-sophisticated form of warfare. The airmen were not Red enough, many felt, and once in the air with a full tank, might disappear, together with their machines.

The Deputy Air Commander, Wang Ping-chang, was criticised during the Cultural Revolution by the Red Guards for "living a corrupt life and exhibiting deplorable behaviour". They accused him of watching Hongkong "yellow" films, of taking along a beautiful nurse with him on his inspection tours, and of keeping sex drugs and pornographic novels under his pillow. When Wu Fa-hsien was promoted to be its commander in 1965, there was much dissatisfaction throughout the reputedly reactionary, pleasure-loving air force, and there is little doubt that he owed his ability to defeat the right-wing elements within it to the strong support he received from Lin Piao.

Yet during the Cultural Revolution there appeared to be little warmth between Wu and Mao, and even less between Wu and Chiang Ch'ing. The Air Force Commander was one of five senior cadres of the regular fighting services whom the Red Guards attacked in January 1967 on her instigation. All five lost their posts, and were only reinstated in the second half of that year. The humiliation of these officers provoked a bitter quarrel between Lin Piao and Mao's wife, Lin Piao declaring:

"There are four kinds of conflict. First, when good man attacks bad man; secondly, when bad men attack each other. These conflicts can be suppressed by the army. The third is when bad man attacks good man – as happened to leaders of the Navy, the Air Force, and the General Logistics Department[2] – bringing first suffering and only later comfort to the good man. The fourth is when good man fights good man."[3]

According to Lin Piao in this open denunciation of Chiang Ch'ing, her attack on the PLA was a case of the bad man fighting the good in the ample shape of Wu and other generals. "Comfort" refers to the backing which restored them to their original posts, and even brought them further offices and titles. A new

105

understanding was then established between Mao and the military, based on the principle enunciated by Lin Piao that: "Those who need not be broken shall not be broken, but any leaders who do not comply with Mao Tsetung's ideology shall be replaced."

After he had regained his position, Wu Fa-hsien published an article in the *People's Daily* on "everlasting loyalty to Chairman Mao, everlasting loyalty to Mao Tsetung's Thought, and everlasting loyalty to Chairman Mao's Revolution of the Proletariat",[4] and wrote another piece of adulation for the *Red Flag* entitled: "Be the Strong Shield of the Revolution of the Proletariat". Wu was energetically "waving the red flag" of the Cultural Revolution in the PLA, and by 1969 his slavish fidelity to Lin Piao had earned him a seat on the Politburo. He was nonetheless licking the wrong boots. He had won not only the hostility of Chiang Ch'ing but the distrust of China's regional commanders, who looked askance at the "Kiangsi Favourites" who had broken traditional barriers and won quick promotion at the expense of men from other provinces. And Wu Fa-hsien was to pay for that with his job.

Why Kiangsi? "Where the leaders are in harmony, the administration is smooth." For the Chinese, this has always been the key to efficient government. Every Chinese ruler, past or present, has cultivated his own trusted confidants and made them the nucleus of his regime. But internal conflict becomes inevitable as time passes, and it may even lead to a life-or-death struggle for power. The ruler, therefore, must not only be certain of the loyalty of his colleagues, but must introduce new and younger men into his faction who consolidate his own position and faithfully perpetuate his own policies.

In earlier days Mao Tsetung was a staunch believer in "Great Hunanism" and selected his lieutenants and successors mainly from men who hailed from Hunan. "If China were Germany, then Hunan would be Prussia," he was fond of saying, and "Those who eat chilli are true revolutionaries." Hunanese food is hot and spicy. He liked to treat his "eastern Prussians" to specialities from their home province, like chillied bitter marrow, and then discuss future plans with them in his own thick Hunanese accent.

Liu Shao-ch'i and the ex-Defence Minister, P'eng Te-huai, were the central figures of this "Great Hunan" clique, and both risked their lives to serve Mao and the party. But when they criticised his policies and refused to accept his Thoughts as incontrovertible gospel, he rounded upon them mercilessly, denounced them as devils, and turned them into outcasts. He then set out to purge the PLA as well as the administration of those that sympathised with these heretics. Many high-ranking officers from Hunan became his targets, in consequence, and he did not speak about "Great Hunanism" any more.

Now any study of the history of the Chinese Communist Party quickly reveals that four provinces – Hunan, Hupeh, Szechuan and Kiangsi – provided the cockpits for much of the early revolutionary agitation in China, and it was from these that thousands of the Red army's first recruits were drawn. The recruits quickly became cadres, and some of the cadres became commanders, but meanwhile the Communists had migrated and extended their territory, so that the second generation of fighting men mainly came from among the broad masses of the peasantry in the north.

The veterans who favoured the policies of Liu Shao-ch'i, and steadily consolidated their mountain-tops until the outbreak of the Cultural Revolution, had been among the original cadres who had fought in the Yangtse Valley and the south, and most of them came from Hunan and Hupeh. Generally speaking, those from Hunan tended to become political commissars, while those from Hupeh tended to become provincial military commanders. The men of the old "southern" generation were therefore important officials, while the Johnny-come-lately northerners, whose blood had bought China for the Communists in the final struggle against the KMT, were by the nature of things in subordinate positions.

After launching the Cultural Revolution, Mao Tsetung sacked more than seventy of the older ideological warlords and high-ranking officers, and suitable successors had to be found. But Mao and Lin Piao did not take advantage of the generation gap to replace many of them with young northerners. Most of the officers who were now given vacant posts in the Military Affairs Commission of the party and in military regions not previously "affiliated" to Mao and Lin Piao had in fact taken part in the Long March. They were chosen from among smaller men who had then been battalion or company commanders or even "little devils" (teenage soldiers) in the First Front Army.

107

They were almost uneducated and had played no role in previous power struggles within the Chinese Communist Party. But they had been trained and brought on by Mao himself during the days of the embattled Kiangsi Soviet in the early thirties, and they enjoyed a close political kinship with Mao and Lin. Sixty per cent of the leaders appointed after the Cultural Revolution were men from Kiangsi Province in whose loyalty and docility their two chiefs consequently had confidence. Military cadres from Kiangsi accounted for more than 40 of the new names on the Central Committee elected by the Ninth Party Congress in 1969. Apart from Wang Tung-hsing, who was already in effective executive control of the party's secret service, and Wu Fa-hsien, who commanded the air force, seven others were worth watching, of whom perhaps the most outstanding was Ting Sheng.

Ting Sheng, Commander of the Canton Military Region, was born of poor peasants in 1912. He joined the army at the age of 18 and was responsible for the personal safety of Mao Tsetung during the Long March. He was a cadre on the First Front Army–115th Division–4th Field Army ladder, and rose to be a regimental commander under Huang Yung-sheng, with whom he mainly served. An expert in protracted assault tactics and guerrilla warfare, "Big-Eyed" Ting is a tall, dark ramrod of a man with a soft, quiet manner, who idolises heroes and is himself a soldier of valour and fortitude. When the 4th Field Army finally overran his home province of Kiangsi in the drive south against the KMT, he refused to stop and see his aged mother during the advance although he passed close to her house, showing the dedicated spirit of the Chinese communist who has true "party nature".

He gained experience in modern warfare as an army commander in Korea, and during the Chinese thrust into India in November 1962 he sent an entire division over a snow-bound 13,000-foot peak to take the enemy in the rear and inflict a stinging defeat upon him beyond the Sela Ridge. This is regarded as one of the most outstanding feats of conventional warfare in the history of the Chinese Communist army. In 1966 Ting was promoted to be Deputy Commander of the Sinkiang Military Region, where Chiang Ch'ing's Red Guards subsequently accused him of suppressing the Cultural Revolution. But shortly after that his former superior, Huang Yung-sheng,

108

was appointed Chief of Staff, and at once arranged for Ting to succeed him as Commander of the Canton Military Region, thus entrusting him with his own stronghold in the Chinese provinces while he himself was in Peking.

Like Ting Sheng, some of the junior 4th Field Army generals owed their basic military allegiance to the Chief of Staff, but more owed it to Lin Piao, or to Mao directly. All gave at least cupboard-loyalty to the Mao–Lin partnership and were anxious that no dispute should break out among their three chiefs By 1970 they had become the new buttress of the regime, powerful within the PLA, the government, the party, the intelligence service and the communications system, and they had been filtered into the military regions of the older warlords, whose natural successors they considered themselves to be. They nonetheless suffered from certain weaknesses. They were not yet a close-knit group, and the Soviet press once called them "a band of ignorant ruffians" who, lacking any strong ideological background, could only support Mao blindly, and after Mao had passed away, Lin Piao; and in 1971 Lin Piao was to be politically "terminated".

Today, moreover, they are no longer young – most of them are between 55 and 60 years old – and while they may hold senior posts in Peking and the provinces, few are in direct command of troops. It is here that the northerners come into play, for the guns that are not in the hands of older veterans of mixed loyalty are today held by a group of generals from the north known as the "battle heroes". Seven out of ten of all divisional commanders and 80 per cent of regimental commanders in the PLA are from the north, and the general pattern is that while the Kiangsi faction have moved into the higher echelons, the northerners command the fighting forces.

The soldiers from the north are of course younger than the high-ranking officials from Kiangsi, and for the most part in their mid-forties. They are not revolutionary veterans of the Long March. They joined the army originally to fight the Japanese. They have no tradition of peasant revolution in their mental make-up, and they have already changed the political outlook of the PLA. They are patriotic, but uninterested in the class struggle. Most of the divisional and regimental commanders in the three southern provinces of Kwangtung, Kwangsi and Hunan are northerners who struck back at the

Maoist Red Guards when they got out of hand in Canton during the Cultural Revolution, and some observers question their loyalty to the Chairman.

But "fame" and "power" are like strong drinks that progressively intoxicate those that drink them – "the man of integrity will sacrifice his life to keep his good name, and the mean man will sacrifice his life for the sake of wealth and power," the ancient philosopher Chuang Tzu has said. The troops counter-attacked the Maoists in Canton because they could not tolerate the loss of their own authority. Bowing to circumstances, therefore, Mao no longer tries to cut back that authority today, and on their side the soldiers themselves have again "hoisted the Great Red Flag" to spread his Thoughts. Mao enjoys the "fame" and the military enjoy the "power". But Mao's fight for influence within the PLA continues, and although he may have sacrificed pieces like Wu Fa-hsien, Kiangsi favourites not dragged down by the fall of Lin Piao will still play a special role as pawns in the game.

10
Huang Yung-sheng: the Speechless Rustic

On 27 March 1968 a rally of one hundred thousand citizens and soldiers in Peking heard Premier Chou En-lai promulgate an order dismissing Yang Ch'eng-wu, the former Acting Chief of General Staff of the PLA, for Mao Tsetung and Lin Piao had decided to appoint Huang Yung-sheng in his place, and by June he was no longer just "Acting".

The young peasant who started life minding buffalo in a Hupeh* village had come a long way. At sixty-two he was a tough, bald, brandy-drinking general, built like a bear, with a cold, slightly canine face, and fond of peppers and Peking opera. By nature, he was impulsively straightforward and uncaring, and had been known to turn up at a meeting with striped pyjama-bottoms peeping from beneath his trouser legs. He took his first step on the revolutionary ladder when he fought in the Hunan uprising of 1927. The Reds were badly mauled by the KMT and the men of Huang's regiment, which had taken heavy casualties, began to desert in groups. Huang's account is characteristically blunt:

"A fellow-soldier from my own village saw me and shouted: 'Are you leaving, Huang? A lot have fled already, and we're going now. How about coming with us?' I was very anxious, and uncertain what to do. Before that, I'd always thought it was easy to be a soldier and make revolution. But after more than a month of painful experience, I was convinced it was no simple matter at all. After all, I might lose my life at any time. I was only nineteen, and hadn't left my home village more than six months before, and my understanding of the whole Chinese revolution and its prospects was incomplete, to say the least..."[1] Huang was nonetheless one of the thousand men with whom Mao fled to the fastnesses of Chingkangshan.

---

* Not Kiangsi, as is commonly believed.

This remnant of the Changsha assault force was constantly waylaid, and many men deserted. Only about 700 reached Sanwan Village, where Mao stopped and reorganised the 400 who agreed to stay with him into a single regiment, and Huang was promoted to squad-commander. Thereafter, these troops were known as Mao's "Sanwan seed-force", and he reposed an especial trust in them. When Huang Yung-sheng was scathingly denounced by Red Guards during the Cultural Revolution, he was not liquidated but promoted. Quite apart from his own power to protect himself, he was more easily forgiven on account of his "Sanwan" background by Mao, who is said to have trained him carefully in "culture, revolutionary theory, strategy and tactics" even in those days.

Huang was a regimental commander on the Long March under Lin Piao, and earned himself a reputation for cunning during an episode in Szechuan, where the main force under Mao and Chu Te was at one point surrounded by the Nationalist enemy. When the two leaders finally extricated themselves and counted heads, Huang and his entire regiment were missing. Presuming that they had been cut to pieces, Mao did not wait for them but continued to move westwards. Huang and his regiment turned up intact a fortnight later, however. He had escaped from the KMT by ordering his men to remove their badges and to pose as Nationalists. As the KMT were assembling a heterogeneous collection of forces against the Communists, including the armies of local warlords, it was difficult to tell friend from foe, and Huang got away with his ruse. The story made him something of an idol, and he was soon given command of the van.

He next won admiration at the crossing of the Tatu River, which was spanned only by a swaying 300-foot bridge of iron chains slung high over a deep gorge. Most of the floorboards of this bridge had been removed by the enemy, who covered what remained from the far bank with two heavy machine-guns. As the KMT were hot on their heels, the Communists sent eighteen volunteers scrambling over the writhing chains to secure the bridge in the face of withering fire which picked most of them off and pitched them into the rapids far below. The defenders also set fire to the planking that was still in position at their end of the bridge, but three survivors among the Reds finally hauled themselves up on to it, charged through the flames, and took

112

out the machine-gun position with hand grenades. It is said that "Ever-Victorious" Huang, badly wounded, was one of the three.

Anti-Communist commentators reject this official version of the crossing, however, and tell a very different story. The Tatu River was defended by the Nationalist 24th Army, which was in fact the feudal force of the Sikang warlord, Liu Wen-hui. Typically, Liu's deputy was his son-in-law, and two of his divisional commanders were his nephews. The 24th Army, which had a wide reputation for incompetence, was derisively called the "Two-Gun Force", for officers and men alike were opium addicts, and while carrying a rifle in one hand were reputed to carry a pipe in the other. They planted their own poppy crops and made money by levying an opium tax on the population at all key points where troops were stationed. Liu paid little attention to orders from the KMT Central Government in Nanking, for he was not dependent upon Chiang Kai-shek for a living.

Having weighed up his chances and decided he could not cross the Tatu River by force with his tired and depleted army, therefore, Mao wrote a letter to Liu (according to anti-Communist sources) asking him to let his column pass over peacefully. If Liu agreed, he urged, they could in future help each other, but if they fought, both would suffer casualties. Moreover, if the KMT caught up with the Communists, Mao's men might well be exterminated, but with no enemy to fight, the Nationalists would then set about establishing an unbreakable hold on Szechuan and Liu's fief in Sikang to the immediate west.

Liu, it is said, finally agreed to let the Red army go through. When the Communists overran all China fourteen years later, warlords and KMT generals and officials who surrendered were usually humiliated, if not executed. But Liu was allowed to keep his pipe and Mao ultimately made him Minister for Forestry.[2] It was Mao's ability to understand and exploit the incongruous patchwork of alliances which opposed him that saved his forces more than once from an abrupt end.

In Yenan, Huang Yung-sheng attended the Red Army University and then joined the Profligate Monk Nieh Jung-chen in expanding the Soviet in the Shansi–Chahar–Hopei Border Region. But after the Japanese surrender he moved into

Manchuria with the faithful Big-Eyed Ting Sheng to wage war on the Nationalists as a regimental commander under Lin Piao. He then followed Lin down the length of China in pursuit of the KMT, and, arrived in the south, was appointed deputy commander of Kwangsi province. This was the beginning of a process that was to make him master of South China and of the great city of Canton, notorious as a crucible of revolution and for its scant respect for Peking. In 1955 he became Commander of the Canton Military Region, which embraces the three extensive provinces of Kwangtung, Kwangsi and Hunan, and three years later Peking nominated T'ao Chu to be its political commissar.

It is laid down that military commanders and political commissars in the Red Army are equal and parallel, but until recently the commissar was always the more important man. T'ao Chu was to rise to be First Secretary of the Central-South Bureau of the Communist Party,* and later, backed by Liu Shao-ch'i himself, to occupy the number four position at the top of the entire Chinese hierarchy – until his star fell. Although Huang and T'ao were both secretaries of the party bureau in Canton, it was T'ao who was the boss.

The two men did not belong to the same mountain-top, but they were close comrades. They had worked together, off and on, for fifteen years, and had both served in Lin Piao's 4th Field Army, where they were respectively known as the "Fighting and Writing Generals". T'ao Chu was often compared to Lu Hsun (the revered revolutionary author who had prudently died in the thirties and so kept his reputation intact). He was a talented writer, and an eloquent master of rhetoric. He published penetrating works on political doctrine, and in any meeting impressed all hearers with his rational analysis, laced with humour, of any particular situation. The reports of Huang the buffalo-boy were, by contrast, embarrassingly tedious, insipid, muddled, and laboriously written in poor Chinese. Frank and sincere in everyday life, and a general who won the affection of his men with much light-hearted fooling and banter, he could be tongue-tied at a formal meeting.

"I am only a rustic," he once said, "and even if you hung me upside down, you wouldn't get a drop of ink out of me. Unlike

---

* Six regional party bureaux covered all China.

all you cultured intellectuals, I minded cattle as a child and was illiterate. I wouldn't be what I am today without the teachings of the party and Chairman Mao. So if I make mistakes when I speak, please don't laugh . . ."[3] Whereupon those present immediately did, for if the eloquent are welcome, the shy earn sympathy, and the best thing about Huang, many said, was his so-called "rustic" character. And he was astute enough to draw attention to it. Mao himself has always devalued intellectuals, and T'ao Chu – the "Lu Hsun of the Army" – disappeared without trace during the Cultural Revolution.

T'ao was accused of being the "Number One Capitalist in the Central-South Bureau" and of harbouring ambitions to build himself an independent ideological kingdom. Red Guards maintained that he had derided the habit of shouting "Ten Thousand Years to Chairman Mao", pointing out that Mao was only human and must die, had called assiduous workers and peasants who buried their noses in the little red book of Mao's Thoughts "monks reading scriptures", and had forbidden men to sing Maoist songs or to quote Mao's words. His left-wing enemies went so far as to accuse him of extolling liberalism and bourgeois thought, and before he fell beneath this wave of indignant if often spurious condemnation, the Red Guards were claiming that Huang Yung-sheng was giving him powerful support in his iniquities.

On 22 January 1967 the Peking *People's Daily* told left-wing revolutionary forces that it was "ten thousand times important" for them to hold power in their hands, and urged them to unite to grasp it. On the same day, Red Guards seized control of Canton from the provincial party authorities, and set up a "Kwangtung Provincial Revolutionary Rebels Joint Committee" in their place. Huang denounced this as a "sham seizure", the new "committee" was challenged by rival "rebels" whom he favoured, and the town was torn open by factional strife.

The Maoist Guards then turned their full wrath upon him. Their papers and wall-posters were full of lurid tales of his corruption and his crimes. He had deposited public funds in a personal bank account in British Hongkong, and with the interest he had bought refrigerators, air-conditioners and record-players, sending them to T'ao Chu and other loose-living cronies as gifts.[4] The diatribe continued during much of that bewildering year. Huang "must be knocked down". He was "a sworn accomplice of T'ao Chu", the "black bandit" whose letters he had published, praised and implicitly obeyed "as if they had been Imperial decrees". He "savagely suppressed the revolutionary rebels, carrying out a white terror" against them, and he "personally spread poison everywhere, revealing himself as a counter-revolutionary double-dealer".[5]

By March, nonetheless, Peking had decreed that a military control committee be set up in Canton under the "Speechless Rustic" to restore order, and he at once screened off all "political, judicial, and public security departments, and newspapers". In April, Premier Chou En-lai arrived in Canton, ostensibly in connection with the Spring Trade Fair but in reality to consolidate Huang Yung-sheng's position and prestige amid the persistent bloodshed and pandemonium, while at the same time urging him to perform the communist confessional act of submitting a written self-criticism to Mao. At the end of June, Huang quietly left for Peking, summoned by the Prime Minister, who then sought to reconcile him with delegates of the revolutionaries who had also come to the capital from Canton. But in the south tempers did not cool, and fighting continued to flicker across Kwangtung. Huang was still "the dog of T'ao Chu", the "butcher of the Cultural Revolution", and the doting father of Huang Chun-ming, the arch-villain of the "July 23 massacre" perpetrated by the "Doctrine Guards".[6]

The main challenge to the left-wing Maoist Red Guards came from the sons of officials in the established hierarchy. They regarded themselves as the natural heirs of the new China, yet every day they saw their parents viciously humiliated by revolutionary street mobs drawn from villages, factories and schools, thrown out of their jobs, and purged. Since it was better to resist than to accept this lamentable fate in turn, they banded together in the "Doctrine Guards" and similar gangs, yelling slogans like "Dragons breed dragons, but rats breed young rats to dig at the castle gate". The confusion was intense, because all Red Guards, whether of the left or right, shouted "Defend Chairman Mao to the death" in public, but while the pro-Mao factions inspired by Chiang Ch'ing tried to wrench power from the old Communist establishment, the right-wing Red Guards were trying to wrench power from them, and were bold enough on occasion to bawl: "Fry Chiang Ch'ing in oil," "Wash

116

Peking in blood," "Destroy all revolutionary organisations." And in Canton the leader of the anti-Mao Red Guards was Huang Chun-ming, the favourite son of Huang Yung-sheng.

In July rival Red Guards fought a pitched battle at the Sun Yat-sen Memorial Hall in Canton, and there were heavy casualties. The "Red Flag" Maoists afterwards reported that the anti-Maoists had seized sticks, crowbars, spears, daggers, bricks, airguns and small-calibre rifles, and had killed thirty of their comrades and wounded four hundred others. "The compound of the Memorial Hall was spattered with blood, and was a most abominable and cruel sight. Confronted with this bloody reality, the rebel fighters picked up bricks and bamboo staves and counter-attacked with a will. But scores of them were dragged into the Hall itself by the right-wing Doctrine Guards, who then closed the windows and tortured them foully. Some were hung up as living targets, and their faces were pricked with daggers, some had their ears or noses slit or cut off or their eyes gouged out, and others were beaten to death. Hair-raising screams and sobs could be heard . . . but while Huang Chun-ming was in Canton attacking Chiang Ch'ing's Red Guards, his father, Huang Yung-sheng, was with Mao and Lin Piao in Peking."[7]

To end the turmoil and stabilise the situation, Chou En-lai finally persuaded the representatives of the mass organisations now so vigorously "making revolution" to accept Huang as head of a preparatory group for the formation of a provincial revolutionary committee, to "support the army and love the people" in four practical ways, and to stop all fighting with weapons.[8] The Red Guards in Canton surrendered their guns to the local troops, and put out posters announcing forgivingly "Huang Yung-sheng is a man of Chairman Mao's headquarters. He has rectified his mistakes, turning truly to the left, and is therefore a good comrade."[9]

Early in November 1967 Huang returned to Canton, and shortly afterwards became Chairman of the new Kwangtung Revolutionary Committee, thanks to the direct support of the Prime Minister. Although theoretically deserving disgrace as an oppressor of Mao's Red Guards, he was restored to full military and political power, and under Chou's continuing protection was later appointed Chief of Staff of the PLA. The Prime Minister had effected a detente between the buffalo-boy and the Maoists, and had bought himself a valuable ally. Soon Huang's name began to appear on official lists of the Chinese hierarchy immediately after the five top men – headed by Mao, Lin, and Chou – who made up the Standing Committee of the Politburo, and above Chiang Ch'ing. But he was evidently convinced that he must maintain his regional power intact if he was to be treated with proper respect and his position consolidated in Peking. So apart from leaving Big-Eyed Ting in Canton as the new commander in his place, he made Liu Hsing-yuan, with whom he had worked from 1951 to 1967, the political commissar of the military region.

Liu, who is now 58 years old, is a veteran from Hunan who took part in the Long March at the age of nineteen. From serving in the First Front Army he became an outstanding political cadre in the 4th Field Army, where his gift for sophistry and flexibility of argument earned him the nickname "Rubbermouth". In 1951 he was posted to Canton, where he served under T'ao Chu and assisted Huang Yungsheng. When T'ao Chu dropped from sight in 1967, it was Rubbermouth who used the current "Three Support and Two Military" campaign[10] to reassert the authority of the PLA over the Red Guards, and once Huang was in Peking he bore the brunt of their attacks. He was accused of being a "venomous snake" leading a life of extravagant decadence, importing all his needs "from mosquito nets to pipes", of ordering that nurses fan him when he was in hospital, and other heinous crimes calculated to appeal to the younger mobs.[11]

In the following year, however, he was still in office and responsible for forming the army's "Mao Tsetung Thought Propaganda Teams" which moved into factories, farms, schools, offices, and social and cultural organisations to conduct classes in the Chairman's Thoughts, and to pass on his latest directives. Ostensibly, the objective of these teams was to strengthen the ideological hold of Mao and Lin Piao upon the provinces, but in fact they became agents for establishing ubiquitous military control over all aspects of national life, until the army articulated the political, financial, economic, industrial, agricultural, educational and social ossiature of the country. In December 1971 Rubbermouth emerged as First Secretary of the Kwangtung Provincial Committee of the cleansed and reconditioned Chinese Communist Party.

But the delicate relationship between Canton and Peking, between Huang's province and Mao's party centre, was reflected in the presence of certain Kiangsi men loyal to Mao rather than to Huang whose main task was to watch Big-Eyed Ting and Rubbermouth Liu in Kwangtung itself, and leading officials in the other provinces of the Canton Military Region like Wei Kuo-ch'ing.

Wei, known as "The King of Kwangsi", backed the anti-Mao Red Guards in his province during the Cultural Revolution and was reportedly responsible for the killing of thousands of pro-Mao "rebels". He was branded as a member of the "black gang" of the revisionist Liu Shao-ch'i, and was accused of keeping back arms destined for North Vietnam, just across the border, in order to use them against the Maoists. He had, in fact, been a subordinate of three arch-villains – Teng Hsiao-p'ing, P'eng Te-huai and T'ao Chu – but Peking did not dare to provoke him too far, for two reasons. One was that the Chinese could not risk a military revolt in this strategic frontier area just north of the Gulf of Tonking. The other was that Kwangsi was the Chuang Autonomous Region, the home of the Chuang ethnic minority of whom Wei was the leader, and there might be a danger of racial strife.

"The King of Kwangsi" survived all attacks, therefore, and emerged from the Cultural Revolution master of his province. It suited Huang to have this deep-rooted element of "anti-Maoism" in the south, for the more precarious the political equilibrium, the more Mao and Lin Piao needed him as a mediator. And the same was true of the other major military regions.

Huang Yung-sheng was originally made Chief of Staff precisely because he was not a fanatical Maoist, but was acceptable to all parties to some degree, and therefore a potential force for compromise and unity at a time when China badly needed good middlemen. To Mao and Lin, he was a comrade from the original "Sanwan seed-force" who could further extend the influence of the old 4th Field Army if properly controlled (he was also a powerful commander with his own base in Canton who would make a bad political enemy). To the more recalcitrant Red warlords in the other big regions, he was nevertheless a man who believed in limiting the power of Mao when it threatened their own local authority in the provinces. To many

Kwangsi favourites, he was now the prestigious Chief of Staff to whom they must largely look for their future. To Chou En-lai he was a "moderate" who had suffered at the hands of Chiang Ch'ing's Red Guards, and whose guns could enhance the Premier's own bargaining position.

He could have been the keystone that kept them all snug – including himself. He might well say he was a "rustic", for the peasant cunning could be glimpsed beneath the soldier, as his striped pyjamas were once glimpsed beneath his army trousers. But whether the lure is land, money or military power, peasants in particular are often betrayed by their own narrow greed. And Huang Yung-sheng proved no exception.

11

The Red Warlords

The most obvious consequence of the Cultural Revolution, whose ostensible purpose was to put the country into the hands of the masses, was the rise to positions of unprecedented power of military leaders who distrusted and personally opposed the whole business. These were the "Maoists" who privately wanted the most un-Maoist of programmes. If they had their way, ideology would be subordinated to economic and military considerations, and the ordinary people would receive fewer sermons on the beauties of the classless society and more of the good things of life.

Ironsides Hsu Shih-yu, Commander of the Nanking Military Region, was the first Communist warlord to block with impunity the attempts of Red Guards and "revolutionary rebels" to "seize power" in his command, and he set the pattern for others who in turn took steps to defuse the Cultural Revolution in their own fiefs, and to keep their local military authority intact. Their natural allies were those administrative and party leaders with a more pragmatic outlook than Mao, and they developed a symbiotic relationship with Premier Chou En-lai and the Money God, Li Hsien-nien, in Peking itself. When the new Politburo was announced in 1969, not only Huang Yung-sheng but two more of the five Red warlords who controlled the most important military regions in China were listed among the full members.

The five warlords were:

Huang Yung-sheng: although Chief of Staff, he was still regarded by the others as the master of Canton Military Region; Politburo member.
Ironsides Hsu Shih-yu: Commander, Nanking Military Region; Politburo member.
Ch'en Hsi-lien: Commander, Shenyang Military Region; Politburo member.
Han Hsien-ch'u: Commander, Foochow Military Region.

Yang Te-chih: Commander, Tsinan Military Region.

All were much reviled by the Red Guards and denounced for suppressing their activities, but emerged from the Cultural Revolution stronger than before. Shenyang, Nanking and Canton alone had some 800,000 troops under command – nearly one-third of the entire PLA – and for the first time their chiefs had a voice in the Politburo. Before the Cultural Revolution, the regions took their orders from Peking, but now they were in a position to affect policy at the centre itself. For the centre was dependent upon them. Huang was at the apex of the army, and the other four were not only the military commanders of their regions, but the heads of their respective provincial revolutionary committees and first secretaries of their respective provincial party committees. They therefore dominated militarily, administratively, and politically. They were dubbed "The Heavenly Kings", and their enhanced authority was an unspoken admission that Peking had had to decentralise.

They were not, however, warlords in the bad old tradition of the twenties, for they were not planning any ruthless expansion of their domains at the expense of neighbours or rivals. They simply wished to be left to run them as local conditions (in their view) demanded. Their solidarity sprang from their common aims, but if there had at any time been a conflict of interests among them, their group would have disintegrated. They posed no threat to Mao. While he lived, they might seek to modify his policies, but not to overthrow Maoism. They did not want to kill the king. They wanted an unwritten Magna Carta.

But three years have passed since the new Politburo was announced and Mao is three years nearer death. It is 1972, and four "Heavenly Kings" are still in place. They are ten to fifteen years younger than the old Chairman, and it is becoming increasingly important to know more about them.

NANKING MILITARY REGION (Anhwei, Chekiang and Kiangsu Provinces)

Hsu Shih-yu (see Chapter 9): the interdependence of Mao and warlord, of king and baron, is accentuated in the case of Ironsides by the fact that his region includes Shanghai, the cradle of the Cultural Revolution and the spiritual home of Maoism. He disposes of about 220,000 men.

SHENYANG MILITARY REGION (Liaoning, Kirin, Heilungkiang Provinces)

Ch'en Hsi-lien, "The Ferocious Tiger", commands a region that takes in the whole of Manchuria, the industrial "northeast" of China on the borders of the Soviet Union, and he has more than 300,000 men under command. His hold on this great fief was further strengthened in 1967 when Tseng Shao-shan was appointed its political commissar. For Tseng had served and fought under the Tiger from 1937 to 1950 and had worked with him in Manchuria for more than a decade. With his promotion, the Tiger gained wings: all political as well as military power was in his hands.

In the early stages of the Cultural Revolution, the pro-Mao Red Guards and rebel workers unleashed a campaign to "seize power" that quickly threw the Manchurian province of Liaoning into a state of semi-chaos. But Tiger Ch'en ordered out three divisions to check Red Guard violence and restore peace, and when in April 1968 rival factions of revolutionaries met in a series of bloody clashes on the boundary of the same province, he despatched tanks and armoured cars to intervene. The rebels heaped abuse on him, but a month later the Liaoning Revolutionary Committee was set up with Ch'en as its chief, and in January 1971, after Mao and Lin Piao had personally attended a meeting of local delegates, the Tiger was elected first secretary of the new party committee with Tseng as his deputy. Mao Yuan-hsin, a nephew of Mao, was included in it as a representative of the masses, but subsequently appeared to add little more than ideological decoration to the functional power of its military bosses.

Ch'en nevertheless had to worry about the infiltration into his command of officers from the 4th Field Army system loyal to Lin Piao.* On the surface, they appeared to cooperate with him painlessly enough, but it was understood that their presence made him a little uneasy, for while the "Heavenly Kings" planned no *coup* against Mao, they were sensitive about any

---

* See first Appendix to Chapter 15.

123

attempt by their overlords in Peking to undermine their own regional authority.

The Tiger, now fifty-nine, was born in a Hupeh village in 1913 and his story is similar to that of the Speechless Rustic, Huang Yung-sheng. The son of a poor family, he minded buffalo as a boy, but when he was only thirteen joined the Communist "children's arson squad". He is a stubborn, truculent man, with a thin smile and a reputation for ruthlessness, courageous yet prudent and full of native guile. When he was commanding West Anhwei Military District during the post-war struggle against the Nationalists, his seventy-year-old mother, much concerned about him, walked more than sixty miles to see him. But he only gave her a bale of cloth and told her to go home the next day. For this demonstration of his strong "party nature" he has been eulogised in the Chinese press. The ideal "new communist man" is not only selfless, but emotionless where family is concerned. Personal feelings, notably love, have been condemned as poisonous bourgeois concepts.

But since war is a product of hostility, the loveless, cold-blooded nature of Tiger Ch'en provided the Communists with an outstanding soldier. He served in the Fourth Front Army of Mao's rival, Chang Kuo-t'ao (except during part of the Long March when he was in the First Front Army), and, while with the 129th Division under the One-Eyed Dragon in the war against Japan, he was cited as the bravest regimental commander in the 8th Route Army (he had just led his men across the Hut'o River in Shansi in a daring raid to blow up a Japanese airfield).

When in 1942 the Japanese threw formidable forces into a major operation to wipe out the troublesome Communist guerrilla bases in North China, Ch'en formed "military work squads" armed with light weapons only and dressed in peasant clothes to mount night ambushes against them, and his present political commissar, Tseng, proved particularly skilful at this type of operation. After the Japanese surrendered, and the Reds began their final southward drive against Chiang Kai-shek, Ch'en distinguished himself as an army corps commander in what was now the 2nd Field Army at the vital crossing of their main obstacle, the Yangtse River.

While Ch'en Yi the Bald launched his 3rd Field Army into the attack opposite Nanking, the One-Eyed Dragon threw his men over the river further west. The KMT are said to have deployed about twenty armed corps to defend the south bank of the Yangtse, and in addition to disposing of naval and air support they were able to concentrate intense artillery fire against anything hostile moving on the water. On 20 April 1949 the Communists crossed the river by night in wooden junks and any other craft they could lay their hands on (for they had no assault boats) and, determined that this must be a do-or-die operation, the ferocious Tiger discarded his flexible guerrilla principles and issued the order: "Advance only. Retreat is impossible." By the morning of the twenty-first, his troops had overrun the KMT gun emplacements, and the main Communist forces poured over the river.

The superstitious claimed that the One-Eyed Dragon and Tiger Ch'en had even changed the wind and ensured darkness for a favourable crossing, for the *I Ching*[1] declares: "Clouds follow the dragon, winds follow the tiger." The KMT defence of the Yangtse proved ineffectual, but it was no small feat for the Communists to ferry two huge armies over its turbulent waters when they disposed of no modern assault equipment and there were 170 armed KMT craft on the river.

Ch'en served in Korea, but he was recalled to Peking to become Commander of Artillery, and was responsible for the heavy shelling of the Nationalist-held island of Quemoy in 1958. Eleven years later he was directing a fight at the other end of the country, for he was Commander of the Shenyang Military Region when Chinese and Russian troops clashed across the Ussuri River on the Sino-Soviet frontier in 1969.

Ch'en declared his unswerving allegiance to Mao during the Cultural Revolution, but the leaders in Peking continued to entrust the defence of the north-east to him for sounder reasons. He was a first-class fighting general who showed little interest in lobbying for more power in the capital, a tiger that rarely left its den. He was content to be warlord of China's biggest military region, and would probably remain manageable enough as long as no one tried to take Manchuria away from him.

FOOCHOW MILITARY REGION (Fukien and Kiangsi Provinces)

Han Hsien-ch'u, the Commander of the Foochow Military Region who has held this post since 1958, is another front-line man, for his fief includes the south-east China coast opposite Formosa, and he is responsible for the immediate defence of the mainland against KMT attack. He comes from the same village in Hupeh* as Tiger Ch'en, is the same age, has the same reputation for ferocity, and like him served in the Fourth Front Army and in the 129th Division under the One-Eyed Dragon. But Han is educated, and only joined up after he had graduated from high school. He also fought in the 4th Field Army under Lin Piao, and commanded the first batch of Chinese "volunteers" to go to Korea, where he became vice-chairman. of the joint Sino–Korean staff. He made a reputation for himself by organising a stubborn defence against the United Nations forces in the autumn of 1951, holding his ground for three months in the face of heavy fire, and earned the title "Hero of the Korean War".

After the outbreak of the Cultural Revolution Han emulated Huang Yung-sheng and the other three Red warlords in Nanking, Shenyang and Tsinan in opposing the Red Guards. "Which headquarters do you belong to?" asked the rebels angrily (meaning which leader and which line – proletarian Mao or revisionist Liu Shao-ch'i). "You send all elements of the 'black gang' to the sanatorium to become fat [on the pretext that] the prisons cannot hold them all, and meanwhile the prisons are used to lock up revolutionary rebels. How sharply contrasted are your love and hate! There have been innumerable armed conflicts in the counties of the Region, and revolutionaries have died by the hundred. The military, with you as their leader, have suppressed the rebels whenever they could, and evaded responsibility when they could not.

"You have accused the cadres of frightening people with Mao Tsetung's works. You have criticised political instructors for reading Mao's quotations to them when they were sick in bed. Why don't you cook them some ginger soup and noodles to eat if you are so concerned with their welfare, yet opposed to offering fighters the spiritual food of Mao's Thought?"[2]

The Red Guards also claimed that Han's son was the leader of the local anti-Mao Red Guards, for, as in the Canton Military Region, most of the children of senior cadres rallied to resist the pro-Mao faction.

---

* Not Hunan, as some say.

When the Red Guards continued to attack Han, Chou En-lai urged him to write a self-criticism. Self-criticism was originally a severe sacrifice, for it meant penning a confession which would be kept on record and could be used against the transgressor whenever evidence was required to justify a purge. But after the Cultural Revolution it lost some of its significance, for few could avoid making mistakes, and all cadres seeking reinstatement went through the process of admitting their crimes and being officially forgiven by Mao and Lin Piao.

Nevertheless, "heroes shed blood, not tears", the Chinese say, and men who carry guns are more obstinate than others. Han refused to capitulate to pressure and in the end only submitted a collective *mea culpa* in the name of all cadres in his Foochow command. His aim was to escape personal responsibility, yet at the same time affirm, after the manner of warlords, that he himself was the Region. Mao and Lin could do nothing to soldiers like Han who refused to be toppled or transferred, and they were forced to compromise with them. In March 1971, accordingly, Han was elected first secretary of the new Fukien party committee.

In his address on this occasion, he emphasised that Fukien was in the forefront of the resistance against the United States, and demanded that vigilance be heightened and that the people of the entire province intensify their preparations for war. It was good patriotic stuff, but when generals cry for men to rally to the defence of the country in the face of a hypothetical threat, they are demanding that soldiers be put in charge of everything and given a free hand. For if there is no danger the military become expendable.

As a result, Communist China has been preparing for years for a war that no one unleashes, and Han is not the only commander who has generated war-fever in order to create an atmosphere in which he could excusably suppress the revolutionary activity of pro-Maoists infiltrated into his command. In his own case he was particularly keen to stunt the local influence of two "left-wing" favourites of Chiang Ch'ing whom he had had to accept as political commissars.*

---

* Ch'eng Shih-ch'ing (since transferred) and Yang Tung-liang.

127

Twenty-five provincial divisions (each a military district) are shared out among ten military regions in metropolitan China, excluding Sinkiang. But, exceptionally, the Tsinan Region only controls one – Shantung. It is not to be disdained, however, for at the time of writing its commander, Yang Te-chih, disposes of 160,000 men. Now sixty-two, Yang was born the son of a poor village blacksmith in Hunan, and was given the sobriquet "Respect-Tiger" or "Tigerlover" (as his elder brother was called "Sea Tiger"). He worked in a coal-mine as a child, and later made his way to the city to be a porter, but when he was eighteen he was involved in the unsuccessful Autumn Harvest Uprising of 1927 with Huang Yung-sheng, and he became one of the original "Sanwan seed-force". He made the Long March in the vanguard with the "Speechless Rustic" and was prominent at the hazardous crossing of the Tatu River. He was with Lin Piao's 115th Division as a regimental commander at the Pinghsingkuan ambush in 1937, and was deputy commander of Chinese "volunteers" in Korea, where the present military chiefs of the Peking and Wuhan Military Regions served under him.* In 1958 he was reduced to the ranks for a spell, as Mao's whim at that time dictated, but was soon restored to the post he had just acquired as commander at Tsinan.

In 1967 the Tigerlover made a tactical error. He paid lip-service to the Cultural Revolution by passively supporting the pro-Mao masses "seizing power" in Shantung. His intention was evidently to compromise with Mao, and his calculation was that the movement was not strong enough to be dangerous and could always be reined in if necessary. In consequence, however, a comparative nonentity in the shape of the vice-mayor of Tsingtao† (which was within the Military Region) was able to make a considerable name for himself as a Maoist "rebel", and when the Shantung Revolutionary Committee was formed with Peking's approval, it was he who was "elected" to be its chairman and thus wielded political power over Yang's considerable army.

The Tigerlover was not going to relinquish control of his fief so easily, however. Mao stepped in to reconcile the two men

---

* Cheng Wei-san and Tseng Szu-yu.   † Wang Hsiao-yu.

and tried to protect the revolutionary, but the Tigerlover felt he had shown enough patience and, choosing his moment, removed the upstart, the Chairman notwithstanding.

If regional warlords meanwhile watched mistrustfully as Lin Piao filtered his comrades from the old 4th Field Army into their strongholds, it was also true that candidates from the commands of the "Five Heavenly Kings" were being slipped into other regions and into positions of influence in Peking itself. Among these moves was the surprising appointment of Pai Hsiang-kuo as Minister for Trade in late 1970. Pai served under Huang Yung-sheng in Canton Military Region,[3] and after Huang became Chief of Staff, he was attached as a military representative (or watchdog) to the ministry. But his promotion to be the head of it was still startling, for it is second only to the Foreign Ministry as a main channel of contact with the outside world, and the Minister is expected to have a sound knowledge of economics, commerce and diplomacy. China's international trade policy, moreover, is often heavily influenced by political considerations.

Two good men were bypassed so that Pai could have the post – the Acting Minister and the Vice-Minister, both of them members of the Central Committee of the party.* His nomination seemed to indicate that top government jobs might increasingly go to soldiers, and that, like Lin Piao, the Chief of Staff was widening his sphere of influence. Between them, they had not done badly. By 1971 the following five generals, all members of the Politburo, held the country's key military posts in the capital:

Huang Yung-sheng: Chief of Staff of the PLA and military chief of all three services

Li Te-sheng: Director of the General Political Department of the PLA

Wu Fa-hsien: Commander of the Air Force

Li Tso-p'eng† : Political Commissar of the Navy

Ch'iu Hui-tso† : Director of the General Logistics Department and controller of the entire military supply service

And all but Li Te-sheng were from the 4th Field Army system.

---

* Lin Hai-yun and Li Ch'iang.
† See appendix to Chapter 11.

However, when Huang also placed his own nominees from the 4th Field Army and the Kiangsi group among the forces of the other "Heavenly Kings", a nasty crack started to develop in this structure. The Red warlords, already contending with men infiltrated among them by Mao and Lin and finding now that one of their own number was doing the same, began to suspect that Huang was ganging up with Lin Piao to ease them out of power. For it was evident that Mao and Lin, at least, accepted their pretensions to autonomy on sufferance and had only compromised with them until a new generation of leaders could replace them, just as Mao had compromised temporarily with the Chinese capitalists when he first declared China a People's Republic.

The trouble was that Huang wore two hats. He was still Chairman of the Kwangtung Revolutionary Committee and the grey eminence of the Canton Military Region, and as such the brother-in-arms of the other four warlords. But he was also the Chief of Staff in Peking and the champion of the newcomers, the "younger" veterans from the stirring days of the Kiangsi Soviet and the 4th Field Army. A bloodless fight for the high ground was on between the five men in Peking from this last group, of whom he was the leader, and the "Heavenly Kings" from the five main regional commands, of whom he was still regarded as the leader. Meanwhile as Chief of Staff he needed Mao to limit the pretensions of the regional commanders, and as a provincial warlord he needed the regional commanders to limit the importunities of the Maoists. And he could no longer be trusted by either side.

In consequence, the day would come when Liu Wen-hui, the opium-smoking feudal warlord whose "two-gun force" let the Communists cross the Tatu River (according to the KMT version) would dine with President Nixon in Peking, while Huang Yung-sheng, the hero who had forced the passage (according to the Communist version), had already been ominously absent from public life for five full months.

12

Boxing the Army Compass

Problems of military power in China are not confined to Peking and the five major regions with which Huang Yung-sheng had such an equivocal relationship. There are in all ten of these semi-autonomous commands, including the Peking Military Region which also appears to exercise control over an eleventh – Sinkiang. The leaders of all these regions were attacked by Red Guards and "revolutionary rebels" during the Cultural Revolution and they all reacted hostilely, sometimes savagely.

PEKING MILITARY REGION (Hopei and Shansi Provinces and Inner Mongolia)

Lin Piao once remarked that Peking and Wuhan Military Regions gave him more headaches than any other area of turbulence, for the Peking commander flouted Chiang Ch'ing, and the Wuhan commander led an open revolt against Peking. But there are those who claim that the Defence Minister secretly encouraged both.

However that may be, the Acting Commander of the Peking Region demanded the right to open fire and to suppress the rebels when they started fighting in the streets, and Chiang Ch'ing was quick to turn on him: "I can see through you, and your claim that mass organisations of thousands of revolutionaries create problems," she cried shrilly. "Suddenly you dare to attack me, Cheng Wei-san, and you must now confess your errors . . . for you have no love for the young Red Guards."[1] But Mao eventually gave way, and the soldiers were told that they could resort to arms to put down the mounting disorders, and to arrest those who resisted them with weapons.

This Cheng, now 58 years old, should in theory be classed with the other Red warlords. He was an outstandingly clever young man from Hupeh, a member of the Ma Huang clique who was promoted to be a divisional political commissar before he was twenty and later served with distinction in Korea.

He is an old comrade-in-arms of Ironsides, the master of Nanking. But by 1971 he was still not confirmed in his post, and his subordinate commands were in the hands of men loyal to Mao and Lin Piao.

WUHAN MILITARY REGION (Hupeh and Honan Provinces)

It was the Commander of Wuhan, not Peking, therefore, whose revolt eventually sobered the leaders of the Cultural Revolution by demonstrating how dangerous the army's antagonism to the Mao-made upheaval really could be.

The central figure in this drama, which was staged in 1967, was a skinny, puny, subtle yet truculent officer with a disfigured face which had earned him the nickname of "Pockmark Ch'en". Ch'en Tsai-tao was no Maoist. He had made his reputation in the Fourth Front Army and the 129th Division. He was another member of the Ma Huang clique, and his most constant chief had been the One-Eyed Dragon, Liu Po-ch'eng. In the first phases of the Cultural Revolution he paid lip-service to the left-wing rebels, but meanwhile he and his political commissar* set about mobilising conservative forces to resist them.

Peking became uneasy, and in February 1967 Mao surreptitiously encouraged the deputy commander of the region to launch a mass campaign to overthrow Pockmark. This man† summoned fifteen senior military cadres to his house for a conference, and secretly registered the proceedings on a miniature tape-recorder in order to be able to play them back to Mao. His voice was later identified as saying: "I can tell you that it is the Military Affairs Commission, not just myself, that is seizing power, for the sanction of the Commission is necessary in order to do so. [Given that sanction] I am capable of succeeding, for I have commanded seven armies in my time, but the call to action must come from your mouths, not just mine . . ."²

Ch'en reacted with ruthless efficiency. By mid-year there were some 400,000 "revolutionary rebels" in Wuhan, but they were still outnumbered by troops loyal to Pockmark, and by a massive organisation of workers and militia called the "One Million Heroes Army" which was stiffened by the "8201 Unit",

---

* Chung Han-hua.   † Li Ying-hsi.

an anti-Maoist PLA formation of divisional strength. These forces proceeded to suppress the leftists and in March alone the "Million Heroes" arrested three thousand of them, disbanding their organisations as "counter-revolutionary". In July Premier Chou En-lai personally ruled that Ch'en was backing the wrong side, and the Minister for Public Security and a representative of the Cultural Revolution Group in the capital* arrived in the triple-city of Wuhan to investigate the matter further.

These two dignitaries duly discovered the true mood of the Wuhan mob and its military leaders when they confirmed the Premier's finding that Ch'en was at fault and that the mass organisations he supported were reactionary. Just after midnight on 20 July a hundred army trucks crammed with men bearing the armbands of the "One Million Heroes Army" and the "8201 Unit" surrounded their hotel. They were seized at gun-point, cursed, kicked and knocked around, and then thrown onto a truck and driven to the local military headquarters through streets patrolled by the PLA and covered by machine-guns on the rooftops. They were put under guard overnight, and hauled out the next day to face a vast demonstration involving 400 trucks, tanks, and even fire-engines packed with men brandishing steel spears or rifles with bayonets fixed, and waving banners bearing the characters "The 8201 Unit of the One Million Heroes Army of Mao Tsetung's Thought". They were then pitched onto a truck again and taken to a local sports ground for more manhandling in public, their insignia were ripped off, and their clothes torn.

By this time the Minister had been painfully injured in the back, and the delegate from the Cultural Revolution Group was in a worse way. He had been pitilessly beaten, he was covered in bruises, his face was badly swollen and one eye was closed. The "Million Heroes" then took over the town, fired Red Guard schools, thrashed and sometimes killed revolutionary rebels. This was not just a case of defiance by a local warlord bent on seeing that nobody "seized power" from him. It was a case of kidnapping and open mutiny against the Maoist leadership. When loyalist troops were ordered to subdue Pockmark's legions and Chou En-lai flew to Wuhan to save the hapless

---

* Hsieh Fu-chih and Wang Li.

133

pair from Peking, he himself only escaped abduction by a ruse. The two men were rescued (or released), and Pockmark was relieved of his post and summoned to the capital, where he was chastised by the Central Committee of the party, obliged to confess his sins, and sentenced to a course of study in the Thoughts of Mao Tsetung.

He received no more severe punishment than that for the armed counter-revolution in Wuhan. Moreover, the deputy commander who had tried to topple him was not given his post but detained in the capital, placed under close surveillance, and also compelled to study Mao's Thoughts. The secret tape-recording of the meeting he had called to plot the overthrow of Ch'en Tsai-tao had fallen into the hands of Huang Yung-sheng. The new Chief of Staff was furious at this conspiracy to undermine military authority and set officer against officer, and bitterly rebuked the leftists at a big meeting in June 1968. "First and foremost we must assure the stability of the army," he stressed. "We must therefore allow men to make mistakes – and also allow them to rectify them. You persistently accuse others of suppressing you. What suppression? To oppose attempts to seize power can be right, for otherwise anyone could seize power . . . and we cannot go on like that."[3]

The man who replaced Pockmark in Wuhan was Tseng Szu-yu, Deputy Commander of the Shenyang Military Region, and although confirmation was not immediately available, it is widely believed that in return Pockmark was subsequently given Tseng's post in Manchuria with the approval of Lin Piao. For just as Mao connived (to say the least) when the deputy commander tried to "make revolution" against Pockmark in order to uphold the extreme Maoist line espoused by Chiang Ch'ing, so Lin Piao is believed to have urged Pockmark to make a firm stand against the rebels that would chasten her.

Pockmark overdid things, and was compelled to perform his act of penance in Peking. He had served his purpose, however. His revolt provoked a spurious and short-lived attempt by the Cultural Revolution Group to purge the whole PLA, but it also stiffened the resistance of local military commanders everywhere to all moves by the Maoists to turn them out into the cold. From then on, Mao sought a compromise rather than a clash with the PLA, which took over the Cultural Revolution and, in doing so, took over the real power.

CHENGTU MILITARY REGION (Szechuan Province including Sikang, and Tibet)

Szechuan and Sikang are the former strongholds of Ho Lung The Moustache, the gallant commander of the 1st Field Army, but after the Cultural Revolution a favourite general of Lin Piao was sent to command the Chengtu Military Region as a whole, and the 4th Field Army once more appeared to dominate the scene.

The one-armed Liang Hsing-ch'u, who joined the Autumn Harvest Uprising in Hunan at the age of seventeen, is now a man of 61, reticent and prudent. In the past his prudence has not, however, inhibited his valour. He has been wounded seventeen times in the Communist cause, and he is deeply respected by the Mao faction, who call him "Night Tiger" after the Model Regiment of the First Front Army. He fought as a divisional commander under Lin Piao for the mastery of Manchuria after the Japanese surrender, retreated with him beyond the Sungari River under heavy pressure from the American-armed Nationalists, and advanced when he attacked again through icy blizzards in a temperature of forty below. A blacksmith as a boy, the Night Tiger is still as hard as nails himself and a keen warrior. He was in Korea, hammering away at heavily-equipped American forces in bitter winter weather, served as deputy to Huang Yung-sheng in the Canton Military Region, and was made Commander of Chengtu in May 1967.

The ground for a take-over by this 4th Field Army nominee had been laid in January of that year, when Ho Lung was publicly disgraced. The commander and political commissar of Chengtu Military Region were the Moustache's men from the old 1st Field Army, and they were both sacked.* But the political commissar was Li Ch'ing-ch'uan, the husband of Ho Lung's niece and a king of the castle in his own right, famous for his blasphemous contention that fertiliser serves more purpose than politics.

Li, whom the Maoists reviled as "Emperor of the South-West", held the key party and PLA posts in Szechuan for ten years before his downfall, and thanks to the patronage of Ho Lung was for many of them the political overseer of Kweichow, Yunnan and Tibet in addition, and a member of the Politburo. With all this

---

* The commander was Huang Hsin-t'ing.

power in his hands, he ruled his personal kingdom like an efficient despot, promoting the loyal with a nod, and punishing critics without pity. His views on doctrinaire Maoism were explicit enough – he is reported to have commented that two of the troubles with students were "too many meetings . . . and too much study of Mao's works". He was accused of complicity in a plot to overthrow the Chairman in February of 1966 which allegedly involved old and treacherous comrades of his like Ho Lung and Teng Hsiao-p'ing, the evicted party secretary-general.

This has not been proved, but it is certain that he fiercely resisted the importunities of an influx of Red Guards from Peking and elsewhere who converged on Szechuan to "seize power". Like Pockmark Ch'en in Wuhan, he inspired the formation of anti-Maoist "Maoist" phalanxes like the local "Production Army" and "Industrial Army" which mauled the visitors mercilessly in a series of bloody clashes that continued even after the PLA intervened to "support the left" (i.e. to restore order). In May 1967 Li was formally dismissed from office, but the announcement was at once followed by a vast protest demonstration in Chengtu, the provincial capital.

It was obvious that his influence could not be destroyed with the stroke of a pen in Peking. Broadcasts continued to complain of the strong "evil wind" of public opinion among the millions of Szechuan who wanted him reinstated, factional fighting intensified, and there were ominous rumours of anti-Maoist guerrillas assembling in the hills. Mao and Lin Piao evidently realised that the appointment of the "Night Tiger" as commander of the region might meet with much passive resistance from the 1st Field Army brotherhood, given his Maoist military past, and the more sympathetic figure of Chang Kuo-hua was therefore brought in at the apex as political commissar.

Chang Kuo-hua was not from the 1st Field – but he was not from the 4th Field Army either. He had served with the 2nd Field Army of the One-Eyed Dragon, and had a reputation as an anti-Maoist. He was warlord of Tibet when the Cultural Revolution broke out, with local political and military power concentrated in his hands, and he fought violently against the "revolutionary rebel" movement's attempts to take over his domain, acting in concert as far as possible with Ho Lung's lieutenants in neighbouring Szechuan.

When Ho Lung fell from grace, Mao summoned Chang to Peking and then re-posted him to Chengtu on the pretext that he should "make revolution elsewhere". The object of Mao and Lin Piao was to separate him from his own troops in Tibet,* and send him to a region in which he would have no loyal armed following on the ground and could not sabotage the Cultural Revolution. He would be under the eye of Liang Hsing-ch'u, and he should prove useful in placating Ho Lung's heretics, to whom he was, of course, acceptable. The situation would therefore be stabilised.

By 1971 these two controlled the provincial revolutionary committee and the provincial party committee. But the game was not played out. Li Ta-chang, one of the old guard in Szechuan, remained vice-chairman of the provincial revolutionary committee and was elected to the Central Committee of the party by the Ninth Congress in April 1969. Li Ch'ing-ch'uan himself reappeared in Peking at the end of 1971 at an official banquet given by the All-China Athletics Federation. Obviously the Ho Lung clique still had a potential for mischief and had to be handled with care where possible. Other leaders of the Moustache's 1st Field Army might have been relentlessly persecuted and compelled to go to ground over a wide area in south-west China, but when Chang Kuo-hua died in February 1972, Li Ta-chang pronounced the eulogy. The mountain-top might have gone, but the silhouette remained.

KUNMING MILITARY REGION (Yunnan and Kweichow Provinces)

Kunming is by tradition a stronghold of the 2nd Field Army of the One-Eyed Dragon that grew out of the old Fourth Front Army of the discredited Chang Kuo-t'ao. As soon as the Cultural Revolution began to gain momentum, therefore, the commander, deputy commander, and political commissar of the region were at once attacked by Mao's rebels. The commander† was dismissed, the commissar‡ was purged and reportedly committed suicide, and military and political power was concentrated in the hands of a confidant of Lin Piao at the head of a new Yunnan Revolutionary Committee. However,

---

* Tibet was only included in Chengtu Military Region in 1971.
  † Ch'in Chi-wei.   ‡ Yen Hung-yen.

this man most inconveniently died, and his two deputies – one a protégé of Premier Chou En-lai, the other a lone senior cadre of the Fourth Front Army enjoying local support from below – were at once at loggerheads.*

Now Peking did not try to solve this problem by putting in a 4th Field Army candidate of Lin Piao. Instead Wang Pi-ch'eng, the second secretary of the Yunnan party committee, was made Acting Commander of the Kunming Military Region. He was a tough general from the 3rd Field Army of Ch'en Yi and his wartime deputy, Su Yu. He had also been deputy commander under Ironsides of the Nanking Military Region, where he had rebuffed the Red Guards, and altogether he had, in theory, a past full of dubious allegiances as far as Mao and Lin Piao were concerned. But like Ironsides he had been defended by K'ang Sheng. "Comrade Wang committed certain mistakes," said K'ang, "but he was frank in his self-criticism. He earned many honours during the War of Liberation, and he should therefore be judged by his entire history and his works, not merely by certain acts."[4]

K'ang Sheng was trying to win both Ironsides Hsu Shih-yu and Wang Pi-ch'eng over in accordance with Mao's plan to cultivate a web of allegiances in the PLA stretching beyond those men loyal to Lin Piao, in the knowledge that the less intransigent cadres from other armies, worried by the rise of the 4th Field veterans, might well be glad to meet him halfway if he favoured them. So a one-time subordinate of Su Yu was given the task of restoring stability to the strategic province of Yunnan, the bulwark of China's south-western defences. And, as will be seen, that was not an isolated case.

LANCHOW MILITARY REGION (Kansu, Shensi, Tsinghai, Ninghsia Provinces)

This vast and strategic expanse of Chinese territory is both the great rear base that serves the "front line" along the hostile Sino–Soviet border to the north, and the hard centre of China's nuclear industry. But again, the vital post of commander of the region was not confided to one of Lin Piao's lieutenants in 1970. P'i Ting-chun is 57, a tall, hefty soldier from Honan who is still called "Little Devil" because he joined the Fourth Front

---

* See Appendix to this chapter for details.

Army at the age of fifteen. His first commander was Ironsides Hsu Shih-yu whom he accompanied on the Long March from the Oyuwan Soviet into the mountains of Szechuan, and once the Fourth Front Army was converted into the 129th Division, he served directly under the One-Eyed Dragon.

In the post-war struggle against the Nationalists, he commanded a regiment in the 3rd Field Army, and after a brilliant diversionary campaign, during which he lured the KMT away from encircled Communist forces by conducting a running fight against overwhelming odds, he was given a division. His immediate superior was Wang Pi-ch'eng and both of them were subordinates of Su Yu.

There is no coincidence here. By 1971 not only these two regional commanders, but at least seven senior cadres in the Lanchow Military Region (including those responsible for safeguarding the nuclear complex) were veterans of the 3rd Field Army and had served under Su Yu, who was now the Vice-Minister for Defence supervising China's nuclear weapons programme.[5]

Su Yu had come to terms with Mao, and these men were paying at least lip-service to Maoism, for the new pattern of 3rd Field Army influence could only develop with the Chairman's consent. And it was shifting the whole balance of military power.

Mao is a great believer in balance (and the imbalance that leads to new balance), and when the dismissal of the double-dealing Yang Ch'eng-wu as Chief of Staff upset the equilibrium of loyalties and rivalries within the PLA, he seems to have seen possibilities of a new counterpoise in Su Yu. Su Yu's career had been uneven up to that moment, for if he had had a good war, he had had an indifferent peace. He is 63 years old, the son of a minor landlord in Hunan, of small build, with a heart-shaped face and wide brows but a strong aquiline nose. His countrymen are well-known for their unyielding toughness, which in Su Yu took the form of a fierce courage on the battlefield, but he is a meditative man by nature, quiet and with a gentle, cultured manner, although alert and quick-witted enough when politics or war demands.

He joined the Communist Youth League as a teenager, led an attack against his teachers at school, and was marked down for arrest by the Kuomintang. He escaped from his home village by hiding under the seat of a train, and joined the Red army in Wuhan. He took part in the Nanchang Uprising in 1927, and was in Mao's mountain stronghold by the time he was nineteen. When the Communists abandoned the Kiangsi Soviet in 1934, Su Yu was among those who remained behind to put up a fight for it against the KMT for as long as possible, and he later became Deputy Commander of the New 4th Army under Ch'en the Bald.

Su proved a masterly general, and many ascribe Ch'en Yi's outstanding successes to him. His right arm had been paralysed by a crippling wound in the thirties, and he nursed a bitter grudge against the KMT. Commanding an army in Kiangsu at 37, he won seven battles in a row, and when Ch'en Yi's forces were regrouped into the 3rd Field Army, Su Yu was at the famous crossing of the Yangtse River and the taking of Nanking and Shanghai. He served consistently with Ch'en Yi and a close bond was forged between them.

There was more than Su Yu's comradeship with Ch'en the Bald in the 3rd Field Army, however, to make Mao hesitate before he gave greater power to this Vice-Minister of Defence who had for so long been ignored. Su Yu had strong feelings about the urgent need to modernise the Chinese army. He accompanied Chou En-lai to the Soviet Union to negotiate arms aid in the early fifties, and when he was Chief of Staff of the PLA between 1954 and 1958, he again went to Moscow, this time with P'eng Te-huai, the Defence Minister who was to fall into disgrace for similar heresies.

But by the time P'eng was sacked, Su Yu had already gone – dismissed on the insistence of Lin Piao for wanting a professional force fit for the electronic age, and so flouting Mao's theories on guerrilla defence and "people's war". He agreed with Khrushchev that "Contemporary national defence is not measured by the number of rifle-carrying soldiers . . . To a country with modern weapons, soldiers no longer form an army, but just a mass of flesh." The Russians respected this practical and perceptive Chinese general, but as the Sino–Soviet friendship which had flowered under Liu Shao-ch'i (but threatened the principles and prejudices of Mao) gave way to distrust and hostility, Su fell from favour in Peking.

Once Mao had rid himself of all leading revisionists like ex-President Liu Shao-ch'i, however, the preoccupation that was Su Yu's undoing – the modernisation of the PLA – could be the making of him. For Mao stopped short of calling the H-bomb ideological anathema. China had to have her own warheads. More than this, Mao had to have them. When Mao made Su Yu responsible for nuclear armament in 1968, Su belonged to none of the groups that had been manoeuvring for mastery of the two scientific and technological bodies that were concerned with it, and he could therefore act as an insulator between Lin Piao and Nieh Jung-chen, the Profligate Monk who was chairman of both of them; and just as his once-suspect views on defence had become an asset, so his once-suspect association with the 3rd Field Army had become a virtue as Mao sought to widen the spectrum of loyalty to himself within the PLA.

By mid-1971 it was therefore possible to define four areas of military power, corresponding approximately to the points of the compass.

In spite of many vociferous complaints in Peking about renewed "militarism" in Japan at the turn of the decade, there were still two main poles of defence in China against two possible aggressors – the Russians in the north and the Americans in the south – and these coincided with the zones of influence of the PLA's two most powerful men of the moment, Lin Piao and Huang Yung-sheng. The undisputed master of East China was Hsu Shih-yu, while in the west Su Yu had become the common denominator of a military group also drawn from the old 3rd Field Army which had been brought in to dilute – possibly to dominate – an explosive mixture of 4th Field Army nominees and of men still loyal to The Moustache and the One-Eyed Dragon; and Mao had reached a pragmatic understanding with both Hsu and Su.

For just as he was anxious to keep the forces within the eternal Washington–Moscow–Peking triangle in equilibrium with himself at the apex, rather than become involved in a bilateral clash with either of his enemies, so the Chairman was developing rival cliques within the PLA into a four-sided figure whose opposing pressures could cancel one another out and keep it stable. But although this experiment in isometrics might work while he lived, would the quadrilateral hold together thereafter, men asked?

And then the figure collapsed, thrown out of balance by the curious fortunes of Marshal Lin Piao.

13
The Fallen Angel

It is October 1970. A modest, seedy, bespectacled little man with brushlike, faintly quizzical eyebrows, addresses a vast crowd at the Gate of Heavenly Peace in Peking in a shrill voice and a thick Hupeh accent as he stumbles through a bunch of notes written in outsize characters. He is Lin Piao, the crown prince of China, prestigious marshal and appointed heir of Chairman Mao himself. He was already the forceful commander of the victorious 4th Field Army more than twenty years ago, but he gives himself no airs. He never yields to anger, shouts or rants, even when he is involved in a stiff argument with subordinates. He is a quiet, plausible man, bad at rallies, good at corner-table persuasion.

A film star says of him: "Lin is like a refined scholar. He carefully puts his cap on straight, and his uniform is always spick and span. He makes you feel that you are a friend of his, and clasps your hand firmly when he greets you. But from the way he walks, you would think he was afraid of stepping on an ant."

As he stands on the rostrum beside the barrel-like figure of Mao at the National Day parade, he resembles a little bird, and his war record shows that the comparison is apt, for it is the nature of little birds to be merciless in attack. When the Communist forces were reorganised to fight the Japanese and Lin Piao was given command of the 115th Division he was the first Red commander to engage the enemy in battle, and he gave the Japanese cause to remember the occasion, for he caught them with their guns down at a place called Pinghsingkuan.

The Great Wall of China, sixteen hundred miles long, is broken by gateways where roads traverse it, and these take the form of fortified "*kuan*" or keeps. Pinghsingkuan therefore was a strategic nerve-end in north-east Shansi through which the Japanese moved on their way south into China proper. On a blustery day in September 1937, Lin Piao observed the intervening terrain from a point ten miles away and stretching out his arms exclaimed: "We shall deal the enemy a heavy blow here." His fragile figure did not look as if it could withstand the wind, but he was in a cheerful and confident mood and his high spirits infected his men.

Divisional headquarters was established under good cover on the forward slope of the range that flanked the highway leading from the Great Wall, but was separated from it by wheatfields in the valley. Lin Piao quickly deployed forward units amid the high, waving corn for a massive ambush, while more troops were sent to seize a temple halfway up the hills on the opposite side of the road, from which its entire length could be controlled. Before the temple or the ridge above it could be secured, however, the grinding rumble of heavy-duty motors was heard, and all took cover. A long Japanese convoy of a hundred trucks began to wind its way through the valley, followed by mounted troops and mules hauling field guns.

Lin Piao's soldiers were lightly armed with rifles, a few clips of ammunition, and a couple of hand-grenades each, and they fixed bayonets in anticipation of close-quarter fighting. When Lin ordered the attack, his available machine-guns and mortars backed up the exploding grenades, and the mounted Japanese fell into disorder. Their infantry quickly retaliated, however, using trucks and ditches for cover; heavy fire was soon cutting swathes through the yellowing wheat, and the valley was filled with drifting smoke. The Chinese Reds then charged the enemy, yelling defiance, and when they reached the highway they fanned out and the battle broke into a confused mêlée of bodies and flashing swords and blood-stained bayonets. A small group of Japanese seized the old temple on the hill opposite, but the Chinese rushed up the slope and wrested it from them.

The enemy could not bring his artillery into play and dared not call for a supporting air-strike with so many men engaged in close combat. The surviving remnant of the Japanese brigade (from the 5th division of General Itagaki) finally scattered, and the Chinese found they had captured fifty field guns, ten tanks and armoured cars, and a hundred other vehicles. Although this victory, won with Lin Piao's "one point, two sides" tactics,[1] could not compare with the most famous of KMT successes against the enemy, it was remarkable as a model ambush executed economically by under-armed troops, and it

143

went further towards establishing Lin Piao's already excellent reputation as a commander in the field.

But in 1970 Lin Piao is a calm, soft-spoken man of 63 without Mao's sense of humour or Chou En-lai's ready tongue. He is polite, earnest, means what he says even if he does not always say what he thinks. He seldom jokes, and he lives austerely. He does not smoke or drink, and if he has an addiction, it is to fried yellow beans which he is persuaded are good for his frequent heavy colds, and which he is quite capable of offering to a guest in the absence of other refreshment. He even calls his crop-haired daughter after them – Tou-tou. His daughter started to make a name for herself as a promising young writer for the revolution, but has slipped into obscurity again.

His home is simple and inelegant (according to an earlier Communist account). The bedroom-study in which he does much of his work is as bare as the exigencies of life could possibly permit. There is a single wooden chair for his own use, and any guests must sit on stools. Two old blankets are neatly folded on a hard bed. The desk is a cheap affair with a map and globe laid out on it,[2] and is lit only by the ceiling lamp. In winter, Lin warms himself at a brazier of coal briquettes.

The room is full of books – Mao, Marx, Lenin, Engels, Stalin – and pinned-up quotations. A photograph of the Chairman hangs on the wall, together with some of his Thoughts. This is where Lin works most of the time, but his wife, Yeh Ch'un, who is herself a member of the Administrative Office of the Military Affairs Commission of the party, runs his routine business here and in the Ministry, and acts as his deputy. In this way she is the counterpart of Chiang Ch'ing, and she is a useful intermediary not only between Lin and generals with whom he does not see eye-to-eye, but between Lin and Mao's charming, ambitious wife whom he personally regards as a political sidewinder.

Why is Lin Piao the chosen successor of Mao, his "closest comrade-in-arms", at this moment? For one thing, he long ago gave his fealty to the Chairman, and for another, he showed during the Cultural Revolution that he did not have the reputation of being China's best strategist for nothing.

Lin Piao's real name was Lin Yu-yung (Lin Piao means "Tiger Cat" Lin) and he hailed from Hupeh, where he was born

144

into a family of nine living in two rooms – he once told Edgar Snow that his father had been the proprietor of a factory, but had been ruined by extortionate taxation. Lin left home at the age of ten to study, joined the youth corps of the Communist Party when he was eighteen, and in 1925 walked some four hundred miles from Changsha to Canton in order to enrol for the entrance examination to the new Whampoa Military Academy. During the Northern Expedition against the warlords, he rose from platoon to company commander, and after Chiang Kai-shek turned on the Communists and their honeymoon with the KMT ended, he fought in the Nanchang Uprising under Chu Te the Cook. Mao Tsetung and Chu Te later fell out over future strategy and Lin Piao staunchly supported Mao against his commander, who was insisting on executing the Central Committee's impractical orders to "seize the towns" while Mao wanted to make revolution in the mountains. Chu Te was soured by this experience, and it was put about that you could not trust men with curved noses like Lin Piao.

Lin was simply being practical, and had not allowed his sentiments to stifle his judgement, but Mao was delighted and began to hold him in high esteem, so that by the time he was twenty-three he was commanding an army corps. With Hades P'eng Te-huai, Lin Piao was Mao's most trusted subordinate commander in the Kiangsi Soviet and on the Long March. When Mao and Chang Kuo-t'ao quarrelled and the Red forces were split in two, it was Hades and Lin Piao who led Mao's half northwards to Yenan, while Mao himself acted as political commissar; once in north Shensi, it was again these two who secured and expanded the key Communist guerrilla base which was to be known as the North-West Border Region.

Lin Piao then became President of the Anti-Japanese Military and Political University at Yenan. The university may have used caves as classrooms and rough walls as blackboards, but it was training cadres to help Mao consolidate his politico–military power, and in a country in which teachers were still venerated by their students, Lin's post promised considerable future influence.

When the Communists began to fight the Japanese, Lin Piao was widely praised for his victory at Pinghsingkuan, but later in 1937 he took a bullet in the chest while commanding the 115th Division against the enemy on the Yellow River, and was

145

rushed back to Yenan. He was not to command troops for six years. However, his troublesome wound later provided him with a pretext for going to Moscow, and he took a team of ten cadres with him to discuss how the Japanese could be contained in Manchuria, for Stalin feared that they might make it their springboard for an assault on the Soviet Union. It suited the Chinese Communists to cooperate with the Russians by extending their own power into the north-east, and Lin Piao established good relations with them. It seems that he was soon fit again, moreover, for he is reported to have taken part in the defence of Leningrad in 1941 as a Soviet lieutenant-colonel.

On his return to Yenan in 1942 to apprise Mao of the results of his mission, he received a warm welcome. He was made president of the party school (accumulating more teacher-student relationships) and helped Mao to inculcate in cadres the concept of a "Chinese" approach to the theory of communism. He then disappeared, and is believed to have spent at least part of the intervening period in Moscow. But in 1945, when the Japanese were on the point of collapse, he again turned up in Yenan.

The Japanese capitulated, and Lin Piao took 20,000 men into Manchuria as the nucleus of what quickly became an extraordinary agglomeration of troops and weapons thrown against the Kuomintang – other elements of the 115th Division from the Profligate Monk's Soviet, units from Ch'en Yi the Bald's army to the south, Mongolian cavalry, disaffected Manchurian detachments, even North Korean contingents. To these were soon added KMT turncoats and captured American weapons as this "North-east Democratic United Army" evolved into Lin Piao's famous 4th Field Army, and Lin found himself with more than 700,000 men under command. Manchuria was taken, Peking compelled to surrender, Tientsin successfully besieged, and subsequently Lin Piao's forces made smooth progress right down the map of China without encountering strong and determined Nationalist resistance anywhere.

In September 1950 the 4th Field Army joined other Communist formations in a "People's Volunteer Army" of 300,000 men that assembled on China's frontier with Korea, and it was Lin Piao who commanded this force when it crossed the Yalu River against the United Nations. After some initial success, however, the "volunteers" were given terrible proof of the

146

impact that a jet-age air force and the fire-power of mechanised troops could have on what Khrushshev had described as "soldiers who no longer formed an army but were just a mass of flesh". The Chinese were physically scattered, morally shattered. Lin Piao soon disappeared, and word was again put about that he had gone to the Soviet Union for medical treatment. Whether he had been wounded again or not, this was plausible enough. His first wound in the fighting against the Japanese had done him permanent damage. He was reputed to have contracted tuberculosis, suffered periodical haemorrhages, and from time to time was completely incapacitated by severe stomach disorders. Although his place as Chinese commander in Korea was taken by Hades P'eng Te-huai, however, Lin Piao had in fact gone no further than Manchuria.

The Chinese had been quick to learn their lesson, it seemed, for he had been withdrawn from the Korean campaign for another operation which was evidently considered at least equally important – the conversion of the Chinese army into something more than that "mass of flesh". While P'eng Te-huai, provided with Soviet arms, struggled to update his forces in the field when they were not actually fighting, Lin Piao was to supervise the business of making sophisticated soldiers out of a million and a half recruits. He was obviously the man for the job. He was perhaps China's best general. He knew his Manchuria. He got on well with the Russians, on whom the Chinese must now rely for everything from automatic weapons to airborne training. And he got on well with Kao Kang, the political and military master of the north-east.

The training programme[3] required 15,000 military and party cadres, most of them junior officers drawn from different field armies or taken straight out of college. The more senior men were army "heroes" (10 per cent of the teaching personnel were colonels and above). The scheme was classified. Military training centres, schools for gunners, engineers, armoured forces, and senior officers' courses were established in the suburbs of cities throughout Manchuria and kept as secret as possible. The recruits began their training in July 1951, Lin was promoted to be Vice-Chairman of the party's Military Affairs Commission a few months later, and he had accomplished his task by 1953. Most of the new blood came from North China, and that is partly why an overwhelming majority of the younger army cadres – many of them holding senior commands – are northerners today. Once again Lin Piao was acting in the role of tutor, and once again benefiting from the teacher-student relationship in terms of future loyalties.

But he nearly tripped. Lin visited Moscow several times during the execution of this plan for the regeneration of the Chinese army, but he was not the only man upon whom the Russians looked with some favour. Kao Kang held Manchuria in his hand, and as Khrushchev later confirmed, Stalin was encouraging him to set up a separate "People's Government" in what would virtually be his own Manchurian kingdom. Stalin wanted to clip Mao's wings, but in March 1953 he died, the new Soviet leaders hastily withdrew from the conspiracy, and the following year Kao Kang was called upon to explain himself in Peking. Liu Shao-ch'i – "pro-Russian" but a patriot who did not believe in parcelling out the provinces of China – led the attack and insisted that, as a deputy of Kao Kang in Manchuria and a man held in high regard in Moscow, Lin Piao must have known of the plot.

Kao Kang was expelled from the party and stripped of all his titles and posts, and it was later announced that he had committed suicide. But Mao strongly defended Lin Piao, for he was anxious not to lose him, and Lin was not only reprieved but made a marshal and a member of the Politburo within a matter of months. His power and influence within the party and army were nonetheless sapped by the hostility of Liu Shao-ch'i and his sympathisers. Lin therefore knew that he must stay close to the Chairman, and for this reason he further cultivated Mao and Maoism, giving his ageing patron resolute support in the successful campaign to ruin Liu which opened ten years later.

The interests of the two men dovetailed. Mao used the army in order to establish his preponderant position in the party, and then as leader of the party he decreed that it must always dominate the army. This did not suit most soldiers at all, and when P'eng Te-huai was Defence Minister the army's resentment was expressed in instances of passive revolt. At one point, for example, the Armoured Force quietly let the post of political commissar fall vacant, and when one was finally appointed, managed to see that there were no vehicles available for his office, so that he could not circulate and interfere in military routine. Similar ploys were practised by subordinate artillery,

148

engineer and infantry units and formations. The generals responsible said plainly on more than one occasion that in their view political commissars no longer suited the requirements of forces preparing for sophisticated modern warfare. They were in the way.

During this difficult period in the late fifties Lin Piao was conspicuous for his loyalty to Mao's concept of a political, revolutionary army. When Hades P'eng Te-huai chastised the Chairman for his policies at the Lu Shan conference in 1959 and was sacked for his temerity, therefore, it was Lin Piao who was given his job. The Tiger Cat at once settled down to the business of earning his future title – "The greatest exponent of the Thoughts of Mao". There was to be profit on both sides, for as Lin indoctrinated the PLA in the teachings of the Chairman, the PLA would become the ideological model that all China must copy. If the army was to be politicised, politics were to be militarised.

Accordingly, Lin launched a campaign within the PLA for the study of Mao's works and stressed the need for a "political breakthrough" in military mentality. He laid down that even while the army was being modernised, the calibre of men was more important than the calibre of weapons (Maoism was their "spiritual atom bomb") and politics must come before training – "Equipment and techniques are important, but the human factor is even more important. For techniques have to be mastered by men." The Liberation Army must undergo both mechanisation and revolutionisation simultaneously, he said later, but "the latter must guide the former". Ranks were abolished, and the soldiers found that they were not only expected to memorise Mao and help with the harvest, but to run their own farms and even factories as part of the drive for that local self-reliance which for the Chairman was to be the very mortar of his ideal China.

Much of this, however, remained a matter of published words and paper statistics, signifying little, for, as we have already noted, grand slams are rare in China, and it is not usual for a winner to pick up all the tricks. Lin Piao may have become Defence Minister, but Liu Shao-ch'i hedged him in with his own men so that he had limited freedom of action. The Chief of Staff* and a large number of senior ministerial cadres were

_____
* Lo Jui-ch'ing.

not Lin's confidants. They were professional-minded generals of P'eng Te-huai's persuasion, and for three years from 1962 to 1965, during which it was given out that Lin Piao was often ill, his functions on the all-important Military Affairs Commission were largely undertaken by Ho Lung The Moustache, as we have seen.

But in September 1965 Lin Piao published his significant article "Long Live the Victory of People's Wars", in which he applied to the whole strategy of world revolution Mao's guerrilla principle that communist insurgents should first dominate the countryside and then surround the towns. The have-nots should rise up and seize the underdeveloped continents of Africa, Asia and Latin America which represented the "countryside", and once they held these they could "encircle" the sophisticated continents of North America and Europe which represented the "towns".

By mid-1966 Mao and Lin had staged a comeback, and the Cultural Revolution had broken upon the astonished millions of China. The appointment of Lin Piao as Mao's heir-designate was by now almost a foregone conclusion, but it would have been a cardinal error to assume that the aims and ideals of these two men were identical, that they were in perfect harmony, that – in short – appearance was reality.

The first discordant note reached the outside world in 1967. The rivalry between Lin Piao and Chiang Ch'ing, Mao's wife, could no longer be concealed. The militants of the Cultural Revolution, of whom Chiang Ch'ing was the jeer-leader, encompassed the downfall not only of military cadres like Wu Fa-hsien, the Air Force Commander, but of Hsiao Hua, chief political commissar of the armed forces and a confidant of Lin Piao who finally fell from grace in August of that year. Five of Hsiao Hua's immediate subordinates were also axed, and the General Political Department of the PLA was decapitated. Chiang Ch'ing's aim became clear. With Hsiao Hua's department smashed, political control of the services should pass to the Cultural Revolution Group within the PLA, of which she was now "adviser". Her military critics must be sacked and replaced with Maoists loyal to her. For since everyone else in the game seemed to be holding a gun, she must have one too.

The move failed, and three prominent members of her own group were subsequently destroyed by Lin Piao,[4] but it must be remembered in all this that Chiang Ch'ing was Mao's left hand, and that the conflict between Lin Piao and herself was the distorted shadow of an unseen divergence of outlook between Lin Piao and her husband.

It was distorted because, unlike his wife, Mao could make use of Lin Piao, the man with the gun, to strengthen his own position in the face of his ideological detractors. And on his side, Lin Piao needed Mao's personal support to strengthen his position in the face of his military rivals, for it cannot be over-emphasised that men do not oppose Mao, but Maoism. When Lin cried out during the Cultural Revolution that all must "read the works of Chairman Mao, listen to the words of Chairman Mao, study the thoughts of Chairman Mao, and be a good fighter for Chairman Mao", he was not fervently endorsing Mao's philosophies, but furthering his own ends and hitting back at Liu Shao-ch'i.

Did he think that Mao's maxims provided a panacea for all of China's ills? "We should not always take the same medicine regardless of the sickness," he once said,[5] showing that he was no dogmatist. The sincerity of his loud and almost obsequious adulation for Mao's military methods could be called into question. His fighting record hardly suggested that he believed in masses rather than machines. He was the first Communist leader to use either tanks or artillery on a big scale, he was the step-father of the Chinese Communist air force, and he was among those disillusioned commanders who saw what machines could do to masses in Korea. It seemed that he might well emerge after Mao's death as a powerful champion of a moderate, international line in Chinese policy. In the past he had stoutly denounced Russian revisionism and called for armed vigilance against possible aggression from the USSR. In the future he might be the first to bury the hatchet with his old contacts in Moscow.

He nevertheless knew that were he not the legitimate successor of Mao, he would have to overcome heavy odds to make himself master of China, for only a minority of military commanders in the provinces would take inconvenient orders from him as plain Lin Piao. He would have to brush away veteran generals who were senior to him or of equal standing, and be strong enough to dismiss those who flouted his directives.

He suffered from the further disadvantage that he himself

was no theoretician and had few admirers among party pundits. He was primarily a calculating Old Guard revolutionary general, a strategist whose political ideology was simply an echo of his master's voice. His main writings were military ("How to Train Soldiers", "Important Principles of Command") and they were required reading within the PLA. The reputation of Chou En-lai was far greater than his, both at home and abroad, and he had also to reckon with the Money God, Vice-Premier Li Hsien-nien, a man loyal to the Prime Minister who held the national purse and enjoyed considerable prestige in the army both as veteran general and treasurer.

The gentle-mannered, somewhat inscrutable crown prince of the Mao regime was known for his craftiness, however, as a man who moved carefully, knew how to make good use of his opportunities, and adapted himself swiftly to the terrain. Furthermore his influence within the PLA was not to be underestimated. He had run three party and army schools and universities across the years, and apart from faithful veterans from the 4th Field Army tradition, he had trained one and a half million new "commanders and fighters" (or officers and men as they were before ranks were abolished) who were now serving all over the country. As the old soldiers of other loyalties faded away, and the younger men came up, Lin Piao's hold on the forces would automatically be strengthened.

But if Mao the theorist could only hold down his antagonists in party and PLA by virtue of his unique position as Mao the Father of the Republic, how could Lin Piao do so – even if he lived long enough to try?

In the event, it was Mao who lived long enough to see him fail.

PART THREE

THE SCENARIO

14

The Storm Signal

Mao has the double standards of all dreamers who realise their dream. He has damned the Chinese intelligentsia black and extolled the ignorant peasantry that brought him to power, yet he has always seen himself as cast in the heroic mould of the conquering yet cultured Chinese poet-king, and capable of even greater things than the illiterate emperors of yesteryear:

> This land so fair
> Makes so many heroes vie to pay homage.
> A pity that Chin Shih Huang and Han Wu
> Could not turn an elegant line
> Tang Tsung and Sung Tsu
> Wrote imperfect verse
> And that darling of Heaven in his day
> Ghenghiz Khan
> Could only bend a bow to shoot eagles.
> All have gone.
> When counting great men
> Still look at today.

He wrote these lines in 1936, sure he would overshadow Chin Shih Huang, the "First Emperor" who had united all China before the birth of Christ, and Han Wu, who had sent his armies to victory in the West. But the dream was evidently already old, for a friend has penned this earlier recollection of him.[1]

"In the spring of 1921, a soft and bewitching night, Mao and I went to a restaurant in Shanghai for supper. When Mao was enlivened with drink, he asked me who in all Chinese history had achieved something great without support or help from anyone. After some thought, I replied that there were only two men, the Emperor Han Kao-tsu [who founded the great Han Dynasty] and Doctor Sun Yat-sen.

" 'Right!' He smashed the table with his fist, upsetting the wine and making the fried prawns jump from his plate. He wiped the wine and the prawns off the table with the sleeve of his cotton jacket, and went on confidently: 'I shall be the third . . .' As we were sipping tea, he found that a pair of copulating flies had drowned in his cup, and nodding and rolling his head about, he burst into lyrical verse – 'Dying under the peony, ever amorous even as a ghost' – in the vein of the lusty and gallant poet . . ."

His vision was born of miserable enough beginnings. He came of a well-to-do peasant family in Hunan, and at first worked hard in the fields, but his father was a drunkard and a tyrant, and Mao left home early. He managed to graduate from normal school in the provincial capital, however, and then went to Peking, where he worked as an assistant librarian in the university and further developed his socialist ideas. Imbued with an extraordinary self-assurance, he was eccentric and aloof, convinced of his destiny. To train his body, he climbed mountains, deliberately going hungry and exposing himself to storms. Once, reading in a newspaper that someone had walked as far as Tibet, he set off on foot around five counties of his native province.

Mao never allowed scruple to blur his vision. In the early days of the revolution he invoked Marx much as a cynical Chinese will display the tablet of an ancestor who is conveniently dead but whose name proves his own legitimacy, and to reassure the Russians further and win their support he erected a hammer-and-sickle flag over his Kiangsi guerrilla base and called it a "Soviet". At that time few Chinese knew who or what "Soviet" was. The tale went around that "Soviet" was the name of a saviour, and some of the peasants began to look for him. Others said "Soviet" was a bandit, and in one part of the neighbouring province of Fukien a reward was offered for his arrest.

Mao realised his dream by doing what was expedient. "His victory was no accident," his enemy Chang Kuo-t'ao has said of him.[2] "He is a very practical man, and has never been bound by doctrine, principle or ideal. Since he was young he has studied and practised the rule of force, the art of seizing power, scheming and strategy, and he has been determined to achieve his ends by hook or by crook." This seems to go too far, but in the name of "people's democracy" and the "dictatorship of the proletariat", Mao has certainly used the gun to become master of all China.

He himself wrote: "Without armed struggle the proletariat and the communist party would have no standing at all in China, and it would be impossible to accomplish any revolutionary task . . . Chiang Kai-shek values the army as his very life. He has held firmly to the vital point that whoever has an army has power, and that war decides everything. In this respect we ought to learn from him . . ."³ Elsewhere he remarked: "Even a gambler must have money to stake, and if he risks it all on a single throw and his luck fails, he cannot gamble any more."⁴

During the Sino–Japanese war, therefore, Mao did not try direct and costly conclusions with the foreign invader, but used the promise of "protracted struggle" against him as a pretext for building up his own Communist armies and expanding the areas under their control, thus accumulating "money to stake" on his coming gamble with Chiang Kai-shek for the mastery of all China. Like Napoleon, Mao did not speak of "victory" or "defeat" so much as of ultimately "winning" or "losing". He has never been fussy about the means to be used. When he kindled the Cultural Revolution he declared: "It is right to rebel! Whatever the adversary supports, we oppose. Whatever the adversary opposes, we support!" Nothing could have been better calculated to fling the dissatisfied young of China into violent rebellion against the established order than this unscrupulous battle-cry.

Has Mao "won" or "lost" since then? To recapitulate briefly: the Cultural Revolution and its aftermath fell into three phases. In the first, the Red Guards and "revolutionary rebels" wrecked the existing "revisionist" structure at the head of which stood Liu Shao-ch'i. In the second, the army was given the mandate to curb excesses and restore order, and it eventually took over the political and administrative control of the country. In the third phase, Mao set out to rebuild the party and to re-establish its ascendancy over the army. But once the new political edifice was up, it could be seen that at every level – Politburo, Central Committee, provincial committee – the army was the strongest single ingredient within the party.

The PLA had become the guiding element in everything. There were army propaganda crews in coal-mines, army "responsible cadres" supervising factories, army political secretaries in the railways, army teams broadcasting to peasants, and army

157

specialists running farms. The ubiquity of the military was becoming a source of discord between soldiers and civil servants, for the PLA and the political cadres led by Premier Chou En-lai were now competing seriously for influence. The Cultural Revolution had nevertheless produced a club of new powerholders whose most important members within the Politburo were Chou En-lai, the Money God Li Hsien-nien, and six senior PLA generals. Facing them were the Mao–Lin partnership and all those in the old Cultural Revolution Group involved in the bid of the "rebel" masses to "seize power". Mao remained undisputed titular chief of the army and the party, but much of his authority had been finessed, and the new men were able to bargain with him from strength.

That does not mean that Mao had lost. He had made his dream come true, and he was still master in Peking. As long as he lived, he would symbolise the unity of China and none would challenge his primacy as Chairman. The formal loyalty even of the Red warlords in the provinces was unquestionable, for they shared with Mao a common determination to safeguard revolutionary China so that the Chinese would never again be subdued and humiliated by foreigners. They would not shatter their own basic solidarity under their chief in Peking, and so tempt the Americans or the Russians to attack.

Down in their great provincial fiefs, however, matters were a little different.

The ancient Chinese strategist Sun Tzu, asked to train the King of Wu's 180 concubines, ordered the two court favourites to be executed when there was indiscipline in the ranks. The chagrined monarch protested, but Sun Tzu said: "When the commander leads the army in the field, he need not obey the sovereign's orders." The ladies died violently and the king, impressed, hired Sun Tzu on a permanent basis. The power game in China was being played out between not only the moderates and the Maoists, the army and the leftists, but Peking and the provinces, for the commanders of military regions subscribed to Sun Tzu's convenient doctrine that the man on the spot must make his own decisions in the light of local circumstance. The sovereign in the capital could only lay down general guidelines.

And the modern military commander was very much the master of the provinces and the "man on the spot". Mao might send out his "instructions", but he had no way of imposing them on the regional warlords, who could adroitly twist his words to suit their own local purpose, and while they praised his policies in Peking, they ruthlessly cut his left-wing revolutionaries down to size in their own bailiwicks.

In December 1970 Mao appeared to have acquiesced to the inevitable. Speaking to the late Edgar Snow, the well-known writer on Chinese affairs, he said that China should learn from the way America developed by decentralising responsibility and wealth among the fifty states. "A central government could not do everything," and China should also depend upon regional and local initiative.[5] This argument was repeated in 1971 in the *People's Daily* and the *Red Flag*, which stressed that two executives were better than one. But it is to be remembered that it did not conflict with Mao's own consistent vision of China as a honeycomb of interlocking, self-sufficient communes inhabited by the new communist jack-of-all-trades who would be peasant–worker–soldier–intellectual. It would only lead to a sharper clash of wills if it were openly translated to mean that Mao's Thought was no longer universal law.

That was not going to happen. The new powerholders continued to echo Mao loudly, while quietly eroding the effective political authority of the Chairman and strengthening local economy in the provinces. They privately recommended that China should increase her commerce with foreign countries, study the technological methods of others, and import machinery, steel, trucks and tractors in quantity to pull the country out of the economic slump into which the Cultural Revolution had plunged it. Politically, their intention was to acquire more autonomy for the regions, to bring back the experienced "old powerholders" of the local bureaucracy and to eliminate the tiresome "rebels" introduced in the turbulent sixties. Militarily, it was, as we have seen, to ensure that a soldier's technical training did not suffer from a surfeit of Mao-study. Industrially, it was to attempt no over-ambitious Great Leap Forward, and, agriculturally, it was to allow the peasants their private plots and their pigs and their profit motive. In short, the new men were advertising Mao's Thought but selling Liu Shao-ch'i's merchandise.

The sly battle for supremacy between "Maoist" and Maoist was not a "power-struggle", therefore, but a conflict of policies that could involve the Communist leaders in ping-pong diplomacy within the Politburo, as it did abroad. And ping-pong diplomacy was necessary, for as the Chinese say, "They could not fight, because they all had each other by the leg". In these circumstances, antagonists do not struggle for an illusory supremacy so much as for a favourable compromise. This means that men must be sacrificed by both sides. That is why Mao could not even rescue Ch'en Po-ta, his trusted personal secretary, from oblivion in 1970.

In that year the polarisation of forces had left Chiang Ch'ing and the rest of the "rebels" out on a limb. But as there could be no question of blaming Mao's wife for the excesses of Red Guard mobs that had discredited the Cultural Revolution and forged an alliance between the new military cliques and Chou En-lai's technocrats, a scapegoat had to be found so that everyone else could exchange at least a Chinese smile again. The scapegoat was Ch'en Po-ta.

Now this squat, ugly, bespectacled ideologist had always praised the thoughts of Mao whole-heartedly, and was formerly the Chairman's speechwriter and the official leader of the Cultural Revolution Group in Peking. He was loyal to Mao and Chiang Ch'ing, and at the Ninth National Congress of the Chinese Communist Party in 1969 he collected his reward – he was elected to the five-man Standing Committee at the top of the Politburo.

But in 1970 a publication called *Cultural Revolutionary Fighting News* described Ch'en Po-ta as the "black puppet-master" of the 16th May Group. This was a fiercely iconoclastic faction of revolutionary rebels that had been unsparing in its attacks on the followers of Chou En-lai and Lin Piao, had allegedly been responsible for burning the British Chancery in Peking, and had sullied the whole movement. It was next disclosed that Ch'en had been a traitor since 1927, when he had been arrested in Nanking by the Kuomintang, had written a "letter of penitence" to procure his release, and had then gone to live in the Soviet Union where he associated with the hated Trotsky–Bukharin clique and plotted with Mao's former "Bolshevik" adversary, Wang Ming.

At a confrontation in April conducted by Chiang Ch'ing and K'ang Sheng, Mao's intelligence chief, Ch'en Po-ta confessed to his "letter of penitence", but denied that he had been engaged in any activity detrimental to the party when in the USSR. His case was passed to Mao for a final verdict, and Mao ruled "Ch'en Po-ta is to be degraded but retained for use".

Four months later, however, the matter was again thrashed out at a second plenary meeting of the Ninth Party Congress; Chiang Ch'ing and K'ang Sheng both came under attack, and the luckless Ch'en Po-ta was politically liquidated. In the following year, the second issue of the official *Red Flag* warned the masses, "The errors of Wang Ming and Liu Shao-ch'i-type sham Marxist political swindlers must be exposed and they themselves must be resisted", and subsequent issues pinpointed the "sham Marxist" of the moment as Ch'en Po-ta. Mao had been compelled to discard Ch'en, who was dismissed as "a radish with a red skin but a white heart", for had he not done so, he might have lost the support of military leaders as well as of important cadres in party and government.

Confidential sources claim that PLA commanders had threatened to block the formation of new party committees in the provinces until Ch'en Po-ta was sacked and China's radicals suitably chastened, and the chronological record upholds their story. The official press first called for the shattered party to be rebuilt in January 1968, but although the Ninth Congress laid down how this should be done in April 1969, not one of the new provincial committees was organised in the eighteen months that followed. Once Ch'en Po-ta had been formally damned and dismissed by the party in August–September 1970, however, all twenty-nine came into being within a year.

That was not the only tactical retreat Mao was obliged to make. Chiang Ch'ing, who had disappeared from the public eye early in 1969, only reappeared in August 1971 when Radio Peking disclosed that she was associated with a new Cultural Group created within Premier Chou En-lai's State Council. Other personalities identified with the extreme left and Chiang Ch'ing's revolutionary activities dropped from sight or were inactive during 1971. This was further evidence that the new men were exerting pressure to rid themselves of those who had urged the "rebels" to seize power. Only Chang Ch'un-ch'iao and Yao Wen-yuan, the Brain and the Trigger-Finger of the "January Revolution" in Shanghai, were still prominent (Ch'en Po-ta having taken the blame for the ultra-democratic "Shanghai Commune").

The new powerholders were determined at the outset that Mao should no longer play dictator, and the regional warlords among them were equally determined to prevent Maoist "rebels" or anyone else from wresting local authority from them. Wary of left-wing demands for collective leadership in the provinces, therefore, the soldiers joined their pragmatic civilian allies in Peking in insisting upon collective leadership within the Politburo. And no one wanted God on a committee. Mao had used Lin Piao and the PLA to impose his own controversial revolutionary policies on China, and had arbitrarily named the sick marshal his heir-designate. But Mao was not a monarch, and Lin was not a Mao, and to many among the moderates and the military this was an intolerable imposition. As these began to flex their muscles, therefore, there were signs that the two leaders were to be reduced to life-size. The Mao–Lin mountain-top was about to be levelled.

Just as the appearance of a professional mediator is a sure sign of strife, so the new prominence of Yeh Chien-ying in the spring of 1971 was like a storm signal. He was soon the only soldier in the Politburo to greet distinguished foreign visitors, who ranged from Emperor Haile Selassie of Ethiopia to Henry Kissinger of the United States. No other army chief showed his face to a foreigner during the enigmatic autumn that followed, and it became obvious that for want of any agreement by now on who was who in the hierarchy, this shrewd conciliator without personal political ambition had been chosen as the sole formal representative of the PLA. But even he was no neutral.

Yeh Chien-ying, "The Dog-Meat Marshal", may at first glance seem an odd choice for his quasi-diplomatic role. He was commissioned at 21, was a senior instructor at the Whampoa Military Academy under Chiang Kai-shek in 1924, and took part in the Nanchang Uprising three years later. He escaped when the insurrection collapsed, spent two years studying tactics in Germany and Russia, and returned to China to join Mao in his Kiangsi Soviet in 1931.

In 1933 he was made Chief of Staff of the First Front Army (subsequently alternating with the One-Eyed Dragon), and it was he who drew up the plan for the Communist break-out and the Long March. He was to prove an impressive strategist with a flair for guerrilla warfare, and when the much-harassed and often dwindling Red columns of those precarious days grew into the vast "Liberation Army" whose millions of men brushed the Nationalists from the Chinese mainland in 1949, he again held that key appointment.

There are more sides to Yeh Chien-ying than plain staff officer, however. They dubbed him the Dog-Meat Marshal because he is a Hakka, descendant of the migrants from north China who moved south to Kwangtung province centuries ago, and who are sometimes called China's gypsies. Hakkas are famous for their love of stewed dog-meat (which comes from a special breed of eating-dog) just as Shanghainese are famous for their curious addiction to rotten bean-curd, and Hunanese – including Mao – for their inordinate fondness for chillis.

But the Hakkas have wandered further than Kwangtung, and they are to be found as far away as Indonesia. The son of a rich merchant who once lived in Singapore, Yeh has a network of relatives and friends and contacts in South-east Asia, and has been regarded as a communist leader of special significance and potential in terms of subversion, infiltration, propaganda, and the fostering of underground activities among Overseas Chinese.

He has a certain reputation in such matters. Once the Red armies had reached Yenan, Yeh threw himself into the task of corrupting the Manchurian troops of the KMT in the area with clandestine propaganda, and was so successful that he must very largely be credited with the kidnapping of Chiang Kai-shek by their commander at Sian in 1936. It was this coup, it will be recollected, that obliged the Generalissimo to agree to a pragmatic alliance with the Communists against the Japanese if he wanted to save his skin. Once the alliance was sealed, the Dog-Meat Marshal was responsible for liaison between the two parties, but used his position to infiltrate and suborn the Nationalists to such good effect that sixteen KMT regiments defected to Mao. He had, somewhat curiously, coupled his military training in Moscow with the study of drama and coaching in the dramatic arts, and perhaps this was part of the pay-off.

He was subsequently involved in the fruitless post-war negotiations between the Communists and the KMT for a lasting reconciliation, and the Americans are no strangers to him. He has travelled widely, but his most regular port of call in the sixties was Hanoi and it is believed that his South-East Asia interests have included Chinese arms aid to North Vietnam.

He shows a talent for the hypocrisies of diplomacy, for concealing the wrong thoughts with the right words, for picking the winning side and so surviving, that is reminiscent of Chou En-lai.

A specialist in Western theories of warfare, he described Soviet military achievements as the "priceless assets of all countries in the Socialist camp" in 1957, but soon afterwards found it expedient to echo Mao's mass line on "people's war" rather than the urgings of those who wanted national defence to be the care of a modern, professional Chinese army. Four years later he was saying "We can defeat the enemy by using close combat, although we have no special weapons", and in 1965 he described the Communist defeat of the KMT as a "victory for Comrade Mao Tsetung's concept of strategy", recommending that it be the subject of "earnest study".

He has also stressed the importance of a "political breakthrough" in the PLA, agreeing loudly with the Maoists that it is more important to be "red" than "expert". His past record as an apparent conformist has not always saved him, however, nor has his ready tongue always pleased. He has a pretty daughter whose husband is a talented pianist,* but when the Red Guards first stormed through the artistic and literary world of China, they set upon this unfortunate man and broke his fingers. Yeh Chien-ying, livid with anger, became a bitter opponent of Chiang Ch'ing and her "rebel" movement, and although he was affable by nature and a military veteran who had remained aloof from party politics, he fell into temporary disfavour.

That was not all he held against the Maoist leadership, and to assume that he has been a faithful *t'ung-chih* of Mao and Lin Piao (on whom he has lavished praise on suitably public occasions) would be dangerous. Ostensibly, theirs has been a classic case of Chinese brotherhood-in-arms, for Yeh was a Fourth Front Army trusty of Mao whose career was for more than twenty years interleaved with that of Lin Piao. However, anti-Communist Chinese claim that close association did more to antagonise the two men than to provide a fixative for friendship, and those who have been close to Yeh say that he dissembles when he takes a "revolutionary" Maoist line. It is quite out of character.

---

* Liu Shih-kun.

At 73 he is a tall, robust man with a supple and serene air, very quiet in manner and fastidious about the cut of his clothes. He is artistic, learned in Chinese classical literature, known for his carefree, sometimes unbridled, behaviour and his love of comfort and enjoyment. He is no Maoist ascetic in search of a selfless millennium, but a keen liver who has been married four times, has a string of houses and a wealthy brother in Hongkong, and is widely known to have been a drinking companion of Chou En-lai (before the Prime Minister cut his own consumption). He has been a dedicated philanderer in his time and is reported to have said – although not in the presence of Emperor Haile Selassie – that Ethiopian women were the best bedfellows in the world (Europeans were the worst). "If Chien-ying can be a Maoist," remarked a friend who held him in affection, "anybody can."

In 1971 he was a member of the Politburo, and Vice-Chairman of the Military Affairs Commission and of the National Defence Council, a skilled negotiator and arbitrator in demand at a time when compromise was necessary both overseas and within the party. He was also one of three Chinese marshals in the Politburo[6] – venerated warriors of the revolution – who for one reason or another had lost some of their enthusiasm for the Mao–Lin leadership, and who respected Chou En-lai. He had no love for Chiang Ch'ing, he had perhaps even less love for Lin Piao, and he could hardly forget that the man who had raised Lin over his head and later made him future master of China in preference to all others was Mao Tsetung.

This was the ominous situation when, in July 1971, President Richard Nixon of the United States of America disclosed that he would pay a visit to the People's Republic of China.

15

While Mao Lives

Two months later the China story suddenly went psychedelic.
ARMY CHIEF HELPS LIU SHAO-CHI ESCAPE, began the string of
demented headlines that stretched from September 1971 until
the following February. MAO DEAD OF HEART ATTACK? – LIN
PIAO KILLED IN PLANE CRASH AFTER COUP BID – LIU SHAO-CHI
DEFECTS TO SOVIET UNION – CHINA'S TOP BRASS SHOT DOWN
OVER MONGOLIA – LIN PIAO TRIES ASSASSINATE MAO – HOW
NIXON SAVED MAO FROM HIS GENERALS.

What had happened? Putting together conflicting foreign
press and intelligence reports, and secret explanations circulated
by Peking for discussion at special meetings of party cadres inside
China, it appears that Lin Piao had tried to murder Mao up
to five times in the previous eighteen months, and, having
failed, had planned to kill him during the National Day parade
in Peking on 1 October. Lin's abortive attempts had included
putting a bomb in his bedroom, planting another on an aircraft
in which the Chairman was flying, and then pumping poison
through the air-conditioner of his railway carriage when the
astute old man evidently concluded it was safer to travel by
train.

Undeterred by these earlier setbacks, he next decided to bomb
Mao's villa in Shanghai, but the local air force commander
lost his nerve and pretended that his only trustworthy pilot for
the job had contracted an eye infection. Lin then sent an
assassin to Mao's office in Peking, but the man was caught,
and since he had been insecure enough to confide his dirty work
to an accomplice, the "Tiger Cat" was most properly betrayed.
The CIA had in any case learned through Israeli intelligence that
Lin was out to liquidate Mao, and President Nixon had arranged
for Dr Henry Kissinger to pass on this vital information at his
first meeting with Chou En-lai in July.

When the National Day parade was subsequently cancelled,
Lin realised that his latest scheme had leaked out, and on

12 September he took Wu Fa-hsien and their personal guards to Mao's home in order to finish off the business without further delay. But Mao was gone. Lin therefore arranged for Huang Yung-sheng to help the revisionist ex-president Liu Shao-ch'i to escape from house arrest in order to create a diversion, and took off in a British-built Trident of the Chinese Air Force with his wife, his son, Wu Fa-hsien and the disgraced Ch'en Po-ta, possibly Huang Yung-sheng, Li Tso-p'eng and Ch'iu Hui-tso, and perhaps even Liu Shao-ch'i, making nine in all. Their destination was Irkutsk in the Soviet Union, but Lin Piao's daughter Tou-tou gave the game away to Chou En-lai, and the Trident was shot down by Chinese fighters or Soviet missiles in the middle of an armed struggle among its fleeing passengers.

There were other gaudy versions of this farrago, of which the most publicised purported to be based on a top-secret document issued by the Central Committee of the party on 13 January 1972 (of which the Chinese Nationalists had somehow obtained a copy). The main attachment to this paper was Lin Piao's own damning "Outline of the Five-Seven-One Project" (of which the Maoists had somehow obtained a copy), a blueprint for a palace coup in which the Maoists would be "bagged in one sweep during a high-level meeting", Mao would be isolated, and Lin would seize power. The operation was not necessarily going to be as painless as that, however. "We may also adopt extraordinary measures, such as poison gas, germ weapons, bombing, car accidents, assassination, kidnap, and small urban guerrilla teams", continued the extracts in KMT English that the Nationalists passed on to the foreign press. The elements of the army and air force that could be counted on for support were listed, and the Soviet Union was to put its weight behind the putsch, even providing a "temporary nuclear protection umbrella".

Allegedly taken to task at the same Central Committee meeting that had sealed the fate of Ch'en Po-ta, and alarmed by subsequent changes in the Peking Military Region that weakened his own hold on North China, Lin Piao was convinced that Mao was planning a "peaceful transition" that would put power back into the hands of Chiang Ch'ing and the Shanghai clique – "the situation is developing towards the 'pen' getting the upper hand", as the "Outline" put it. His answer was "revolution by violence", and the whole document read like a penny shocker for those of tender years. Lin himself was referred to as "The Chief" by the plotters, and his wife was "The Viscountess". Mao was codenamed "B-52", the forces of revolution were the "United Fleet", and the Maoists on the Politburo were "enemy battleships".

The facts behind all these fine-spun yarns were that Lin Piao had not been seen in public since June 1971, and the other army leaders allegedly involved were not seen after September. A Chinese Air Force Trident crashed in Mongolia on the 13th of that month and, according to the Russians, was found to contain the bodies of eight men and one woman (but all were said to be under fifty). Army leave was stopped, the air force was grounded, civil aviation schedules were cut or suspended altogether, and the National Day parade was cancelled. These events prompted speculation that Mao's successor had died or was at least seriously ill, or that Mao himself was dead. But any claim that the rest of the blood-and-thunder was fact could, it seemed, only be based on the argument that it made such preposterous fiction.

It was nonetheless hyperbole that told an underlying truth. It is communist practice to damn men as devils incarnate when they are to be discarded for their deviations. Their real crimes are never heinous enough, and the world has been regaled ever since the Russian revolution with hair-raising accounts of the diabolical treachery of Marxists who have simply made the mistake of belonging to the minority, or who could conveniently serve as scapegoats for this or that piece of human stupidity (since the god of the moment on top of the pile must always appear infallible). It is suddenly found that, like Ch'en Po-ta, they have all along been Trotskyist plants or American spies, or saboteurs paid by the British Imperialists, have cleverly concealed their sins for the past forty years, and have only just been unmasked. The astonished onlooker is left with the impression that in the communist world all honest heroes are gullible morons and it is the villains who are the geniuses. Mao, it is implied, was as big a booby as a judge of men as Lin Piao was a bungler as an assassin. But once it was whispered that Lin was the would-be killer of Mao it was obvious that, on the contrary, he was the quarry.

A vicious paper offensive opened up against a nameless miscreant who was nevertheless quickly identified as the unfortunate heir of the Chairman. He was "the chieftain of the opportunist line" with "illicit connections abroad", an "ambitionist" involved in a "criminal conspiracy to restore capitalism". The main organs of the Maoist press accused him of twisting Mao's requirements for evaluating party cadres by emphasising "drive" without regard for whether the drive was directed towards proletarian ends or not. Editorials rebuked him for "despising the masses and extolling genius", for he had written that Mao's Thought had not grown spontaneously from the working millions, but was the product of Mao's own superhuman mind, and could be "transformed into a great material force".

Newspapers hit out savagely at all "wild talk about 'genius' that is nothing more than the philosophy of the bourgeois ambitionist . . . the dialectic of history will always punish those who so grossly depart from the truth".[1] "There has never been any saviour of the world," stressed Radio Changsha, "the creation of history depends only on ourselves."[2] As for transforming thought into material force, the *Red Flag* remarked obliquely, "Liu Shao-ch'i confused matter and consciousness, in an attempt to replace social being with man's thinking. This is substituting sham for genuine."[3]

Lin Piao, it was clear by the winter of 1971, headed a short list of distinguished battle casualties suffered in a fierce struggle within the Politburo over the party "line", and since the "line" takes in every aspect of national and ideological policy, experts argued somewhat futilely as to where exactly he had made his mistake and drawn down upon himself the royal wrath. His "opportunism" was said to have been accompanied by "mountain-top mentality, sectarianism and splittism", he had glorified the power of the army, yet divided its allegiances, and like Ch'en Po-ta he must be held responsible for the deliberate excesses of the 16th May Group which had discredited the Cultural Revolution. He had opposed Chiang Ch'ing, he had "simplified and vulgarised" Mao's Thoughts in his pocket bible, and he had isolated Mao from the Chinese people.

Perhaps he had also sabotaged agriculture by taking the wrong stand in the current dispute over mechanisation? Or sabotaged industry by taking the wrong stand in the dispute over the priorities to be given to steel and electronics? Or forged secret ties with the Russians, or angered Mao by opposing ping-pong diplomacy and the Nixon visit? One was reminded of the Buddhist parable of the six blind men who were asked to describe an elephant. One touched its tusk and said that an elephant was like a carrot, one touched its ear and said that an elephant was like a winnowing basket, another touched its tail and said an elephant was like a piece of rope, and so on. But the "line", like the elephant, is the sum of its parts.

None of the speculation explained why the cautious and able Lin Piao should try so inefficiently to murder the 77-year-old master who had raised him up to be his heir, why Mao should disown his faithful crown prince or Tou-tou betray her father, or how Mao himself had been so slow to discover that Lin Piao had "castrated" his ideas in the little red book of *Quotations* he first put out in 1964. The case against Lin was flimsy, and smelled of wholesale perjury.

Even if they had not seen eye to eye and Mao had suspected Lin of hidden Soviet sympathies or of planning to "go "revisionist" after his death, the fact remained that there was no other general in all China whom he could trust more than the Tiger Cat. Ch'en Po-ta had been his "pen". Lin Piao had been his "gun"; and now he had lost both. Furthermore, Lin had been attacked for extolling Mao's genius, for pursuing Mao's revolutionary policy of putting politics before firing practice in the army and factory production in industry. In short, his enemies were sniping at him for ultra-Maoism, which meant that they were aiming off to hit Mao himself.

Lin's introduction to the *Quotations* disappeared, and so did his portrait, his famous tract "Long Live the Victory of People's Wars", and the draft constitution that appointed him as Mao's successor. But there were also fewer pictures and busts and slogans of Mao to be seen. It may be argued that the Chairman himself approved, for he had told Edgar Snow at the end of 1970 that the "cult of the personality" had gone too far. It can also be argued that no one could have sacked Lin Piao but Mao. In neither case did he have any choice in the matter, however, whatever his feelings.

Lin Piao was a sacrifice, not a villain cringing before the righteous anger of a wronged patron. Chou En-lai and the new powerholders among the regional warlords had set out to curtail the blind worship of Mao, to strip Lin of his synthetic supremacy as Mao's appointed heir, and to leave the Chairman dependent upon their goodwill and cooperation. And Mao was forced to strike a bargain with them – a bargain moreover that was also much to the taste of Chiang Ch'ing. The sensational stories circulated about his successor's sins were designed to enable him to ditch Lin Piao with dignity – had not the ingrate tried to kill him? – for if the PLA was to hold the power, Mao was to have the face.

Mao's Thought remained the official gospel of Communist China, the Maoists would still pour out millions of words in their struggle to create a socialist society, could warn troops against being "arrogant and complacent" and urge them to understand that there must be "collective leadership" at all levels in the provinces, not just soldiers issuing arbitrary and impractical parade-ground orders to the civilians. Local army units formally placed themselves under the supervision of local party organisations, and commanders agreed that the party must control the gun.

Why not? In 1972, 20 provincial party committees out of 29 were still headed by soldiers. Regional military bosses could afford to go through the motions of political submission gracefully – and in so doing, shed some of the minor supervisory chores that had tied down too many troops in communes and factories throughout the country. The Cultural Revolution was over and Lin Piao, the one marshal who had espoused it, had been "politically liquidated". His whereabouts were unknown.

Lin Piao had not been the only one to go. His faithful Air Force Commander, Wu Fa-hsien, had paid the price of his ill-advised loyalty towards the heir-designate. But it would be a mistake to believe that the sudden disappearance from the Peking scene in September 1971 of Huang Yung-sheng and his two other senior deputy chiefs of staff automatically proves that they also were members of some murderous cabal against Mao masterminded by Lin Piao. Lin and the "Speechless Rustic" were only dominoes in the same doomed row in the sense that they were the *grand patrons* of the 4th Field Army veterans, whose overriding position in the hierarchy others were anxious to undermine. Huang had little sympathy with Lin, the armed underwriter of the Cultural Revolution which had plunged his Canton fief into bloody confusion. It was not Mao who was the prime mover against Huang and his fellow-powerholders in the Politburo; it was, as far as can be judged, the warlord with whom Mao had concluded an unwritten "Chinese contract" – Ironsides Hsu Shih-yu of Nanking.

The amiable Huang Yung-sheng was the victim of short-sighted ambition. The peasant from Hupeh was too limited of vision, it seems, to realise that if he used his position as Chief of Staff to expand his own regional power to a point where he topped all others, he would be the first target for their underkill – the process whereby men of average strength combine to tear down a giant before he can trample them.

By the autumn of 1971, the relationship between the Defence Minister and the Chief of Staff was no longer orthodox. The five key men at the apex of the military machine in Peking who held in their hands the destinies of five vital services – the General Political Department, the Army, the Navy, the Air Force, and the General Logistics Department – were naturally subordinate to the Defence Minister. But although he was one of them, Huang had short-circuited Lin Piao's authority by making all the others (except Li Te-sheng of the Political Department) deputy chiefs of staff under him. From being their equal, he had become their direct superior, and he had meanwhile taken three trusted lieutenants from his former fief of Canton and appointed them deputy chiefs of staff also.

In the provinces, he could now count on the loyalty not only of the three provincial armies in Canton Military Region, which was still a semi-independent kingdom, but on most of the officers and men in three more armies in the Wuhan, Lanchow and Chengtu Military Regions. And he had further extended his network by judiciously transferring officers from these formations elsewhere, including two who had been made Commander of Sinkiang Military Region and political commissar of Tibet respectively.*

He was becoming dangerously powerful, and at the same time curiously reluctant to grant important posts to subordinates of Hsu Shih-yu in particular (the other "Heavenly Kings" of Foochow, Shenyang and Tsinan were more favoured). It appears, therefore, that Ironsides led a concerted move against him. Nor was it difficult for the four Red warlords to persuade Chou En-lai in turn that his one-time protégé had temporarily outlived his usefulness as C-of-S, for Chou was

* See first appendix to this chapter.

above all anxious to preserve a stable balance of forces within the PLA, and no friend of any man whose personal ambition rocked it. If Mao could sanction the removal of Lin Piao, Chou could arrange the suspension of Huang Yung-sheng.

With Lin and Huang gone, some 4th Field Army nominees were demoted. Others, like Liang Hsing-ch'u, the Commander of Chengtu Military Region, fell quiet. The pro-Lin "Night Tiger" was the only local leader who did not fly to Peking in February 1972 when the plane bearing the ashes of his political commissar, Chang Kuo-hua, was met at the airport by Chou En-lai and a special mourning ceremony was held on the spot. Comparable honour had been shown hitherto only to the mayor of Shanghai for whom Yao Wen-yuan had written until he died in 1965 (page 20).

Peking was paying singular tribute to a veteran of the 2nd Field Army of the One-Eyed Dragon who had in his day been the warlord of Tibet. Moreover, his were the second obsequies of note within two months. On 11 January, Ch'en the Bald, the veteran commander of the 3rd Field Army, had been given a state funeral personally attended by Chairman Mao at which Chou En-lai read a fulsome oration over the remains of the man who had defied the Red Guards so blatantly but had more recently been described as "loyal and correct". "We should learn from the revolutionary spirit of Comrade Ch'en Yi," declaimed the Prime Minister, "and transform our grief into strength." His death was a "great loss" to the party and the army. Li Te-sheng The Bayonet presided over the ceremonies which were attended not only by dignitaries as different as Chiang Ch'ing and Chu Te the Cook, but by men loyal to Chou En-lai who had been written off as losers, like the Profligate Monk Nieh Jung-chen and Slow March Hsu Hsiang-ch'ien.

By this time the signs were obvious. The veterans of the 2nd and, even more, of the 3rd Field Army were gaining strength. The man of the moment was Chou En-lai. New faces were already beginning to come into the foreground in Peking. But it was their background that was interesting.

Wu Te, now Acting Chairman of the Peking Revolutionary Committee, had been secretary-general of the Profligate Monk's northern Soviet in the forties, and a labour leader under the influence of Liu Shao-ch'i. Hua Kuo-feng, civilian chief of the

Hunan revolutionary and party committees who had fought a lone battle against the local pro-Lin military, had been transferred to the capital where he was officially described as one of the "leaders of the party and government" and could well aspire to the Politburo.

Hua Kuo-feng was listed above Keng Piao,* but this 63-year-old Hunanese who was in his time chief of staff of Nieh the Profligate Monk and deputy commander to Yang Te-chih, the Red warlord of Tsinan, must not be underestimated. From being an able and trusted general, he became in less stirring times a diplomat and later a vice-minister for foreign affairs close to Liu Shao-ch'i. Foreign expert and soldier, he was respected for combining "pen" and "sword", and in 1971 was appointed director of the party's International Liaison Department. This made him a back-room policy-maker senior to any official in the Foreign Ministry, including not only Ch'iao Kuan-hua, the vice-minister who led the first Chinese delegation to the United Nations, but the new minister himself, Chi P'eng-fei.†

The past of all these men pointed the way that the internal struggle for China was to go. Ch'iao Kuan-hua, who first welcomed President Nixon when he arrived in Shanghai and flew with him to Peking, is of bourgeois stock, a well-educated, quick-witted linguist with a phenomenal memory which has earned him the nickname "Foreign Affairs Think-Tank". Both he and his wife (now dead) were professional associates of long standing of Premier Chou En-lai. Their son was a leader of anti-Mao Red Guards during the Cultural Revolution and associated with the sons of men like Ho Lung The Moustache, Ch'en Yi, and Li Ch'ing-ch'uan the "Emperor of the Southwest".

Chi P'eng-fei also came of a well-to-do family, studied medicine, and after rallying to the Kiangsi Soviet and making the Long March as a doctor, became director of medical services in Yenan. At 62 he is a cautious, thrifty man, approachable and possessed of a nice dry humour but essentially quiet and correct in manner, and he never allows himself to be swept away by his own flow of speech. He has always observed the letter of party law, and even the Red Guards left him alone.

---

* See second appendix to this chapter.
† See second appendix to this chapter.

But the qualifications that earned him the post of Foreign Minister when Ch'en Yi died were political, rather than personal.

In 1939 he gave up his medical duties and became political commissar of the first column of the New 4th Army. This brought him into close contact with Liu Shao-ch'i and also with Ch'en Yi, its commander, whom he followed when the formation was converted into the 3rd Field Army. For the Prime Minister, therefore, he was another valuable link between the State Council and 3rd Field Army veterans, to whom he could talk as campaigner to campaigner – explaining, for example, the desirability of receiving Richard Nixon, "Boss of the Imperialist Aggressors", to soldiers instinctively distrustful of smart-aleck diplomacy like Su Yu and Hsu Shih-yu, and winning them over for his chief.

For this is the core of the matter. Mao might have been reduced to man-size, Lin Piao eliminated, Huang Yung-sheng halted in his stride, but Chou En-lai was assuming the complex reins of power among elbowing generals and rival political factions soured by the betrayals of the Cultural Revolution, and his overriding problem was unity.

16

While Mao Lives (Continued)

Above all, Chou needed "men for all seasons", ex-generals with complicated careers who had served in different Red armies and had friends in rival camps. His long-term strategy was self-evidently to round off, if not to level, the more forbidding military mountain-tops, and like Mao's earlier moves to broaden his own base within the PLA, this automatically brought out of the shadows men from the field armies of other marshals whose lack of affection for Lin Piao had once been a blemish but was now a blessing.

For the first time in 22 years, accordingly, a general not drawn from the old 4th Field Army was officially listed in May 1972 as the commander "responsible" for the Canton Military Garrison. T'an Chih-keng,* who distinguished himself in the ruthless struggle for Suchow during the winter of 1948, was a veteran of the New 4th Army and the 3rd Field Army, and had served with Su Yu, Wang P'i-cheng (now in Kunming), and Foreign Minister Chi P'eng-fei under the overall command of Ch'en Yi the Bald. His surprise appointment was obviously calculated to weaken the hold of the 4th Field Army brotherhood on the Canton Military Region and correspondingly strengthen the hand of Chou En-lai.

Similarly, by June 1972 "Tigerlover" Yang Te-chih, the Red warlord of Tsinan Military Region, had been assigned as a senior subordinate (and almost certainly deputy commander) a full general from the 1st Field Army named Chang Tsung-hsun* who had a long record of loyalty to the outlawed marshal, Ho Lung The Moustache. To add to his sins, Chang Tsung-hsun had also accompanied Hades P'eng Te-huai to Russia in 1959, and subsequently served as deputy to the doomed Chief of Staff, Lo Jui-ch'ing. Hades had been sacked in 1959, Lo Jui-ch'ing had gone the way of Hades in 1965, and Chang the way of Lo Jui-ch'ing in 1967. Yet by mid-1972 some analysts

---

* See appendix to this chapter.

already forecast that he might even be restored to his former post on the general staff in the capital.

While Chou En-lai might favour other formations, however, he did not turn his back on the 4th Field Army. Since his business was unity, his business was with everyone. Even when the crisis broke in Peking in 1971, therefore, Pai Hsiang-kuo,* Huang Yung-sheng's trusted lieutenant from Canton who had risen to be Minister of Trade under his patronage, continued a planned tour abroad during which he opened a new era in commercial relations with France, signed a trade agreement with Italy – the first between China and a Common Market country – and another with Algeria. He was now to be accounted one of Chou En-lai's "friends from the 4th Field Army".

In "making friends in order to isolate the enemy", as he had once phrased it, Chou might one day put the discarded Speechless Rustic Huang Yung-sheng himself back on the board, if he is still alive, for in China heads rarely roll *à la russe*, and although it is customary to think that the power game in a communist country is best explained in terms like "liquidate", "purge" or "Siberia", the essential difference between politics in Peking and politics in the Anglo-Saxon capitals is that the struggle takes place within one party instead of two. Some losers disappear for ever, but most simply "step aside", drop from sight when defeated, and may reappear again later, much as a Nixon or a Wilson may do in the West.

In mid-1972, when Lin Piao had been written off as dead, diplomats in Peking reported that the Speechless Rustic and his immediate deputies were safely in gaol or under house arrest in the capital, poring compulsorily over the works of Mao. During the previous year articles had already been published urging cadres not to make the mistake of confusing those guilty of the transgression of "mountain-top-ism" with "ambitionists" implicated in criminal counter-revolutionary plots. The first had not conspired with the second – they had been exploited by them. The erring Huang was not to be confused with the evil Lin Piao, it was implied. Two of these articles appeared in the Shenyang and Nanking Military Regions, and it was evident that even Ironsides sought only to clip Huang's wings, not to stamp him into the dirt.[1]

---

* See appendix to this chapter.

There was a good reason for this. A domesticated Huang Yung-sheng might yet be needed. The 4th Field Army mountain had not dissolved into thin air because the top had been levelled. It might have grown out of a heterogeneous collection of units in Manchuria, but commanders and formations with a history of loyalty to Lin Piao or Hung Yung-sheng or both held solid positions across the map of China. If Huang commanded the allegiance of the Canton Military Region, Huang and Lin shared popularity in at least four armies elsewhere, and Lin himself was still the hero not only of the faithful 38th in Peking, but of subordinate "commanders and fighters" in no fewer than three more armies in Manchuria. At his headquarters in the Shenyang Military Region, Ch'en Hsi-lien had had to work with eight immediate subordinates from 4th Field Army placed there by the Tiger Cat.*

The campaign to smear Lin Piao was meeting with resistance. Since he and his accomplices were never named, but only referred to obliquely by such phrases as "Liu Shao-ch'i-type political swindlers", Lin's supporters could attack others under the anonymous cloak of this ambiguous epithet. A broadcast from Manchuria accusing "political charlatans" of "instigating one section of the masses to fight another" and of "harbouring bitter hatred for the great People's Liberation Army" fitted Chiang Ch'ing far better than it fitted Lin Piao. Others that denounced sinners of "well-to-do origin" who had "forged foreign links" and were now "stabbing Chairman Mao in the back" were far more applicable to Chou En-lai, the mandarin's son, than to the marshal from Hupeh who had been born into a family of nine living in two rooms.

It was also proving peculiarly difficult to persuade the more cautious Chinese to join the chorus of condemnation against the fallen Lin, to "beat the dog already in the water", as the vernacular brutally puts it. For the dog was demigod yesterday and none could be absolutely sure that he was dead or down today. The Cultural Revolution had taught a sharp lesson. In 1967 the cadres of the disgraced Liu Shao-ch'i were being hunted down relentlessly by Red Guards, and "revolutionary rebels" were all the rage, but three years later the Red Guards had been sent down to the farms, the "rebels" had been shorn of all but

---

* See first appendix to Chapter 15.

178

token authority, and the cadres and soldiers they had so pitilessly reviled once more held all the local power in their hands.

The Red Guards had been urged to weed out an unregenerate "small handful" of revisionists, the masses were now being asked to flay a "small handful" of supporters of Lin Piao, and no one could be sure which "small handful" would be the quarry next. In these unsteady circumstances, prudent men were as reluctant to beat the dog in the water as they were to jump in and haul him out.

Moreover, Chou En-lai, the sly conciliator with the impeccable stage sincerity, was now facing his biggest challenge. For he had to establish a new equilibrium among the disparate forces in play. He did not, therefore, want the followers of Huang Yung-sheng to fall too low any more than he wanted Hsu Shih-yu to become another Huang Yung-sheng. There was already a basis for comparison between the two men. Huang had climbed to the top as master of the Canton Military Region at a time when the 4th Field Army was in the ascendant. Ironsides was the master of the Nanking Military Region at a time when the 3rd Field Army was in the ascendant. Like the Speechless Rustic, Ironsides had been extending his military influence across the country, and he could do so in the face of the Chief of Staff's reluctance to post his men to other regions, for, thanks to their "understanding", he had the support of the Chairman himself.

By the end of 1971, Ironsides had drawn closer to Su Yu in the west, where they shared loyal lieutenants from the old 3rd Field Army in the commanders of Kunming and Lanchow Military Regions. Three of his deputies in Nanking had taken up key posts in Wuhan Military Region since the previous year, and a fourth had reportedly been made commander of the air force in Shenyang Military Region. His crack 31st Army was transferred to Manchuria to support Tiger Ch'en and offset the 4th Field Army presence. One of his close comrades-in-arms was made Deputy Commander of the Peking Military Region, and his 27th Army transferred to the capital from Inner Mongolia. At the same time a fifth protégé of Ironsides in Nanking, Chang Ts'ai-ch'ien, was appointed Deputy Chief of Staff of the PLA in the capital.[2]

This little-known veteran from the New 4th Army and the

3rd Field Army, who had also served under the Money God Li Hsien-nien in the war against Japan, personified a new trend. After the "black" September of 1971 he came increasingly to the fore and was to be seen on formal occasions with foreign guests and to be heard chastising the Americans to visiting military leaders from North Korea. These were obvious signs of fortune's favour, and odds were laid that he would be the next Chief of Staff. Meanwhile another 3rd Field Army man who had been close to Ironsides and Li Hsien-nien began to represent the air force in public as deputy commander, and seemed to have taken the place of Wu Fa-hsien. A third – though a Maoist this time – replaced Li Tso-p'eng on formal occasions for the navy, of which he was commander.* Neither had been prominent before.

It was evident that on his side Chou En-lai wanted to clear Peking as a cockpit for rivalry, for politically these were lesser men who could not aspire to the ambitions of a Huang Yung-sheng nor provoke jealousy in others. If there had to be a chief of staff at this stage, let him be a man who would be below the commanders in the provinces in terms of power, so that he could be above them in terms of position without being tempted to think big. In this way Chou could achieve the balance he wanted – with himself at the centre of the field of force.

Paradoxically, however, the danger of this policy was that the Red warlords seemed to agree with it, and that it could only produce a team of proxies in Peking. Although both were at least nominally members of the Politburo, neither Ironsides nor Tiger Ch'en appeared during this period, and it looked as if regional military chiefs had decided only to commit pawns to the power game in the capital. The explanation for this could be simple. Peking had not always proved a healthy place for high-ranking soldiers. There had been a faster turnover in chiefs of staff of the PLA than in any top job in government or party. If Lin Piao could be laid low, why not they? But a military commander who stayed in his own provincial fief was like the "Ferocious Tiger" in his Manchurian lair. Given the rivalry within the PLA as further incentive, the situation was encouraging provincial commanders to strengthen their own

---

* K'uang Jen-nung and Hsiao Ching-kuang. See appendix to this chapter.

mountain-tops, while military authority at the centre grew weaker, and this would not bind closer the 29 Chinas of China, but shake them looser.

In Peking a docked tail was trying to wag the monstrous body of the republic, and the guiding dictum that politics must control the gun had deteriorated into a meaningless closed circle of words reading "party-leads-army-leads-party-leads-army-leads . . ." Only nine out of the 21 full members of the Politburo were known still to be active,[3] and this rump committee was held together by an uneasy truce between Chou En-lai and his "moderate" Peking partners, Li Hsien-nien and Yeh Chien-ying, on one side, and Chiang Ch'ing and the two Shanghai supporters of the Maoist revolutionary line on the other.

The Prime Minister might control the gun through his allies-of-convenience among the provincial warlords, but the gun is not an argument for all circumstances. With Lin Piao eliminated Chiang Ch'ing was now listed third in the Politburo after Chou En-lai, and her henchmen were in fifth and sixth places. She was being more consistently praised in press and radio than any Chinese leader other than Mao, and small wonder, for Yao Wen-yuan had been described by Chou himself as "head of propaganda", which would mean that he coordinated the entire national culture – all the words, and the pictures that were worth ten thousand words.

Moreover, although Mao might have lost much of his hold on the army, he still controlled the T'e Wu. Chou En-lai might be the man of the moment but he was not the master of China yet. He was therefore careful to compromise with Mao in order to get his own way, to argue the Chairman into setting his seal on his own policies, and he very typically stressed to the Chinese millions and the world outside that the decision to invite President Nixon to Peking had been taken by Mao himself.

But Chou was acting like the fox that puts on the tiger's skin in order to scare the other animals. Mao set the mood for the meeting by receiving the President with a ready enough smile in his own home on the first day of his visit, but although he had no love for the Russians, his reservations about turning his benign glance on the Americans were mirrored in the behaviour of those closest to him.

The leftist leaders in Shanghai had protested when Dr Henry Kissinger first came to China. There had reportedly been an angry exchange between Chou and Chiang Ch'ing over the visit, and part of the army had agreed with Mao's wife. When President Nixon arrived in Shanghai, in consequence, Chang Ch'un-ch'iao and Yao Wen-yuan failed to greet him, let alone accompany him to Peking. Nor was Chiang Ch'ing waiting at the state guest house to welcome him to the capital, as she had welcomed previous distinguished visitors. Instead, the Chinese solved the problem of her reluctance to appear with an exquisite finesse – she met the Nixons at the performance of the ballet *The Red Detachment of Women* in her role as patron of the Chinese revolutionary theatre rather than as the wife of Mao Tsetung. "The Brain" conducted his American guests around when they returned to Shanghai later, but the "Trigger-Finger" did not see them on any occasion.

The wary Premier responded by limiting the list of Chinese who met the Nixons to those who obviously had business with them or whose presence would provoke no angry comment from the Maoists, and then took the last trick. When he flew back to the capital from Shanghai after the Americans had left, he was given a triumphal welcome by thousands of Chinese Communists of all persuasions – including both Chiang Ch'ing and Yao Wen-yuan. The Maoists had surrendered. Most exceptionally, Chou's portrait appeared, large and alone, in the official press. Even Lin Piao at the height of his popularity as Mao's closest comrade-in-arms had never been granted that honour.

It began to seem that while the prominence of Chiang Ch'ing and the Shanghai revolutionaries gave Mao face, the pen also was proving to have its limits as a weapon. Had the Maoists lost out altogether? Mao had "liberated" China by launching a "people's war" against the Kuomintang, and he was convinced that the world could be liberated by the same method. In 1969 the new constitution, which enshrined his Thought as gospel and formally made Lin Piao his heir, had also solemnly committed the party to uniting with all oppressed peoples in order to "overthrow imperialism headed by the United States, modern revisionism with the Soviet revisionist renegade clique as its centre, and the reactionaries of all countries . . ."

By the following year, however, China had begun to turn

upon the world her Mona Lisa smile, and in 1971 Peking had invented ping-pong diplomacy, the People's Republic had joined the United Nations, and Mr Richard Nixon had laid plans to visit its capital. It was Liu Shao-ch'i who had urged that while China was weak, she must compromise with America and Russia, curtail her economic aid to the governments in the have-not continents and her arms aid to the "liberation movements" that were fighting against them. Had Mao's revolutionary dictum been consigned to the trash-can?

It must be remembered that a "people's war" is an armed insurrection which, by definition, must be fought by the natives of a country, not by foreigners. China urges that Laotians must overthrow Laotians, and she therefore encourages them with tracts, not troops. The Chinese do not send their armies abroad except – as in the case of the Korean War – when their frontiers appear to be threatened.

Ping-pong diplomacy and "people's wars" could therefore be regarded as two sides of the same coin. The new power-holders led by Chou En-lai might want to make it up with the world. Mao might want permanent world revolution. But as long as the have-nots fought to the last Vietnamese, Indonesian, or Birmingham black, and China only cheered them on from the sidelines, the two policies could coexist and even complement each other. It might appear that the Chinese were tripping over themselves when they tried to establish closer relations with Malaysia on a state-to-state basis and simultaneously supported the armed Malaysian communist terrorists in the jungle, but that depended on how adroitly they manoeuvred. For in theory the threat of increased (or a hint of decreased) terrorism might in itself be a persuasive argument when China set out to make friends and influence governments.

Meanwhile, the aggressive alternatives to smiling diplomacy were distinctly dangerous. The PLA already had enough on its hands. It was running the administration, mending the economy, preparing for a possible attack by the Soviet Union or the United States. The Red warlords were nursing their military power in their own regions, and in the frontier provinces in north and south China their men were deployed for the defence of the homeland.

Mao might have told the late Pandit Nehru that even if half of the people in the world were to be annihilated in a nuclear war, the other half would remain, Imperialism would be "razed to the ground" and Socialism supervene, but he knew that in spite of her huge population, China herself was horribly vulnerable. In the regions along her border with the Soviet Union were located her biggest arsenal, her aircraft factories, her nuclear development centres and testing grounds, her main refineries, the heavy industries of Manchuria, and important hydro-electric plants. From this area came her petroleum, and much of her iron, steel and coal. Generals might rattle their sabres and demand greater mobilisation of the masses in order to strengthen their own hold on the country, but China could risk no war at home, let alone a military adventure abroad.

Mao, therefore, bowed to circumstance, as he had bowed to circumstance over the fall of Lin Piao. To pacify indignant militants, the Nixon visit was equated by implication with his insistence in 1940 that China must preserve her hypocritical alliance with Chiang Kai-shek in order to defeat the greater enemy, Japan. First things first. This time the Russians and the Japanese must be neutralised, and the more distant Americans, like the hapless Nationalists, could presumably be dealt with later.

Whatever the face-saving compromises reached, however, it became evident on 1 July 1972, the 51st anniversary of the Chinese Communist Party, that China's fine appearance of unity before a watchful world concealed a reality of persistent political wrangling. In previous years, the Republic's three principal journals had carried special editorials for the occasion, and Communist leaders had often appeared at commemorative gatherings. But in 1972 the momentous day passed unmarked by a single relevant article or speech.

It was clear that even if (as was suspected) a high-level conference had been held just before the anniversary, the differences expressed at it had been sharp enough to stop a strong, unequivocal and quotable "line" from emerging. The party was still burdened with the incongruous by-products of its Ninth Congress in April 1969: a Politburo with more vacancies than survivors; a plenum packed with soldiers, too many of whom were supporters of Lin Piao; and a draft constitution which named that fallen angel as Mao's successor. And it was certain that (quite apart from all other possible bones of contention) the Maoists, the military and the moderates could not easily agree on just who and what should replace these anachronisms.

By 28 July it nevertheless looked as if Peking might be ready to put an end to the whole artificial situation. Breaking an embarrassed, ten-month-long silence, the Chinese finally "confirmed" that Lin Piao had "attempted a *coup d'état* and tried to assassinate Mao Tsetung", and when this "plot was foiled", he had "fled on 12 September towards the Soviet Union in a plane which crashed in the People's Republic of Mongolia". Whether the announcement was true or not was almost beside the point (it had apparently been forgotten that Russian experts had declared that no corpse more than fifty years old had been found in the wreckage of the Trident). The 65-year-old Lin Piao was officially dead, and presumably the empty chairs held by his faction could at last be refilled, starting with his own post of Defence Minister.

Three nights later those who believed that Lin had plotted against Mao because "the pen" was "getting the upper hand", could see how unlikely that was. The occasion was a banquet held in the Great Hall of the People in Peking to celebrate the 45th anniversary of the Red Army, and it was attended by the entire Chinese Communist leadership, less Mao. The main address was delivered by Chou En-lai's close comrade, Yeh Chien-ying, the "Dog-Meat Marshal". Among the distinguished guests were more than twenty victims of the Cultural Revolution who had come in from the cold for the first time, and the most prominent among these was Ch'en Yun, a trusted minister of Chou En-lai who had in former days stood in for him as acting premier when he travelled abroad.

But Ch'en Yun was not the only *revenant* of interest. The occasion could also be described as the fifth anniversary of the "Wuhan Incident", the armed rebellion against the Maoists in which "Pockmark" Ch'en Tsai-tao and his "Million Heroes Army" had kidnapped and beaten up two high-ranking emissaries from the capital. Yet there at the banquet was "Pockmark" himself, and with him was his former political commissar and closest henchman in that lamentable affair, which had shaken all China and sabotaged Mao's Cultural Revolution. Neither had been heard of for half a decade.

The scene, with its numerous Banquos back from the political grave, showed how far the pragmatic Prime Minister had advanced, and the trend was underlined in the official editorials published to mark the anniversary, for they shamelessly stressed the importance to a soldier of soldiering – "a mass campaign for military training" was "gaining momentum". Discarded generals condemned to outer darkness for using the "Big Military Contest" of the sixties as a pretext for keeping their men busy with machine-guns rather than Mao's Thought may have permitted themselves a small smile (two of them were also at the banquet).

This was only one side of the story, however. The hand of the Maoists could be plainly seen in an editorial of the *Red Flag* calling for all to study once more Mao's famous "resolution" at the Kut'ien Conference in 1929, in which he had propounded his thesis that "the party commands the gun". Mao had then enumerated the many sins and deviations to which socialist soldiers were exposed, warning all against developing a "purely military viewpoint", against "small-group mentality", the "mentality of the hired hand" who believes he is "only responsible to his senior officer and not to the revolution", and who puts "the interest of the individual and of the small clique above that of the whole". The revival of this forty-three-year-old discourse was doubtless an attack on Lin Piao and recalcitrants of the 4th Field Army, but through them it was an attack on all soldiers who did not toe the party "line".

It may only have been a matter of words, the work of China's propagandists and not China's powerholders. But the words would carry their own political weight as long as the Chairman lived. Mao might find himself in the condition known to chess players as *Zugzwang*, and be obliged to move as others dictated, but he was still a powerful piece that could at the same time limit the moves of the adversary. The name of the game would be the same when he was taken from the board, but not the game itself. What, then, would happen when Mao died?

When Mao Dies

What happens when the Chairman goes? Who succeeds when Mao fails? It would be absurd to try and produce precise, computerised answers to these questions, for computers take no account of the accidents of history. Chou En-lai may die before Mao. Two devoted *t'ung-chih* may fall out over a woman. But it is possible to set the scenario and explain the hazards involved.

The hazards are all the same hazard in different forms – the danger of going by appearances. Even the Chinese loyalty system becomes brittle with age, and the continuity of close relationships fragile. By the time Huang Yung-sheng had defied the Red Guards in Canton, for example, the fact that he had been one of the "Sanwan seed-force" might have inclined Mao to clemency, but was no longer a guarantee of royal favour. Membership of the Ma Huang clique that created the rival Oyuwan Soviet had far more meaning.

Again, the literal "truth" in China – proved by quoting from the texts of Communist speeches and writings – is no more truth than a "Maoist" is a Maoist. To analysts who deal solely in this commodity we owe the dogmatic assertions that it was the Chairman himself who personally decided to put an end to his own glorification, to sack Lin Piao, to invite President Nixon to China. These statements are all true on paper. And they are all totally misleading.

From this it is only one step to the elementary mistake of confusing position with power. It may be objected that this book has given no more than passing mention to men like Tung Pi-wu, Acting President of the Republic during the Nixon visit, and does not even name Kuo Mo-jo at all, although he may well be chairman of the next National People's Congress if he is still alive. But while their titles may sound impressive, in terms of power these are nonentities.

The most deceptive element of all in the scenario is Mao

himself, for Mao is a living paradox. Mao the Chairman and Father of the Republic is sacrosanct, his seal on a decision gives it the force of law, and he is the greatest single unifying factor in all China. But Mao, the revolutionary who believes that "one must divide into two", has been largely isolated and neutralised by moderates as the greatest single disruptive influence in the country. And he will remain a paradox after death, for as his disruptive influence fades, unity should be easier to achieve, but the prestigious leader who united the people behind him (or his opponents against him) will also have gone. His departure, as Mao might put it himself, will move China from a position of balance to one of imbalance from which a new balance must eventually emerge.

Chou En-lai is the most obvious candidate for the succession – the perilous honour first enjoyed by the ill-fated Liu Shao-ch'i and then by the disgraced Lin Piao. If he survives, he may have to move with exceptional care to achieve that new balance, and if he does not survive, this will be even more true of Li Hsien-nien or whichever other "moderate" assumes the task. For when Mao is no longer there, Chou's orders and policy decisions will not be heavy with the cachet of the Chairman's formal approval, and therefore incontestable. Moreover, the warlords will no longer be automatically drawn to him by their mutual anxiety to curb the unrivalled influence of their intimidating captive. It is war that unites men, not peace. When militant Maoism has lost Mao, the generals may be chary of committing themselves to a point where Chou can put a lock on them, and regional bosses like Ironsides Hsu Shih-yu may only agree to cooperate with Peking as long as they are not obliged to make any sacrifice of power in their provinces.

Chou is not Mao, Yeh Chien-ying is only acceptable to the PLA as the senior soldier in Peking just because he commands nothing and cannot control the regions, and if the Prime Minister promotes a newcomer, like Deputy Chief of Staff Chang Ts'ai-ch'ien, to a position of greater power, he may be looked upon by the old warlords in the provinces as a mere upstart. Yet somehow Chou must gain the close support of these military barons without letting them climb on his back, and establish collective leadership at all levels that will give his civilian cadres in party and administration a stronger hold on the country. Until he does, China will continue to have a truncated leadership at the centre facing strong, semi-autonomous army authority on the regional mountain-tops outside. As the distinguished soldiers and administrators who had fallen during the Cultural Revolution began to appear again in Peking in 1972, it became evident that he was already seeking to solve this problem – as well as to outface Chiang Ch'ing and the Maoists with their own victims.

Chou En-lai nonetheless told President Nixon that China had too many elderly leaders and could learn from the United States in this respect. Did he already see himself defeated by the generation gap? Part of his problem would appear to be that the board will still be dominated by the same pieces when Mao dies – "Night Tiger", "Ferocious Tiger", "Tigerlover", "Ironsides", the "Dog-Meat Marshal", the "One-Eyed Dragon" and the rest of the ageing warriors of the revolution. It was significant that when the Russians reported that all nine people killed in the Trident crash were under fifty, China-watchers could at once say with certainty that no one of real consequence could have been on board. Apart from the few who may have been compromised in the Lin Piao drama, the "Kiangsi Favourites" from the Long March may give Chou room to manoeuvre, for they are good "Red capital" with excellent revolutionary records, they have no mountain-tops of their own, and with Mao dead they will belong to no one man – Chou Hsing,* the Prime Minister's confidant in Yunnan, is typical of them. Yet even they are no longer young.

However, these are all difficulties that Chou En-lai can over-come. The generation gap in the Chinese army is a myth for which Mao is largely responsible. The younger commanders – northerners prominent among them – are just not revolutionaries. Their greatest military experience was the Korean War, in which they served an entire political spectrum of generals ranging from Lin Piao to "Hades" P'eng Te-huai. Their loyalties are secular, however. In the Cultural Revolution they obeyed orders, even orders from Chiang Ch'ing, but they could not rise to prominence during the tumultuous years in which Mao struggled to impose his idealistic line on the nation and "politics commanded all". For Mao could place no confidence in them. They were apolitical instruments, not ideological dis-

* See appendix to Chapter 12.

189

ciples. Once Mao goes, they can quickly come to the fore in a less exigent political atmosphere, for they will be attracted to the moderate leadership, and the moderate leadership will need them.

Their emergence could be one of many natural adjustments to bring new stability to China, for the human paradox in the situation – Mao-the-master and Mao-the-captive – is a false weight that produces a false equilibrium as long as he is alive. When he dies, it may well be as if a magnet had been withdrawn. The political law of gravity will operate freely again, and the various elements in play shift according to their normal values to find their own level. The imbalance Mao leaves must precipitate a new pattern of power and should make it easier – not more difficult – for Chou En-lai to gather most of that power into his hands.

In the first place, he should be able to slide one of them into the invisible, many-fingered glove with which Mao maintains a secret grasp on China's eight hundred millions – the T'e Wu. The only big questionmark here is Chou's relationship with the "Devil's Clutch", Wang Tung-hsing. Otherwise he should have little trouble. Chou himself is an old undercover comrade from his Shanghai days. He is understood to be close to Yu Sang, the number three man in the organisation who was constantly with him during the Nixon visit. It was also the Prime Minister who had Chou Hsing made a Vice-Minister of Public Security in earlier years, and he could now bring this tried man to the top of the T'e Wu if he chose. K'ang Sheng, the overall chief, was known to be sick in 1972, and the collapse of the Cultural Revolution which had carried him to the number five position in the Politburo meant that once more the uneven graph of his career would dip. If he outlived Mao, he would again become a policeman rather than a politician, and he would need a new master.

Not a new mistress. Chiang Ch'ing and her left-wing Maoist faction will have a purpose to serve as the authentic voice of pure revolutionary Marxism–Leninism that must continue for a while to denounce Russian revisionism, and maintain China's position as the sacred repository of the One True Faith within the international communist movement. But her power will have died with her husband, and it is to be expected that she will only last as long as her words are needed to cover Chou En-lai's own deviationist acts.

190

It follows that the strictly pragmatic alliance-of-convenience between the Maoist leadership and the fundamentally anti-Maoist commanders among 3rd Field Army veterans like Su Yu and Ironsides Hsu Shih-yu will come to an end with Mao. Their relationship with Chou should therefore lose its ambiguity. Moreover, the Prime Minister's demand for unity is clearly echoed by China's generals, who do not forget that more than 40 Russian divisions are deployed along their northern frontiers. All know that China must have a central political and administrative authority, and that central authority must have a chief. Who more suitable than the moderate Chou En-lai? Or his lieutenant, the Money God, Li Hsien-nien, if Chou should die?

The moment must produce the man whom Chou needs as a strong Minister of Defence at the apex of the PLA. Ironsides and Su Yu come to mind as outstanding candidates. Yeh Chien-ying could fade into the background, and a younger general could be appointed Chief of Staff. It should also be possible to hold a new party congress and to elect a new Central Committee (if this could not be done while Mao still lived), and the warlords who had been sitting in their fiefs to protect their own mountain-tops could then sit on the Politburo and protect them from there instead. With collective leadership a reality, the conflicting lines of power between Peking and the provinces would become parallel rails on which the Chinese state would run.

Chou's alliance with the soldiers, once Mao is no longer there to unite them against him, must be founded on the identity of aims that marks the true *t'ung-chih*. And here Mao will have made matters easier by launching the Cultural Revolution, for although its effects may be far-reaching and China may never be quite the same again, the commanders of the PLA and most of the cadres in party and government at least agree that they do not want a second such revolution. The revolutionary heroes of China do not forget their humiliation at the hands of grubby youngsters, and it is today a mark of respectability to have been mauled by Red Guards – much as it is a mark of respectability among Asian politicians of the post-war period to have done time in a colonial gaol before their countries won independence from the West.

The Cultural Revolution sowed a deep distrust of starry-eyed socialists in the minds of most men, discrediting Maoism and isolating Mao himself from the millions even as their voices prudently recited his Thoughts. At the beginning of 1972, Chou the "moderate" was already dangerously popular. For where it was possible for China-watching agencies to find out what the man-in-the-street thought of his masters, the almost invariable answer was that the idealistic Mao was a dictator divorced from the immediate desires of the masses, his wife was a nonentity, Lin Piao was an obscure military hero of yesterday, but Chou En-lai was the hero of today.

China should quickly find a new balance and achieve a new unity, therefore, if Chou gives the country more of his own commonsense form of communist administration; and he surely will. When President Nixon arrived in Peking, the ideological smog was already lifting. There was more in the shops, the clothes ration had been increased by 50 per cent, and villagers in the south were asking their relatives across the border in Hongkong to send them radio sets or bicycles, where before they would have asked for cooking oil or cotton cloth. What was the political policy in their village? "One man one pig!" was the triumphant stock reply. Democracy had nothing on revisionism, it seemed. A communist remarked confidently in Hongkong: "We followed Mao's way for twenty years and it did not succeed. So we are turning away from it, and you will see, the next generation of Chinese here will be able to go back across the border to China and live there perfectly happily."

If Liu Shao-ch'i could use the "Mao line" as a label to disguise his own revisionist policies between 1959 and 1965 while Mao lived, Chou will certainly be able to do so when Mao dies. A pragmatic programme that will raise living standards, leave the soldier to his rifle practice, the factory hand to work his press and the farmer to breed his hens, can be the basis of a contract with the Red warlords which will in return enable the Premier's cadres to hold a fair share of local administrative and party power in the provinces as well as Peking.

In foreign affairs it may mean smiling diplomacy with an increasingly dangerous smile, for with Mao out of play, Chou En-lai will be free to balance a rapprochement with the Russians against China's expanding relations with the West, and set Peking firmly at the apex of the super-power triangle with the option of taking concerted action with Moscow against the rest.

192

Bound closer by similar revisionist policies, they might even between them be able to put together the shattered monolith of international communism once more.

While China remains weak, divided and exhausted by the upheavals of the Maoist era, Chou En-lai and his comrades will doubtless play for time. But although the tears of the Prime Minister may have softened the hearts of anti-Communist Chinese leaders in Chungking thirty years ago, no one catches him crying before them now. Once China is a united and stable nuclear super-power, with special standing in the United Nations as the champion of the underdog and special standing among all "liberation movements" as the champion of world revolution, he may stop smiling altogether. Chinese leaders do not differ over communist aims. They only differ over the method and the speed with which those aims are to be achieved.

The fundamental mistake made by the visionary Mao has been to forget that people are only human. His Utopia, like all those before it, therefore, must remain a dream. His Thought will doubtless be buried more slowly than his body, but even if he is venerated as a communist god and his words are preserved as gospel, they will only suffer the fate of all gospels – to be quoted as literal "truth" in order to justify a heresy. In January 1972 an article published in the *Red Flag* demonstrated how neat the double-think of Chou En-lai and the moderate powerholders could be when it came to misusing Mao, for it was headed "A Sharp Weapon to Criticise Revisionism"[1] and it cited thirty-year-old writings of the Chairman, in which in fact he urged not only that the party must "develop the economy and ensure the supplies", but must also "give consideration to both public and private interests". In wartime 1942, that may have made good guerrilla sense. In peacetime 1972, it was straight revisionism.

It seems reasonable to suppose that no single military mountain-top will try to seize power in China, where even Lin Piao could not consolidate his position, and that the army and government will also crush any move by left-wing extremists to mount a second Maoist revolution. The political heirs of the Chairman must therefore be men like Chou En-lai and Li Hsien-nien, Hsu Shih-yu and Su Yu, at the head of a collective leadership combining the civilian pragmatists loyal to the Prime Minister and the Red warlords of China's military regions.

But whoever rules in Peking, or however numerous the rulers, the main spiritual successor of Mao Tsetung is likely to be the one man (disgraced or even dead himself) who above all has personified the creeping revisionism the old Chairman so hates but cannot halt – the renegade, traitor, scab and political swindler, ex-President Liu Shao-ch'i.

18

Postscript from Peking

Outside there is a November nip in the air, and autumn tints match the upcurling roof of the Gate of Heavenly Peace across the square. Here in the vast neo-classical Great Hall of the People, however, the Chinese Prime Minister dispenses measured warmth to Sir Alec Douglas-Home. Introduced to Chou En-lai in my turn,* I am treated briefly to the soft, tireless grasp of the professional handshaker but despite his curt, practised backchat his eyes seem blurred with fatigue. Ping-pong diplomacy evidently takes its toll of Chou, as he processes an endless succession of visitors and weaves them into the fabric of his foreign policy. Yet at 74 he still radiates a marvellously controlled mental vigour, and in Peking one senses that he is the power, if not the glory. A great corps of comrades and cadres will go down with him if he ever falls.

But there is no sign of that. At the banquet thrown for the fiftieth birthday of Prince Norodom Sihanouk of Cambodia, I watched Chou En-lai move down the line of guests, immediately followed by three "moderate" confidants – Yeh Chien-ying, the Dog-Meat Marshal, the Money God Li Hsien-nien, and Chi P'eng-fei, Chen the Bald's successor as Chinese Foreign Minister. The Maoist left wing was represented by a subordinate figure, and Chiang Ch'ing herself put in only a brief appearance in the background.

Chou appears to be neutralising the potential of the extremist "Shanghai Mafia" that championed the Cultural Revolution with the purposeful circumspection of an acupuncturist sticking needles into a patient in order to kill pain, not provoke it. Recently, and for the first time, Chiang Ch'ing was placed below the Dog-Meat Marshal in an official list of the Politburo, and although the Prime Minister is said to have hinted to

* As a correspondent of the *Observer* accompanying the British Foreign Secretary.

visiting American editors that Yao Wen-yuan, the Trigger-Finger, might be the successor of Mao, Chinese cadres to whom I speak dismiss this disagreeable prediction as a ridiculous, faintly exasperating *canard de Pékin* whenever I ask if there is a vestige of truth in it.

The Cultural Revolution itself is as embarrassing as the skeleton of a saint in the cupboard for, while it was fathered by Mao himself, it developed its own regrettable characteristics. Talking to us last week in Shanghai, a leading member of the Municipal Revolutionary Committee skipped all mention of the creation of the "Shanghai Commune" when the masses seized power in 1967, for it would be condemned as "ultra-democratic" today and it implicated leading left-wing Politburo members like Yao Wen-yuan himself.

This cadre also neatly concealed a disastrous slump in output during that interlude of near-anarchy by referring to the spectacular increase in shipbuilding achieved solely in the past two years as progress "since the beginning of the Cultural Revolution". Officials are deeply apologetic about the burning of the British Chancery at the height of the turmoil, but blame it on to "sycophants" like Ch'en Po-ta around the wretched Lin Piao, who deliberately set out to discredit the whole movement. "We ourselves were blind, we did not know what was happening," one of them pleaded to me.

The term "Cultural Revolution", with all its connotations of mass action and violent change, is merely a semantic amulet that the Chinese are careful to wear in their speech. We are tactfully told that it is not over, but "entering a new phase". The "face" of the Maoists is not destroyed, therefore, but simply ages prematurely, as the power of the moderates is consolidated.

The effects of that great upheaval of the sixties are not to be underestimated, however. At a bucolic "May 7 Cadre School" outside Peking I have met men and women from the backbone of the bureaucracy – chairbound officials, ranking members of revolutionary committees, and senior school-teachers – who were not only humbly studying Engels and Mao in the dirt courtyard of a farm, but feeding the pigs, working the fields of grain and vegetables, and, during part of their six-month sojourn "down in the country", living and labouring side by side with the neighbouring peasants themselves.

196

All the rank and file of the civil service and party hierarchy are in theory being systematically fed through these schools, in which they are conditioned to identify themselves with the minds and miseries of the millions, to "heighten their consciousness of the class struggle" and "cultivate the mass line view" – in short, to learn the hard way what life is like at the proletarian rice-roots. The Cultural Revolution has also left its influence on education, so that today theory is wedded to practice. At the universities of both Shanghai and Peking I found that the years of academic study had been cut by two, and the student could move from blackboard to bench-lathe and back again.

The most advertised claim of all is that there is greater "participation of the masses" in revolutionary and party committees and it is impressed upon me, for example, that seven out of every ten members on the Municipal Revolutionary Committee of Shanghai are now "workers and intellectuals". The power of the PLA in everything from provincial government to sheet-metal shop, it is emphasised, has correspondingly waned. A civilian cadre is quick to remark that the number of military "responsibles" at a local shipyard has dropped from twenty to three, and the same tale is told wherever one goes.

However, the high verbal polish given by cadres to the Chinese scene can often obscure the underlying reality. In Peking University, four out of fifteen members of the standing committee are still army "commanders" (while "student participation" is non-existent), and there are more uniforms about than the predigested statistics fed to foreigners suggest.

In a paved chamber the size of a tennis court 25 feet below a Peking shopping-street, part of a fantastic labyrinth of tunnels through which three million citizens must be dispersed to the suburbs in case of air attack, a leading cadre of the PLA takes over the press briefing when the questions get tough, and barks an unequivocal answer at us when asked if any Russians have been allowed to see these shelters. "They would steal our military secrets," he says bluntly. "They have a million troops on our border, and they are plotting aggression against us" – and I recall how Han Hsien-ch'u, Commander of Foochow Military Region, reminded the masses of the pre-eminent role of the soldier by warning them 18 months ago that his command was in the forefront of the resistance against the United States (p. 127).

197

On the eve of my arrival in China, it was disclosed that three more ministries in the State Council had been given to soldiers, and that the new Minister for Public Security was a certain Li Chen. But Li Chen was a general in the old 2nd Field Army. His commander was the One-Eyed Dragon, Liu Po-ch'eng, his direct chief as a subordinate political commissar was the disgraced secretary-general of the party, Teng Hsiao-p'ing, and he subsequently served under the Ferocious Tiger, Ch'en Hsi-lien, in Manchuria. Here was the reality behind the face-saving facade of "mass participation".

Meanwhile Ironsides Hsu Shih-yu has reappeared in the news, listed as "Member of the Politburo, First Secretary of the Party Committee for Kiangsu Province, Chairman of the Revolutionary Committee of Kiangsu Province", as well as "Commander of Nanking Military Units", and it is evident that the claim that "the party commands the gun" should still be taken with a pinch of powder, even if the downfall of Lin Piao has been a traumatic blow for the PLA.

And his death. "For," a responsible cadre tells me here, after giving me yet another graphic version of Lin's iniquitous plotting, "I can assure you that he is quite definitely dead." "Were Huang Yung-sheng and the deputy chiefs of staff aboard the aircraft in which he fled?" I ask quickly. "No," comes the categorical answer, and my next question – what happened to these officers, are they also dead? – is elliptically answered before I can ask it. "It is doubtful even if Lin Piao would have been executed, had he been caught. Chairman Mao has said 'you cannot chop off the top of a man as you can a leek'. He may turn out to have been innocent, or he may be redeemable. He may have to undergo a course of ideological rectification, or he may be sent down to live with and learn from the peasants for a time. But no more."

As earlier suspicions that Huang Yung-sheng and his missing deputies of the 4th Field Army brotherhood would surface again are reinforced, pieces almost literally continue to drop into place. For a little later it is revealed that Rubbermouth Liu Hsing-yuan, whom the Speechless Rustic left to hold the fort for him as political commissar of Canton Military Region when he himself moved to Peking as Chief of Staff, has re-appeared after an ill-omened absence as a leading member of the provincial revolutionary committee of Szechuan, and is thus reunited with his own former troops who were earlier transferred there from Kwangtung.

It is obviously worth taking this question of the resurrection of dubious soldiers further, and as our "Shanghai" saloon hoots its way down the Peking–Tientsin road towards the headquarters of the 196th Infantry Division, I ask the Chinese cadre beside the driver with calculated suddenness: "Given the 'Wuhan Incident', how could Ch'en Tsai-tao turn up bold as brass at the official banquet held to celebrate Army Day in Peking this year?" The cadre swings around to give me a long look and a short answer. "Why shouldn't he?" he counters coldly. "He is an excellent comrade. A man may rectify his mistakes."

"Mistakes" was a revealing definition for the acts of a Regional Commander who had openly defied Peking and kidnapped the Minister for Public Security, but it was not the first time it had been used in this connection. It will be recollected that, as the new Chief of Staff, Huang Yung-sheng himself had been furious at learning from a secret tape-recording of the original plot to overthrow Pockmark Ch'en in 1967, and had later rebuked a rally of leftists with the words "First and foremost we must assure the stability of the army. We must therefore allow men to make mistakes – and also allow them to rectify them . . ." (p. 134).

At the headquarters of the 196th Division we are nonetheless given the impression that while the fallen may return from oblivion, the old mountain-tops – the cliques in the 4th Field Army among them – are being systematically eroded by mass cross-postings of commanders and recruits. In this formation, I am told, there are troops from provinces as far apart as Shansi, Kwangtung, and Chekiang. But when I ask the four men sharing my table at lunch in the mess where they come from, they all reply "Hopei" – and so does the deputy commander of the division, who is our host.

A regimental political commissar tells how his brigade started as twelve men, three rifles and a red flag in Shansi during the war against the Japanese. "Then the veterans of this division were all in the Shansi–Chahar–Hopei Soviet?" "Yes." "And your overall commander was Nieh Jung-chen?" A sudden smile from the deputy-commander – "Yes, Nieh Jung-chen." The heirs of the old North China Liberation Army, in fact, are still in place around Peking twenty-three years after Chiang Kai-shek fled to Formosa and the War of Liberation ended. And the semi-legendary chief of that Army was the Profligate Monk, one of Chou En-lai's closest and most trusted comrades.

Chou En-lai knows how to use his friends, as he knows how to misuse his foes, but a man who seeks to keep his balance on as precarious a pile of political bric-à-brac as the Chinese power structure represents today makes no abrupt gestures. Changes therefore take place slowly. Mao's face still gazes down from the wall of every office, and official buildings are decorated with plaques bearing his strictures and exhortations in huge, simplified characters. His portrait is being quietly removed from less formal settings, however, and the great statue of him that stood in Sian has gone. His button is on many breasts, but far from all, and his teachings, it is stressed, are not to be memorised from a little red missal but studied along with those of Marx, Lenin and Engels.

The soldiers are less obtrusive in factory and farm, the cadres go to "May 7" schools to rake muck with the masses, the students are given a more imaginative "revolutionary" syllabus – but they must still take entrance examinations to universities, once contemptuously abolished as bourgeois anachronisms, however impeccable their proletarian background. Like Confucius, Chou En-lai seeks a middle way. We ask an experienced and intelligent cadre what is the best thing the regime has done for China and his curiously negative answer is "get rid of Liu Shao-ch'i and Lin Piao". But the logic of this soon becomes evident. The twin barrage against Liu the "capitalist" and Lin Piao the bogus "ultra-leftist" hits extremists of right and left who are Chou's natural enemies. This forces the masses to feel their way down the centre-line.

Officials constantly warn one that everything is "still experimental". For if a commune gives extra pay to star workers, it may be accused of offering capitalistic "material incentives". But if it refuses to grant "reasonable rewards" to the virtuous, it will be guilty of ultra-leftist "egalitarianism". Stuck with a bonus fund, what do the cadres do? "We are still discussing it," replies a leading member of the revolutionary committee running a turbo-generator plant in Chekiang Province, after a slight pause. "And meanwhile we are dividing up the bonus money equally among all the workers."

The same debate goes on in the farming communes, but these are not the mindless anthills they were supposed to become in 1958. "Seven per cent of all the arable land here has been allotted to the peasants for their private use," a cadre explains at Hsu Hang Commune outside Shanghai. "And that means," a mother of five tells me, pointing to a fenced patch in which two curiously smooth pigs and six scruffy hens are segregated from disciplined rows of vegetables by a bamboo hedge, "that we have half a *mou*, not counting the bit of garden that goes with the house." A *mou* is one-sixth of an acre. The seven members of the family raise four pigs annually on this plot, whose total output, sold to the commune or on the local free market, earns them nearly £60 a year over and above the £200 they are paid for their collective labour in one of the commune's production teams.

Prices and wages have hardly moved in fourteen years, but although this is in many ways a touchingly poor and backward country, the crowds in the streets of Peking look well-fed and reasonably relaxed, the stores are full of shoppers, and great flocks of bicycles – expensive at £25 each or more – skim along the streets of a capital which now boasts nearly one pair of wheels for every two pairs of legs. Sewing machines, transistor radios, and watches are in demand. People are putting out flowers, even buying goldfish to keep.

For Mao Tsetung, every period of consolidation like this has been no more than a breathing space, justifying the next dash forward towards the ultimate classless society, and just as one car too many will one day bring New York to a standstill, they say, one bicycle too many in Peking – or the affluence it suggests – could goad the Maoists into another revolutionary paroxysm against "spontaneous capitalism" in China. But today that is an outside chance.

Heirs Apparent? Here in the capital itself it seems even more evident than elsewhere that Chou En-lai and the "moderates" in Politburo and PLA must be the future masters of China – men at the top of a pyramid of power from whom faceless and nameless *t'ung-chih*, as yet unheard of and unphotographed in the West, stretch down to the very base as their successors.

But earlier on this misty November evening, I stood in an empty, echoing auditorium within the Great Hall of the People which waits, year after year, to seat the delegates to the next

National People's Congress – the long overdue superparliament of representatives from all over the country that none dares to convene – while outside a nationwide chorus of placards chanted "*Mao Chu Hsi Wan Sui* – Ten Thousand Years to Chairman Mao" – in gold on red or red on white. And it seemed obvious that harmonious collective leadership and an end to disputes over pragmatic policies and ping-pong diplomacy would come only "when", as discreet imperial mandarins used to say of ageing emperors, "ten thousand years have passed".

D.B.
Peking
3 November 1972

APPENDIXES

APPENDIXES

The Politburo

The Political Bureau of the Chinese Communist Party, as announced in April 1969.

Note: After Chairman Mao and Vice-Chairman Lin Piao, all names are listed according to their strokes, i.e. in a Chinese equivalent of alphabetical order.

Standing Committee

Mao Tsetung	Chairman.
Lin Piao	Vice-Chairman.
Ch'en Po-ta	Mao's personal secretary.
Chou En-lai	Prime Minister.
K'ang Sheng	Chief of Intelligence and Secret Police Services.

Full Members

Yen Ch'un	Wife of Lin Piao.
Yeh Chien-ying	Former Chief of Staff, PLA.
Liu Po-ch'eng	Former Commander of the 2nd Field Army.
Chiang Ch'ing	Wife of Mao Tsetung.
Chu Te	Former Commander-in-Chief, PLA.
Hsu Shih-yu	Commander, Nanking Military Region.
Ch'en Hsi-lien	Commander, Shenyang Military Region.
Li Hsien-nien	Vice-Premier and Minister of Finance.
Li Tso-p'eng	Political Commissar of the Navy.
Wu Fa-hsien	Commander of the Air Force.
Chang Ch'un-ch'iao	First Secretary, Shanghai Party Committee.
Ch'iu Hui-tso	Director of General Logistics Department, PLA.
Yao Wen-yuan	Second Secretary, Shanghai Party Committee.
Huang Yung-sheng	Chief of Staff, PLA.
Tung Pi-wu	Vice-Chairman of the Republic.
Hsieh Fu-chih	First Secretary of the Peking Party Committee, and Minister for Public Security.

Alternate Members

Chi Teng-k'uei	Alternate Secretary, Honan Provincial Party Committee.

Li Hsueh-feng	Chairman, Hopei Provincial Revolutionary Committee.
Li Te-sheng	Director of the General Political Department, PLA.
Wang Tung-hsing	Chief of the Security Department of the Military Affairs Commission and Vice-Minister for Public Security.

Total: 21 full members and four alternate members.

POWER CHART

(Subject to change during the period of constant reorganisation that began with the Cultural Revolution)

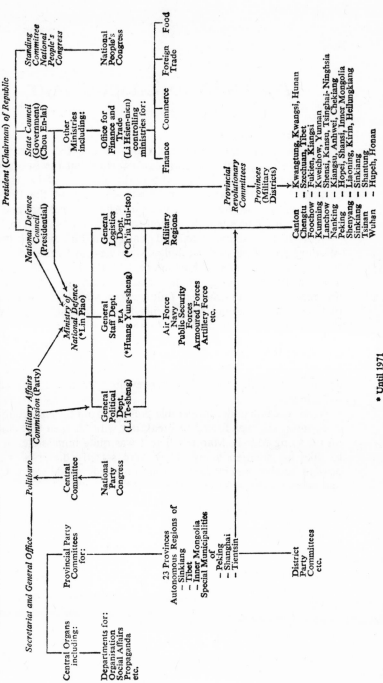

* Until 1971

Appendix to Chapter Two

Mao's Marriages and Family

There is a further version, put about by the Red Guards, that Yao Wen-yuan is not the son-in-law of Mao, but the husband of Mao's niece, Wang Hai-jung, who is the daughter of his younger brother. Wang Hai-jung is the Deputy-Director of the Protocol Department in the Ministry of Foreign Affairs in Peking, and was a member of China's first delegation to the United Nations in 1971.

Apart from his first wife, and Yang K'ai-hui, the mother of An-ying, An-ch'ing and An-lung, Mao was also married to Ho Tze-ch'eng, the woman whom he sent to the Soviet Union from Yenan as mentally sick before he met Chiang Ch'ing. Ho Tze-ch'eng was the wife of a hunch-back tailor whom Mao killed at the time that he was assembling his guerrilla forces on Chingkangshan in Kiangsi, and before he made the Long March in 1934. He took her as his own wife, and she bore him several children. But Mao had no time for children while he was fighting against the Kuomintang and struggling for power within the Communist movement, and in fact teasingly called them "counter-revolutionaries" as they were a hindrance.

When he came under intolerable pressure from the encircling KMT in Kiangsi, and was forced to break out with his men and embark on the Long March, Mao felt that it was quite impossible for him to take his children along. They were secretly dispersed among peasant families, and by the time the Communists had overrun China and peace had been restored, they could not be traced. On the Long March itself, Ho Tze-ch'eng gave birth to a daughter, although wounded by KMT bombers. There are unconfirmed reports that she is living in Hangchow, and that this "Miss Long March" looks after her.

Appendix to Chapter Eleven

1. LI TSO-P'ENG. One of two favourite generals of Lin Piao who lost an arm during the Long March (the other was Liang Hsing-ch'u, Commander of the Chengtu Military Region). Li was a battalion commander in the Model Regiment of the First Front Army, and distinguished himself by fighting a stiff battle against the veteran Nationalist commander Hsueh Yueh in Kweichow, south-west China, enabling the main force of the Red Army to break free of a threat of encirclement (Lung Shu-chin, currently Commander of Sinkiang Military Region, served with him at this time). When the war against Japan ended and the Communists began their final struggle with the Nationalists for the domination of China, Li accompanied Lin Piao to the north-east and took part in three campaigns in which they not only fought according to Lin Piao's tactics (often launching human sea attacks against the KMT after concentrating overwhelming forces against a smaller enemy) but instituted land reform, confiscated properties from landlords, and recruited, trained, and armed the peasantry in a bid to consolidate their hold on Manchuria before the KMT could break it.

They fared badly in two violent battles in which Chiang Yung-hui, now Deputy Commander of Shenyang Military Region, was wounded in the eye, and extricated themselves with difficulty. Li realised that they had been defeated because they and their men had no real comprehension of modern fire-power, and commented afterwards: "It is absurd to recall now, but we were really ignorant. The green and red tracer was flying, and the night sky was full of flares and incendiaries, and it was just like a firework show on National Day." But the men were cut to ribbons before they could get to close quarters with the enemy, for they depended far too much on hand-to-hand combat, he admitted. He did not lose his fighting spirit, however, and he write an essay in 1965 containing the much-publicised Maoist dictum for those who want to launch their own "people's war"; "tactically pit ten against one, strategically one against ten" (i.e. beat a far bigger enemy by concentrating your small forces against an even smaller section of his).*

* *Fighting under the command of Comrade Lin Piao*, an article originally published in the *Chinese Youth* in Peking, 1957, volume 20, later reprinted in Lin Piao's selected works and circulated by the Chih Luen Press in Hongkong (1970).

In 1949 Li was put in command of the 43rd Army and after the capture of Tientsin, advanced south to Kwangtung and Kwangsi provinces with the 4th Field Army. In January 1950 Lin Piao gave him the direction of the assault landing against the KMT on Hainan Island, and in April several hundred junks carried thirty thousand men on what was the greatest amphibious operation ever undertaken by the Red Army. Under Li and Han Hsien-ch'u (now Commander of Foochow Military Region), the attack succeeded and the island, today an important Chinese air and naval base opposite North Vietnam, was taken. In 1962 Li was made Deputy Commander of the Chinese Navy, and acquired control of it as political commissar in 1967.

2. CH'IU HUI-TSO has in the past enjoyed a close relationship with Huang Yung-sheng. During the war against Japan, they served together in the Shansi–Chahar–Hopei Soviet under the command of the Profligate Monk, Nieh Jung-chen, and later in Manchuria. In 1949 Ch'iu was appointed Political Commissar of the 45th Army in the 4th Field Army which was at the taking of Tientsin, and participated in the drive south to Hunan and Kwangsi. There he assisted T'ao Chu, now disgraced but in 1950 Political Commissar of the 4th Field Army, to carry out a stringent land reform programme during which countless landlords were pitilessly slaughtered. Ch'iu became Director of the Political Department of Kwangtung Military District when Lung Shu-chin, now the military commander in Sinkiang, was military commander there. They both belonged to a small circle of men close to Huang Yung-sheng.

Appendix to Chapter Twelve

1. On the death of T'an Fu-jen, head of the Yunnan Revolutionary Committee and Political Commissar of the Kunming Military Region, a struggle for influence developed between Chou Hsing, Governor of Yunnan and First Secretary of the Yunnan Party Committee, and Ch'en K'ang, Deputy Commander of the Kunming Military Region.

Sixty-six year old Chou Hsing is from Kiangsi, close to Chou En-lai and, to a lesser degree, to Mao Tsetung himself. He began life as a shop apprentice, but was filled with revolutionary zeal at an early age and organised the Peasants' Association in his home village. He led a local revolt, started his own group of guerrillas as their self-appointed leader, and finally joined the Chinese Communist Party. Stern, stubborn, pokerfaced, Chou Hsing earned Mao's appreciation when in his role of vice-chief of security he executed an order to hunt down and destroy KMT subversives of the "Anti-Bolshevik League" who had been responsible for a major mutiny in the Kiangsi Soviet.

After the Long March, Chou Hsing was in charge of intelligence work in the North-West Border Region which was Mao's head-quarters, and in 1949 he became director of the Public Security Bureau in Nanking. Supported by Chou En-lai, he was appointed Vice-Minister of Public Security in 1954 and held the post for four years. After a short spell as Political Commissar of Shenyang Military Region he was sent to Yunnan in 1965, evidently to keep an eye on Ho Lung and the 1st Field Army veterans, and to organise offensive intelligence operations across the frontier into South-East Asia. He was not known to be trusted by either Lin Piao or Huang.

Ch'en K'ang is fifty-six, and while Chou Hsing has a First Front Army background, Ch'en is among the veterans of the Fourth Front Army and the 2nd Field Army of the One-Eyed Dragon, Liu Po-ch'eng. When the commander and political commissar of Kunming Military Region were both eliminated, he found himself in an isolated and exposed position, but he survived and continued to enjoy considerable prestige among the local military.

Appendixes to Chapter Fifteen

THE RISING POWER OF THE 4TH FIELD ARMY
BEFORE SEPTEMBER 1971

Defence Minister and Vice-Chairman of the Communist Party:
Lin Piao.
Chief of Staff of the PLA: Huang Yung-sheng.

Key service chiefs named deputy chiefs of staff:

Li Te-sheng, General Political Department (not 4th Field Army).
Wu Fa-hsien, Air Force Commander.
Li Tso-p'eng, Political Commissar of the Navy.
Ch'iu Hui-tso, Director of General Logistics Department.

Three subordinates of Huang from Canton named deputy chiefs of
staff:

Yen Chung-ch'uan.
Wen Yu-ch'eng.
Pai Hsiang-kuo.

Canton Military Region: 41st, 42nd, 43rd, and 55th Armies loyal
to Huang.
Wuhan Military Region: 43rd (elements from Canton) and 54th
Armies loyal to Huang.
Lanchow Military Region: 47th Army loyal to Lin Piao and Huang
Yung-sheng.
Chengtu Military Region: 50th Army loyal to Lin Piao and Huang.
Jen Jung, ex-43rd Army cadre posted as political commissar to
Tibet, loyal to Huang.
Sinkiang Military Region: Lung Shu-chin, ex-43rd Army cadre
posted as regional commander to Sinkiang, loyal to Huang.
Shenyang Military Region: 39th, 40th, and 46th Armies loyal to
Lin Piao. Eight 4th Field Army deputies posted by Lin Piao
to the headquarters of Ch'en Hsi-lien, the regional commander,
were:

Chang Yung-hui   deputy commander.
Hsiao Chuan-fu   deputy commander.

Teng Yueh	deputy commander.
Wang Yang	deputy commander.
Chang Feng	deputy commander.
Li Shao-yuan	deputy political commissar.
Liu Kuang-t'ao	deputy political commissar.
Tseng Kuo-hua	deputy political commissar.

NEW FACES IN THE FOREGROUND IN PEKING

1. Wu Te Born in Hopei in 1914, Wu Te graduated in Peking, and first came to notice when he led a workers' strike at Tang Shan in 1935. K'ang Sheng trained him as a secret agent in Yenan in 1940, and he became a political commissar in the Eighth Route Army and secretary-general of the political department in the northern Soviet created by Nieh Jung-chen. When the north was cleared of the KMT in 1948–1949, he continued to concentrate on organising labour, and he was a member of the executive committee of the All China Federation of Trade Unions until 1953. This work brought him into sympathetic contact with Liu Shao-ch'i whose own field of revolutionary work had been urban labour rather than Mao's peasantry.

After the "liberation" Wu Te filled a variety of posts ranging from Vice-Minister for the Fuel Industry in 1950 to Political Commissar of Kirin Military District in Manchuria in 1958. He was appointed Deputy Mayor of Peking in 1966, and Acting Mayor when P'eng Chen was purged in the early stages of the Cultural Revolution. In the following year Wu was elected Vice-Chairman of the Peking Revolutionary Committee, and at the Ninth Congress in April 1969 he was made a full member of the Central Committee of the party. He was prominent during President Nixon's visit to China in February 1972, when he was described as Acting Chairman of the Peking Revolutionary Committee, and it was predicted that he would be a candidate for membership of the next Politburo.

2. Hua Kuo-feng Little is known about this relative newcomer, who first appeared as Vice-Governor of Hunan in 1958. He was the provincial deputy for Hunan at the last National People's Congress in 1964 and made chief commander of the Irrigation District Construction Command in Mao's own home county of Shaoshan in 1966. But when he became Acting Chairman of the Hunan Revolutionary Committee and first secretary of the provincial party committee it was clear that he was no Maoist, for he was soon involved in a struggle for political supremacy with local military leaders who had strongly supported Lin Piao during the Cultural Revolution. Hua Kuo-feng's transfer to the capital, disclosed in

November 1971, and his high rating in the hierarchy may make him a candidate for the Politburo.

3. KENG PIAO Born in Hunan in 1909, Keng Piao attended the Whampoa Military Academy with Lin Piao, took part in the Long March, and was promoted to be a divisional chief of staff after his regiment had led the successful assault on Tsunyi in January 1935. After the war against Japan he served with Nieh Jung-chen, who was his early patron, and later with Lin Piao. In 1948 he was a deputy corps commander under Yang Te-chih in North China. In 1950 he joined the Foreign Ministry, held a succession of diplomatic posts abroad, and was a Vice-Minister for Foreign Affairs from 1960 to 1963.

He was known for his sympathy for Liu Shao-ch'i and for Teng Hsiao-p'ing, the disgraced Party Secretary-General, but his good relations with Ch'en Yi and Nieh Jung-chen persuaded Chou En-lai to protect him during the Cultural Revolution, and as ambassador to Albania he was the first Chinese head of mission to be sent out again into the field (all had been withdrawn except the ambassador to Cairo). In 1969 he was made a full member of the Central Committee of the party although Chi P'eng-fei, who was to become Foreign Minister in succession to Ch'en Yi, was not even an alternative member. Then in 1971 it was revealed that he had accompanied Chou En-lai to Hanoi in the very senior capacity of Director of the International Liaison Department of the party. He also, therefore, might well aspire to the Politburo.

4. CH'IAO KUAN-HUA Now 64 years old, Ch'iao was born in Kiangsu of a well-to-do family, graduated at Tsinghua University in Peking where he took political science, and at the age of twenty-two joined the Communist Party. He then went to Germany where he studied military science, and today he speaks both German and English well. He returned to China in 1937 when war was declared against Japan. He worked as a journalist during this period, ultimately becoming the director for all South China of the official Communist *Hsinhua* News Agency, and Chou En-lai, whose approval he earned for his grasp of international affairs and his phenomenal memory, used his services during the confidential negotiations in Chungking between the Communists on one hand and the KMT and the Americans on the other.

In 1949 he was appointed Vice-Chairman of the Foreign Policy Committee in the Ministry of Foreign Affairs. This was the beginning of his career with the ministry. He travelled widely and was first seen at the United Nations as early as 1950, for he was an adviser on a special Chinese delegation to the Security Council over the question of Formosa. He accompanied Chou En-lai to the Bandung Conference in 1955, and on at least a score of other visits to foreign countries. He also accompanied Liu Shao-ch'i on an official visit to North Korea in 1963, and Ch'en Yi to Djakarta in 1964, having just been made a Vice-Minister for Foreign Affairs.

Ch'iao's wife, Kung P'eng, was a senior official of the Foreign Ministry before she died in 1970, and had been not only Director of Information but Director of the Ministry's Intelligence Department. Their son (Ch'iao Chung-huai or Ch'iao Ting-huai) was an anti-Maoist Red Guard leader during the Cultural Revolution, and the position of Ch'iao and his wife became delicate. But Chou En-lai stood by them. On his return to Peking after leading the first Chinese delegation to the United Nations in 1971, Ch'iao was given a welcome only second to that accorded to Chou En-lai when he returned to the capital after seeing the Nixons off at the end of their visit to China in the following February.

5. CHI P'ENG-FEI 62-year-old Chi P'eng-fei is a native of Shensi who began his career in military medicine in the army of the warlord, Feng Yu-hsiang, which moved into Kiangsi to attack Mao's forces but mutinied and joined the Communists in 1931. As noted, he took part in the Long March, and became director of the medical department of the Revolutionary Military Council in Yenan. In the autumn of 1939 he was made political commissar of Ch'en Yi's "Northward Advance Column" in the New 4th Army, and by 1950 was the deputy political commissar of a corps in the 3rd Field Army under Ch'en Yi's overall command. After the civil war he served as ambassador to East Germany and was made a Vice-Minister for Foreign affairs in 1955. He has also accompanied Chou En-lai on official trips abroad, and was with Liu Shao-ch'i in North Korea in 1963. From 1969 onwards he was effectively acting Foreign Minister in the absence of Ch'en Yi, and early in 1971 was officially confirmed as such. When Ch'en Yi died in January 1972, Chi P'eng-fei succeeded him as Foreign Minister.

Appendix to Chapter Sixteen

NOTES ON PERSONALITIES

1. T'AN CHIH-KENG   In 1941 the relationship between T'an and prominent Chinese leaders who then served with the New 4th Army was as follows:

Army Commander	Ch'en Yi.
Army Political Commissar	Liu Shao-ch'i.
Divisional Commander	Su Yu.
Divisional Political Commissar	Chi P'eng-fei (now Foreign Minister).
Brigade Group Commander	Wang Pi-ch'eng (now Commander of Kunming Military Region).
Regimental Commander	T'an Chih-keng.

When the New 4th Army was reorganised as the 3rd Field Army under Ch'en Yi, T'an, as noted, distinguished himself in the famous Huai-Hai campaign of 1948–1949 directed by Ch'en the Bald and the One-Eyed Dragon, Liu Po-ch'eng. After the defeat of the KMT, he served in Korea. He was subsequently appointed Chief of Staff of the 23rd Army in Heilungkiang, Manchuria, and in 1966 was given command of it.

2. CHANG TSUNG-HSUN   Born in Shensi in 1898. Chang graduated from the Whampoa Military Academy in 1925, and when Mao's original "Sanwan seed-force" assembled on Chingkangshan two years later, he was considerably senior to the Speechless Rustic, Huang Yung-sheng. He took part in the Long March, commanded a brigade of the 120th Division under Ho Lung The Moustache in the war against Japan, and rose to be his deputy commander in the 1st Field Army in January 1949. In 1954 he became Deputy Chief of Staff of the PLA and a member of the National Defence Council, and one year afterwards was promoted to full general.

Chang attended the funeral of Stalin, and accompanied Hades P'eng Te-huai to Russia, East Europe and Mongolia in 1959, returning to China just two months before Hades launched the attack on Mao's policies which provoked his dismissal from the post

216

of Minister of Defence. Five years later Chang was a prominent subordinate of Lo Jui-ch'ing when, with the connivance of Ho Lung and in defiance of Lin Piao, the Chief of Staff used the "Big Military Contest" organised for the PLA throughout the country as a device for ensuring that soldiers devoted their time to military training rather than political indoctrination. Chang himself became Chairman of a preparatory committee for extending this idea by promoting "Military Contests among Friendly Armies of Socialist Countries", but in the following year Lo Jui-ch'ing was sacked, and two years later Chang also fell from sight. He re-emerged as deputy commander (?) of Yang Te-chih, the Red warlord of Tsinan Military Region, in mid-1972.

3. PAI HSIANG-KUO   Little is known of this general's earlier career. Prior to 1970 he was for many years a political commissar of the 41st Army, which was under the direct command of Lin Piao until 1949, and later under Huang Yung-sheng. During the Cultural Revolution, Pai became a vice-chairman of the Kwangtung Provincial Revolutionary Committee and Chairman of the Swatow Administrative Regional Revolutionary Committee.

He was transferred to Peking in 1970 as the military "responsible" in the Ministry of Trade, and in December of that year was referred to for the first time as having become the Minister. He subsequently led trade delegations to Ceylon, Rumania and, as noted, France, Italy and Algeria. He has been described as well-briefed and well-informed by those who have negotiated with him, and, although he had theoretically plunged into the world of commercial exchanges, he was still wearing his military uniform in 1972. In terms of loyalties, he has been closer in the past to Huang Yung-sheng than to Lin Piao.

4. K'UANG JEN-NUNG   A veteran of the 4th Field Army, K'uang was for a long time close to Ch'en Yi, to Hsu Shih-yu and Li Hsien-nien. He served in the famous Suchow campaign at the end of 1948, when he distinguished himself by mobilising hundreds of thousands of peasants in support of the red guerrilla armies, and was subsequently appointed commander of the garrison of Tsinan. He directed the China Civil Aviation Administration under the aegis of Chou En-lai during the fifties, and this took him to Moscow, Hanoi and Ulan Bator, and later to Indonesia and Pakistan. He was made a lieutenant-general in 1964, and Deputy Commander of the Air Force in 1968.

5. HSIAO CHING-KUANG   Born in Changsha in 1904, Hsiao was a schoolmate of Mao Tsetung whom Mao once jokingly said he had

217

made Commander of the Navy because he had in his day been a ferryman on the Yangtse. But Hsiao studied in Moscow for four years in the early twenties, and was then with Lin Piao at the Whampoa Military Academy. He joined the Northern Expedition, but again went to Russia for military and political studies for a further three years when the Communists and KMT split. He returned to China and eventually joined Mao in the Kiangsi Soviet, took part in the Long March, and after the Communists had reached Yenan, became for a time Chief of Staff of the Eighth Route Army in the war against the Japanese.

After a series of interim posts, he was made Commander of Naval Headquarters in 1950 and a Vice-Minister for National Defence in 1954. His career thereafter was marked by contact with the Russians until the Sino-Soviet quarrel began coming to a head in 1958. Just as K'uang had been obscured by Wu Fa-hsien, Hsiao was obscured by Li Tso-p'eng until the second half of 1971. Their appearance in public thereafter underlined that Wu and Li had fallen from favour, and that they might now achieve a new importance themselves, possibly becoming members of the Politburo. But while Chou trusts K'uang, he distrusts Hsiao, and Hsiao's new prominence seemed to indicate that Chou was according Mao a face-saving *quid pro quo*.

Chapter Notes

CHAPTER 1: LADIES FIRST

1 Talk by Liu Shao-ch'i at the forum of industrialists and merchants in April 1949, quoted in part in the *People's Daily*, 15 August 1967.
2 Talk by Liu Shao-ch'i delivered in July 1951, quoted in part in the *People's Daily*, 18 August 1967.
3 *Mao Tsetung Chu Tso Hsuan Tu* (2nd volume) on agricultural co-operatives.
4 The *People Daily*, 26 May 1967.
5 The *People's Daily*, 24 May 1967.
6 "The Cultural Revolution Close Up", by A. Zhelokhovtsev, *Novy Mir*, Moscow, March 1968 (adapted from translation in *Joint Publications Research Service* No. 45701, 17 June 1968, Washington D.C.).

CHAPTER 2: THE BRAIN AND THE TRIGGER-FINGER

1 Chou En-lai was speaking to Kweichow rebels on 2 March 1967, according to the Bulgarian news agency, BTA.
2 T'ao Chu was a former First Secretary of the Central-South Bureau of the Chinese Communist Party. He was an advocate of free expression of natural emotion, and he wrote two books entitled, *Thoughts, Feelings and Literary Talent*, and *Ideals, Integrity and the Spiritual Life*. During the Cultural Revolution these books were branded as anti-party and anti-Maoist "poisonous weeds".
3 When Mao held his sixth rally of Red Guards in Peking, Li Na (also known as Hsiao Li) appeared as a representative of the PLA and stood with high-ranking officers. She had been planted in the PLA by Chiang Ch'ing, who had arranged for her to be given a responsible position on the *Liberation Army Daily*. She was at her most active in 1968, but as far as is known she has not appeared in public since October of that year.

4 Remark by Mao in 1959 at the Eighth Plenum of the Chinese Communist Party – *China Monthly*, 1 May 1968, Hongkong.

CHAPTER 3: THE FIVE SMILES OF CHOU EN-LAI

1 Yao Ch'ien, author of *Wen Chun Meng*.
2 *Eleven Years with Vice-Chairman Chou*, by Lung Fei-fu.
3 The successive leaders of the Chinese Communist Party concerned were Ch'en Tu-hsiu, Chu Ch'iu-pai, Li Li-san, Wang Ming (Ch'en Shao-yu).
4 Chou Hsiao-yen, professor of singing at the Shanghai Music Academy, and Sun Wei-shih, Director of the Chinese Youth Arts Institute (wife of the Deputy Foreign Minister, Hsu Yi-hsin, who was associated with Chiang Ch'ing in Yenan before she attached herself to Mao Tsetung).
5 The system of secret agents within the Communist underground was completely independent, and the "Red Squad" had a special place within it. Its members were not subject to strict routine discipline and were given large sums of money to spend, but they were obliged to execute any party orders they received, which were usually to kidnap, murder, or perform acts of terrorism.
6 Chou En-lai, on 27 January 1967, in a discussion with the Revolutionary Rebel Organisation of the railway system.
7 "Revolutionary correspondence" published in October 1967.
8 Speech by Chou En-lai at the People's Palace in Peking where he received representatives from the Manchurian provinces on 28 September 1967.
9 Ch'en Yun, Nieh Jung-chen, Ch'en Yi, Li Fu-ch'un.

CHAPTER 4: LI HSIEN-NIEN: THE MONEY GOD

1 From the *Peking Commune* of 26 May 1967.
2 Quotations from "Profile of Li Hsien-nien" by Gordon A. Bennett in the *Far Eastern Economic Review*, 14 March 1968. (Translated from Red Guard posters.)

CHAPTER 7: THE BARREL OF THE GUN

1 This guidance was contained in a report published in the *People's Daily* in December 1969 on party-building in the Peking Hsinhua Printing Works.

CHAPTER 8: THE MOUNTAIN-TOPS

1 Original text published in the *People's Daily* and *Kuang Ming Jih Pao*, 31 October 1957.
2 The opera singer was Yuan Hsueh-fen, the dancer Tai Ai-lien.
3 Tseng Shao-shan, Political Commissar of Shenyang Military Region (Manchuria), Li Te-sheng, Director of the General Political Department of the PLA, and Ch'en Hsi-lien, Commander of the Shenyang Military Region, are all ex-2nd Field Army cadres.

CHAPTER 9: THREE "COMRADES"
Part One: "Ironsides" Hsu Shih-yu

1 The Three Heavenly Guardians are Huang Yung-sheng, quondam Chief of Staff of the PLA; Hsu Shih-yu, Commander of Nanking Military Region; and Ch'en Hsi-lien, Commander of Shenyang Military Region.
2 During the Sino-Japanese War, Hsueh Yueh three times defeated the enemy to win the "Three Great Victories of Changsha".
3 Li Te, Chief of Staff, and Huang Ch'ao, Secretary, both of the Fourth Front Army, and other capable subordinates of Chang Kuo-t'ao, were secretly executed in Sinkiang by Mao Tsetung, according to Chang Kuo-t'ao (*My Reminiscences*, by Chang Kuo-t'ao).
4 Nanking is the third largest of China's military regions.
5 From October 1966 to January 1967 a Japanese academic named Mineo Nakajima made an extensive tour of Canton, Peking, Nanking, Shanghai and Changsha to observe the Cultural Revolution. While collecting material he was harassed and followed by Red Guards, and in Canton he was finally arrested and questioned by the Public Security Department. On his return to Japan, he published a long article entitled "The truth about Mao Tsetung's departure from Peking" in the *Chuo Kooron* (March 1967). It gave a detailed analysis of the situation in Communist China at that time, and created a considerable stir.
6 From *North Shensi Labour Camp*, by Su Wei-ch'uan, published by Asia Press, Hongkong. Su Wei-ch'uan was a party member for thirteen years and served with the "North-West Labour Reform Brigade" in Yenan.

221

7 The *Red Flag*, No. 16, 23 November 1967.

Part Two: The Two-edged Bayonet

1 The Kuomintang Government had divided the country into "Clearance Districts" for the purpose of purging it progressively of Communists. But the deputy commander of the 17th Clearance District, Kuo Hsun-ch'i alias Kuo Chih-hsun, was in fact a Communist secret agent. This account is taken from *The T'e Wu Duel in the Hsiang Yang Campaign* by Huang Min, published in 1970 in Hongkong. Huang Min was himself an intelligence officer at Kuomintang headquarters in Wuhan who was detached to take part in the operations in the Hsiang Yang sector.

Part Three: The Kiangsi Favourites

1 Published on 13 February 1964, and included in a Red Guard booklet entitled *Mao Tsetung's Thought* in April 1967.
2 The other officers were: Ch'iu Hui-tso, Director of the General Logistics Department, PLA; Li Tso-p'eng, First Political Commissar, Chinese Navy; Wang Hung-k'un, Senior Political Commissar, Chinese Navy; and Chang Hsiu-ch'uan, Senior Political Commissar, Chinese Navy.
3 Talk by Lin Piao to leaders of the Wuhan Military Region on 9 August 1967. Published in a Red Guard magazine *Chu River Film Unit – The East is Red* in September 1967.
4 *People's Daily*, 13 August 1967.

CHAPTER 10: HUANG YUNG-SHENG: THE SPEECHLESS RUSTIC

1 *The Flying Red Flag*, volume 3, page 3, published in October 1959 by the Chinese Youth Publications Company.
2 *Wan Jen*, volume 19, page 25, published in Hongkong on 5 February 1970, quoting from *Hsi Nan Pao Wei Chan Pei Kung T'e Ch'ai K'ua* of San Lang.
3 Huang Yung-sheng's speech at a meeting of cultural representatives of the South China Military Region in Canton in March 1952. It was published in *Wan Jen*, volume 22, page 5.
4 Published in the newspaper of the 3rd Command Headquarters of the Red Guards in Canton on 24 August 1967.

5 *Red Flag of the South China Teachers' Training College*, 29 August 1967.
6 "Doctrine Guards" is short for the "Mao Tsetung Doctrine Red Guards of Canton".
7 Published in the newspaper of the Mao group Red Guards in Canton, *Chu River Film Productions: The East is Red*.
8 The "Support the Army and Love the People" campaign called for:
   (a) a halt to all armed struggles and the surrender of all weapons to the PLA
   (b) a ban on seizing weapons from the PLA
   (c) support for the PLA in maintaining order and the smooth running of communications, and no interference in the execution of its duties
   (d) all prisoners to be freed unconditionally and immediately by all rival organisations.
9 Joint publication of *Wuhan Steel Second Headquarters* and *Chu River Film Productions: The East is Red*, 13 September 1968.
10 The "Three Support and Two Military" campaign called upon the PLA (a) to support industrial production, agricultural production, and revolutionary left-wing groups struggling to seize power, and (b) to exercise military control and intensify political and military training.
11 *January Storm*, a pamphlet published on 28 August 1967 by the Canton Red Revolutionary Rebel Joint Headquarters.

CHAPTER 11: THE RED WARLORDS

1 The *I Ching* is an ancient work of divination.
2 The *Lung Ch'i Red Guards*, published on 5 August 1968 by the Mao Tsetung Thought Red Guards Propaganda Team of the Fukien Revolutionary Committee.
3 Pai Hsiang-kuo was the Political Commissar of the 41st Army, stationed at Swatow, Kwangtung Province, before the Cultural Revolution. See also appendix to Chapter 16.

CHAPTER 12: BOXING THE ARMY COMPASS

1 *Peking Aerial Navigation College Red Flag*, No. 108, 12 June 1968.
2 *Wuhan Steel 2nd Headquarters* and *Chu River Film Productions: The East is Red* joint publication.

3 From *Red Headquarter Bulletin*, No. 4–5, published on 12 July 1968 in Canton, and other sources.
4 Quoted in a Red Guard bulletin in March 1968.
5 Among the ex-3rd Field Army generals transferred to Lanchow Military Region were: Huang Ching-yao, ex-Commander of Shensi Military District (1967), Hu Wei, the ex-Deputy Commander of Shensi Military District, these men both "supported the left" during the Cultural Revolution, and Fang Sheng-p'u, responsible for the defence of the nuclear weapons plant (he was formerly Deputy Commander of the Air Force in Lanchow).

CHAPTER 13: THE FALLEN ANGEL

1 Taken from a personal account by Li T'ien-yu, deceased Deputy Chief of Staff, published in *Kang Tieh Tzu Ti Ping*, Peking, Vol. Two, February 1958. New China News Agency republished the account in August 1965.
   "One Point" refers to a deployment of forces for attack with a narrow spearhead and a long column behind it. The spearhead is directed at the weak point of the enemy's defences, and once this is penetrated the force then breaks apart to attack from "two sides", "three sides" or even more.
2 *Huo Chu T'ung Hsin* (Torch Bulletin), No. 1, July 1968.
3 From *Ten Thousand miles behind the Iron Curtain* by Pei Lu, published 1959, Hongkong.
4 Between September 1967 and April 1969 three members of the Cultural Revolution Group were dismissed: Wang Li, Kuan Feng, Ch'i Pen-yu.
5 *Kung Tso T'ung Hsin* (Work Bulletin), Peking, No. 20, 22 May 1961.

CHAPTER 14: THE STORM SIGNAL

1 Extract from an article entitled "Mao Tsetung and Chu Te" by Li Ang, published in the 190th issue of *Prospect* in Hongkong, 1 January 1970. Li Ang was a member of the Chinese Communist Party who first met Mao at the congress convened in Shanghai in 1921. Later he withdrew from the party.
2 Translated from an advance extract of Chang Kuo-t'ao's memoirs published in issue No. 68 of *China Monthly*, Hongkong, 1 January 1969.
3 "Problems of War and Strategy", from the *Selected Works of Mao Tsetung*, Vol. II.

4 "On Protracted War", from the *Selected Works of Mao Tsetung,* Vol. II.
5 "A conversation with Mao Tsetung" by Edgar Snow, *Life* Magazine, 30 April 1971.
6 Before ranks were abolished, China's ten Marshals were: Lin Piao, Chu Te, Liu Po-ch'eng, Yeh Chien-Ying (all members of the Politburo), Nieh Jung-chen and Hsu Hsiang-ch'ien (obliged to write self-criticisms confessing grave errors during the Cultural Revolution, but protected by Chou En-lai and not necessarily out of the power game), Ho Lung and P'eng Te-huai (in disgrace), Lo Jung-huan and Ch'en Yi (deceased).

CHAPTER 15: WHILE MAO LIVES

1 *People's Daily,* 20 October 1971.
2 Changsha Radio broadcast, 29 October 1971.
3 *Red Flag,* No. 11, 1971.

CHAPTER 16: WHILE MAO LIVES (CONTINUED)

1 *Red Flag,* December 1971, published these two articles: "Strengthen the Proletarian Party Power", from the Writing Group of the Liaoning Provincial Party Committee, and "Raise the Party's Excellent Working Style", from the Writing Group of the Kiangsu Provincial Party Committee.
2 Hsu Shih-yu's men were: Wang Pi-ch'eng, Commander of Kunming Military Region, and P'i Ting-chun, Commander of Lanchow Military Region.
Deputies transferred from Nanking to Wuhan Military Region:
　Wang Liu-sheng, Political Commissar.
　Hsieh Sheng-kun, Deputy Commander.
　Lin Wei-hsien, Deputy Political Commissar.
Air Force Commander, Shenyang Military Region: Ts'ai Yung (reported).
Deputy Commander, Peking Military Region: Yu T'ai-chung.
First Deputy Chief of Staff in Peking: Chang Ts'ai-ch'ien.
3 Active members of the Politburo, as listed, were:
　Mao Tsetung
　Chou En-lai
　Chiang Ch'ing
　Yeh Chien-ying
　Chang Ch'un-ch'iao
　Yao Wen-yuan

Li Hsien-nien
Tung Pi-wu (Acting President of the Republic)
Ch'en Hsi-lien.
(Hsu Shin-yu's name appeared again in October 1972.)

CHAPTER 17: WHEN MAO DIES

1 *Red Flag*, 1 January 1972, "A Sharp Weapon to Criticise
Revisionism", by the Writing Group of the Heilungkiang provincial party committee, quoting from Mao Tsetung's "Economic
and Financial Problems in the Anti-Japanese War".

List of Published Sources

CHINESE-LANGUAGE

Published in Peking and Shanghai

Books

Mao Tsetung Hsuan Chi, People's Press, Peking.
Kuan-yu Kuo-chi Kung Ch'an Chu-i Yun-tung Tsung Lu-hsien-ti Lun Chan, People's Press, Peking.
Yung-yuan Tu-ch'u Cheng-chih, People's Press, Peking.
Kung Nung Ping Hsueh Che-hsueh Yung Che-hsueh, People's Press, Peking.
Tao-ch'u Shih Hung Ch'i, China Youth Press, Peking.
Nu-li Hsueh-hao Mao Tsetung Ssu-hsiang, Hsin Hua Shop, Peking.
"San-Pa" Hsien-shang-ti K'ai Ko, Liberation Army Literature and Art Press, Peking.
Ch'ao-hsien T'ung-hsin Pao-kao Hsuan, People's Literature Press, Peking.
Sheng-huo Tsai Ying-hsiung-men Chung-chien, by Pa Chin, People's Literature Press, Peking.
Tai-yang Chao Tsai Sang Chien Ho Shang, by Ting Ling, People's Literature Press, Peking.
Jen Min Chieh-yang Chun-ti 30 Nien, by Huang Tao, People's Press, Peking.
Lun Kung Ch'an Tang Tang-yuan-ti Hsiu-yang, by Liu Shao-ch'i, People's Press, Peking.

Newspapers and Magazines

Hung Ch'i, Renmin Ribao, Chieh-fang Chun Pao, Kuang Ming Ribao, Wen-i Pao (Nos. 250, 252), *Wen Hui Pao* (Shanghai), *Ta Kung Pao* (Shanghai).
Jen Min Shou-ts'e, printed by *Ta Kung Pao*, Shanghai.
Hung Ch'i P'iao P'iao, China Youth Press, Peking.
Hsing Huo Liao Yuan (Nos. 6 and 7), People's Literature Press, Peking.
Red Guard publications, bulletins, etc.

Published in Hongkong

Books (General)

Chung Kung Shih Nien, Yu Luen Press.
Lin Piao Chuan Chi, Chih Luen Press.
Chung Kung Wen-hua Ta Ko-ming Tzu-liao Hui-p'ien (No. 1), by Ting Wang, Ming Pao Press.
Lun Chung Kung-ti Chun-shih Fa-chan, by Shih Ch'eng-chih, Yu Luen Press.
Wo-ti Hui-i, by Chang Kuo T'ao, Ming Pao Monthly (1969–1971).
Chang Kuo T'ao Fu-jen Hui-i Lu, by Yang Tzu Lieh, Chih Luen Press.
Wo yu Hung Chun, by Kung Ch'u, Nan Feng Press.
Tou-cheng 18 Nien, by Smarlo, Chih Luen Press.
"Chiu Ta" I-hou-ti Mao Cheng-ch'uan, Chen Pao Press.
San-shih Nien Lai-ti Chung Kung, by Ku Kuan Chiao, Asia Press.
Shen-pei Nu-kung Ying, by Su Wei Ch'uan, Asia Press.
T'ieh Mu Chien Hsing I-wan Li, by Pei Lu, Freedom Press.
Hsiang Fan Chan-i Chung-ti T'e Wu Chan, by Huang Min, Wan Jen Tsa-chih (Nos. 131, 132, 133).
Chung Kung Wen-i Tsung Pi-p'an, by Ting Sen, Asia Press.
Chung Kung Chun-jen Chih (Chinese edition of *Mao's Generals*), by Huang Chen Hsia, Research Institute of Contemporary History, Hongkong.

Books (Left-wing)

Chin Ling Ch'un Meng, by T'ang Jen, Wen Tsung Press.
Shih Nien Nei Chan, by T'ang Jen, Wen Tsung Press.
Pa Nien K'ang Chan, by T'ang Jen, Wen Tsung Press.
Hsueh Jou Ch'ang Ch'eng, by T'ang Jen, Wen Tsung Press.
Chou Pan T'an Ping Lu, by Chen Shao Chiao.
Kuan Nei Liaotung I Chu Ch'i, by Chen Shao Chiao.
Chin Ling Ts'an-chao Chi, by Chen Shao Chiao.
Chu-lu Shen Chuan K'ang, by Chen Shao Chiao.
Hsi-pei Ch'un-fa Chi, by Chen Shao Chiao.

Newspapers and Magazines

Ta Kung Pao, Wen Hui Pao, and other Hongkong papers.
China Monthly, Yu Luen Press.
Ming Pao Yueh Han, Ming Pao Press.
Ming Pao Chou Han, Ming Pao Press.
Chan Wang, Chih Luen Press.
Wan Jen Tsa-chih, Yu Luen Press.

Published in Taiwan

Chung Kung Jen Ming Lu, International Relations Research Center.
Fei Tang K'ung-chih Fang-shih Yu Kung-tso Fang-fa, No. 6 Bureau Central Committee of the Kuomintang.
Chao Fei Chi Shih, by Hsueh Yueh, Wen Hsing Book Shop, Taipei.

Published in Canton

Ti Ssu Chun Chi Shih, by Chang Fa K'uei, Huai Yuan Book Shop, Canton.

ENGLISH-LANGUAGE

Books

A Doak Barnett, *China After Mao*, Oxford University Press and Princeton University Press.
C. P. Fitzgerald, *Revolution in China*, The Cresset Press, London.
Alexander L. George, *The Chinese Communist Army in Action*, Columbia University Press.
K. S. Karol, *China – the Other Communism*, Heinemann, London.
John Wilson Lewis (ed.), *Party Leadership and Revolutionary Power in China*, Cambridge University Press.
F. F. Liu, *A Military History of Modern China*, Princeton University Press.
Henry McAleavy, *The Modern History of China*, Weidenfeld and Nicolson, London.
Edgar O'Ballance, *The Red Army of China*, Faber and Faber, London.
George Paloczi-Horvath, *Mao Tse-tung: Emperor of the Blue Ants*, Secker and Warburg, London.
Robert Payne, *Mao Tse-tung, Ruler of Red China*, London.
Robert Payne, *Chiang Kai-shek*, Weybright and Talley, New York.
Stuart Schram, *Mao Tse-tung*, Pelican Books, London.
Benjamin I. Schwartz, *Chinese Communism and the Rise of Mao*, Harvard University Press.
Edgar Snow, *Red Star over China*, Victor Gollancz, London.
Dick Wilson, *The Long March*, Hamish Hamilton, London.

Other Publications

The China Quarterly, London (including "The Field Army in Chinese Communist Military Politics" by William Whitson, issue No. 37 of January–March 1969).
The Far Eastern Economic Review, Hongkong (including profile of

Li Hsien-nien by Gordon A. Bennett, published 13 March 1968).

Who's Who in Communist China, Union Research Institute, Hongkong.

China News Analysis, Hongkong.

Current Scene (American. Ceased publication July 1970.)

China Reporting Service (American).

The Selected Works of Mao Tse-tung, Foreign Language Press, Peking.

Index

Africa: Chou En-lai on, 36
Afro-Asian Conf. (Bandung), 27
agricultural cooperatives, 8–9, 36
Air Force, Chinese, 103–4
All-China Federation of Democratic Women, 6–7
Anti-Japanese Military and Political University, 3, 43, 89, 145
Autumn Harvest Uprising, xxvii, 71

"Bayonet, The": see Li Te-sheng
"Brain, The": see Chang Ch'un-ch'iao

Canton Military Garrison, 176
Canton Military Region, 172
Central Intelligence Agency, 166
Central News Agency for all East China, 23
Chang Ch'un-ch'iao, 19 fn., 23–6, 161
Chang Kuo-hua, 136–7, 173
Chang Kuo-t'ao, 40–1, 43, 73–4, 79, 87–9, 124, 137, 145, 156
Chang Shao-ch'ing: see K'ang Sheng
Chang Ts'ai-ch'ien, 188
Chang Tsung-hsun, 176, 216
Ch'en Hsi-lien, 46, 87, 97, 102, 121, 123-5, 178
Ch'en K'ang, 211
Ch'en Po-ta, 92, 160–1, 167, 170, 196
Ch'en Tsai-tao, 132–4, 185, 199
Ch'en Yi, 43, 53–4, 75–6, 80, 91, 124, 146, 173, 176

Ch'en Yun, 44 fn., 185
Ch'eng Shih-ch'ing, 127 fn.
Cheng Wei-san, 87, 128 fn., 131–2
Chengtu Military Region, 135–7
Chiang Ch'ing: marriage to T'ang Na, 1; liaison with film director, 1–2; at Yenan, 3; lecturer at Lu Hsun Academy of Arts, 4; encounter with Mao, 5; children, 6; compared with Communist leaders' wives, 6–7; bitterness towards, 10; "rectification of theatre", 10–12; Cultural Revolution, 12–16, 20–1; interplay with PLA, 23; Cultural Revolution, 25–6, 33–5, 51, 92, 105, 116, 150–1, 160, 164, 181–2, 195; comparison with Mme Chou, 31
Chiang Kai-shek, xxvi, xxvii, 29–30, 49, 70, 72, 145, 157, 163
Chiang Yung-hui, 209
Ch'iao Kuan-hua, 174, 214–5
Ch'in Chi-wei, 137 fn.
Chi P'eng-fei, 174–6, 195, 215
Ching Ping, xiii–xiv
Ch'iu Hui-tso, 129, 167, 210
Chou En-lai: international outlook, xxvi; wife, 7, 31; on Paris Commune, 18; five smiles, 27; flexibility, 28; early years, 29; dedication, appointed Prime Minister, 30; liaison in Germany, 31; leader of Shanghai intelligence net-

231

233